GRAPHIC SAMPLER

Samson Threatening His Father-in-Law. *Print from restrike album, after the Rembrandt painting.*

GRAPHIC SAMPLER

Compiled by

RENATA V. SHAW

Prints and Photographs Division

LIBRARY OF CONGRESS   WASHINGTON   1979

Library of Congress Cataloging in Publication Data

Main entry under title:

Graphic sampler.

  1. Prints—Addresses, essays, lectures.
2. Drawing—Addresses, essays, lectures.
3. Popular culture—Illustrations—Addresses,
essays, lectures. 4. Architectural drawing—
Addresses, essays, lectures. I. Shaw, Renata V.
II. United States. Library of Congress. Prints
and Photographs Division.
NE400.G7   760′.074′0153   79–12124
ISBN 0–8444–0309–1

Frontispiece: Samson Threatening His Father-in-Law.
Print from restrike album, after the Rembrandt painting.

For sale by the Superintendent of Documents, U.S. Government Printing Office
Washington, D.C. 20402
Stock Number 030–000–00092–7

This book is dedicated to Edgar Breitenbach,
Chief of the Prints and Photographs Division from 1956 to 1973,
whose enthusiasm and interest in the graphic arts
inspired many of the essays in this volume.

Preface

With this *Graphic Sampler,* the Prints and Photographs Division presents to its friends a representative selection of images from the vast and diverse collections in its custody. The choice of subject matter studied by the twelve authors has been suggested either by the rediscovery of a group of drawings or prints hitherto unrecognized beyond a small circle of staff members or by the arrival of a new and interesting acquisition.

The first section of essays deals with pictures created between the end of the fifteenth century and the year 1800. A wide variety of techniques are represented here, ranging from an engraving on parchment to chiaroscuro woodcuts, from copper engravings and etchings to pen-and-ink drawings. These images were produced in continental Europe, in England, and in the United States. Many were not produced for aesthetic reasons alone but were created to foster religious devotion, to enhance the fame of artists through reproductive engravings, or to provide decorative patterns for use by goldsmiths, cabinetmakers, printers, and other artisans.

Also covered in this initial section are series of popular prints—those of street cries, for example—which served as souvenirs and collectors' items at the time of publication. This graphic folk art increases in interest and value with time because it documents clothing, customs, and trades long since vanished from our daily experience. Pen-and-ink sketches of guild days celebrated in Norwich also afford us a glimpse of eighteenth-century daily life still rooted in medieval English tradition.

Architectural plans explored in this section range from a royal project in Italy to designs for domestic buildings in the United States. These carefully executed pen-and-wash drawings exemplify the work of professional architects of the eighteenth century. The work of the Italian Francisco La Vega, as well as that of Benjamin Latrobe, is permeated by the ideals of neoclassicism spreading from the continent of Europe throughout the Western world.

Prints and drawings of the nineteenth century are investigated in the second section of essays. The first article is devoted to forty-nine Rembrandt restrikes which the author attempts to place in their proper time frame. Rembrandt etchings enjoyed a revival of popularity in the beginning of the nineteenth century; thus the correct identification of restrikes becomes a challenging puzzle for the print connoisseur. In the following article we return to Benjamin Latrobe, whose contribution to the design of the U.S. Capitol forms a well-documented chapter in the building's history. The Library is fortunate in owning a unique watercolor rendering of Latrobe's exterior view of the Capitol.

The invention of lithography in 1798 brought a new versatile technique to the aid of book illustrators, advertising artists, political cartoonists, and publishers of historical and popular prints, who welcomed a quick and inexpensive method of getting their pictures to the public. Several articles explore the use of this new vehicle of printmaking. The one on Nicolas-Toussaint Charlet, a French illustrator, explains how he used images to express his enthusiasm for Napoleon in hundreds of lively scenes of day-to-day life during the reign of Bonaparte. In Germany the new method was put to the service of politics. The Library's two broadsides announcing the rise of Prussia were produced to advise neighboring countries of an imminent power struggle among the nations of Europe.

In the United States lithography was used to advantage in the newly developing field of commercial advertising of luxury goods. Examples of this are the colorful tobacco labels treated in the fourth article in this section. These images mirror the social concerns of the middle of the nineteenth century, the artists having borrowed freely from bookplates, fashion illustrations, and newspapers of the day. Lithographed letterheads also made their first appearance during this period. These tiny pictures of American cities are of historical interest because they capture the cityscapes at a specific period and state of growth possibly not documented in any other pictorial source. In contrast to these small images, large-size lithographic posters were used to advertise the performing arts.

The most spectacular advertisements were those announcing the latest events in the world of opera, vaudeville, music hall, and circus.

Schools used lithographic wall charts as aids to object teaching. Industrial entrepreneurs and manufacturers of elegant consumer goods used lithographic advertisements to publicize items ranging from locomotives and pistols to gas "smoothing-irons," bicycles, and sewing machines. The pictorial essay on women, the last article in this section, makes use of many of these lithographs because they mirror different facets of the daily activities of the American woman in the second half of the nineteenth century.

The two other essays in this section are devoted to original drawings. The Leutze sketchbooks reveal the working methods of an American artist who based his murals for the U.S. Capitol on studies made in the American West, while a more exotic selection of eyewitness accounts is the Library's collection of Yokohama-e, Japanese ink-and-wash drawings of the first Americans who landed in Japan with Commodore Perry in 1853. These images from the Orient furnish an entertaining and revealing view of the way Westerners appeared to Japanese observers. The drawings were converted into popular woodcuts, and many different editions were published in the 1850s before the novelty of the subject matter wore off.

The third section of essays describes prints, drawings, cartoons, and posters from the turn of the century to the 1960s. Six of these essays are devoted to individual artists. John Singer Sargent used the lithographic medium to develop pictorial ideas later to be translated into larger works. William Glackens appears in this sampler as artist-reporter of the Spanish-American War. His drawings of the troops in action capture the time and place of the dramatic events and point to his later career as a prominent painter of the Ashcan school. The Austrian-American composer Arnold Schönberg is discussed here as painter of a small work called *Vision*. This portrait from 1910 is typical of the expressionist style of the period. It is also the visual equivalent of the trends in contemporary music. Clifford Kennedy Berryman's career as political cartoonist spans over fifty years of American history, from the 1890s, when cartoons first became regular features in American newspapers, through the Truman era. His pictorial commentary on Washington politics and the international scene provides a visual record of the major issues of the first half of the twentieth century. Fritz Eichenberg's work focuses on the graphic interpretation of some of the seminal writers of the nineteenth and twentieth centuries. His woodcuts capture the essence of a story and translate it into pictorial form. In the essay included here, Eichenberg explains his working methods and shows us the development of an idea from quick, sketchy notation to final finished solution. Max Beckmannn's lithographic sheets for his "Day and Dream" series are an expressionistic interpretation of scenes from his life. The artist remains deliberately enigmatic, leaving the explanation of his pictures to the imagination of the viewer.

Two articles in this section document the somewhat more lively and topical mood of contemporary images. One on Mexican graphic art of the twentieth century shows how the graphic work involved brings the national concerns of the country into sharp focus. Pre-Columbian and Western stylistic elements are fused into a Mexican indigenous expression interpretive of native subjects and the aspirations of the people. Modern graphic art has here succeeded in filling an artistic as well as a social need. No discussion of twentieth-century visual art is complete without some reference to advertising art, which touches the imagination of more individuals than any other visual art form of our times. Appropriately, the last short essay in the section describes a motion-picture poster of Charlie Chaplin.

Although there is no common subject, medium or purpose readily available to help us fit the graphics explored by our authors into a comprehensive pattern, it is the joy of the Prints and Photographs Division that its collections are rich and inexhaustible. This abundance is reflected in the final article on the Library's architectural collections, which discusses the advantages offered to researchers in a special subject area by our unparalleled graphic collections. As is so amply demonstrated here, they can be explored from many different points of view and continually offer the user ever new and fresh images for his inspiration.

Contents

I PRINTS AND DRAWINGS FROM THE
FIFTEENTH CENTURY TO 1800

2

Israhel van Meckenem's Man of Sorrows

BY EDGAR BREITENBACH

When the Library acquired the Gardiner Greene Hubbard Collection in 1898, its first important donation in the field of graphic arts, it received, among many other treasures, a fifteenth-century engraving, the significance of which was not immediately recognized.[1] Its subject is the Man of Sorrows—the dead Christ before the cross, his head resting on his right shoulder, his arms crossed over his body. The background is covered with hatched lines, except for the Greek initials IS (Iesos) on the left and XC (Christos) on the right. The inscription on the titulus is somewhat garbled, indicating that the engraver was not acquainted with Greek letters. It should read: *"O Basileus tes doxes"* (King of Glory).

The Man of Sorrows does not represent a historic moment in the life of Christ, but is rather a symbolic image, a summing up of his Passion. It has its origins in Byzantine art and was transmitted to Italy in the twelfth century and hence to the rest of Europe.

The engraving is printed on parchment, a material rarely used for prints and always indicative of a special purpose. There are wide margins around the print, painted in the manner of a miniature. The motifs consist of precious stones and flowers on three sides, while at the bottom there is an inscription in gold letters which reads *"Orate pro magistro Rutgero de Venlo/Canonico Gereonis, sacre pagine licentiato."*

Rutger de Venlo was a prominent faculty member of Cologne University. The matricula of the university mentions him on a number of occasions.[2] A

Man of Sorrows. *Engraved by Israhel van Meckenem (ca. 1444–1503). From the Prints and Photographs Division. LC–USZ62–49294.*

3

native of Louvain, he entered the University of Cologne in 1491 (or possibly in 1489) and there became magister in 1494 and professor in 1500. His reputation grew steadily, until in 1518 he was elevated to the rank of canon of both the *Stift* St. Gereon and of St. Ursula, the latter a famous secular convent for the daughters of the high nobility of the Rhineland.[3] Finally, in 1519 he became *Rektor*, the elected head of the university. Rutger de Venlo died on April 29, 1525. The obsequies took place on May 18, and it is assumed that the print was made for this occasion, most likely in compliance with the canon's will. It was customary among the clergy of St. Gereon to leave money to the *Stift* as an offering to the priests for memorial masses celebrated for their benefit when deceased.[4]

We can now return to our print, first to establish the artist and then to trace the history of the subject matter. In the fairly large body of literature on the iconography of the Man of Sorrows,[5] most scholars mention this print, and some reproduce it. The engraver is Israhel van Meckenem (ca. 1444–1503), who created more images of the Man of Sorrows than any of his German contemporaries. It has been described by Max Lehrs in his catalog of Israhel van Meckenem's prints under No. 166.[6] Lehrs knew two states of the print, generally assumed to have been made about 1495.[7] According to Fritz Koreny,[8] the Library's copy is a late impression of a hitherto unknown third state, apparently made after Israhel's death. At that time the plate was so worn that it was re-engraved within the contours of Israhel's original design, a testimony to the immense popularity of the print. I assume that the inscription underneath the plate seen in the earlier states was eliminated in the process, for reasons I shall discuss later.

Israhel's print is not original, but, as the inscription (seen on the second state) indicates, a faithful rendering of a picture that shows a vision of Christ, which, according to legend, appeared to Pope Gregory the Great. On Israhel's other print of the same image, the place where the picture is kept is given: the church of Santa Croce in Gerusalemme in Rome.

In a brilliant essay Carlo Bertelli recently traced the history of this picture, which is actually a small, portable mosaic. Bertelli makes it highly plausible that the mosaic was made in a Latin outpost of the Byzantine empire during the late thirteenth or early fourteenth century. It was presented to the monastery of St. Catherine on Mount Sinai and later taken from there by Raimondello Orsini del Balzo, Count of Lecce, when he visited the Sinai in 1380 or 1381.[9] He in turn presented it to Santa Croce in 1385 or 1386. There the mosaic joined the

Man of Sorrows. *Second state. Israhel van Meckenem. Courtesy Cabinet des Estampes, Bibliothèqe nationale.*

great treasure of relics displayed in the subterranean "chapel Jerusalem," the pavement of which covers earth brought from Golgotha. "Even the 'Gregorian' mosaic, as a replica of a well-known icon in the church of the Holy Sepulchre in Jerusalem . . ., enhanced the ideal connections of the 'chapel Jerusalem' with the Holy City. In fact, it might have been presented precisely to this shrine just because of its connections with the *Sepulchrum Domini*." [10]

The church of Santa Croce was taken over in 1371 by the Carthusian monks, who established a charterhouse next to it. It should be realized that religious institutions have their secular, as well as their spiritual, aspects. Services to the faithful, buildings and their upkeep, growth in general, all require a steady income. In the late Middle Ages such income was derived from land and houses owned by a church (rents, tithes, agricultural products) and from gifts of parishioners and pilgrims.

To attract people, relics and reputedly miracle-working images were of enormous importance, particularly if papal blessings and indulgences had been bestowed on them. It was the latter that the errant faithful were seeking. The urgent desire to free oneself from sin and thus shorten the pains of purgatory manifested itself most strongly in the rumor circulating in December 1299 that anyone visiting St. Peter's on New Year's Day of the new century would receive full absolution. Pope Boniface VIII felt compelled to give substance to the rumor, thus starting the tradition of the Jubilee Years, which at that time were intended to celebrate the beginning of each century. But the enormous success of this event, from the point of view of both clergy and laity, prompted Clement VI to pronounce 1350 as the second Jubilee Year.[11] Two papal bulls are connected with this year, a genuine one of 1343, *Unigenitus Dei filius,* and a spurious one, *Ad memoriam reducendo,* which was widely circulated. Concocted sometime between 1350 and the Jubilee Year of 1400, it nevertheless claimed Clement VI as its author. This bull contains two passages of importance to our subject. It mentions for the first time the nonpatriarchal basilicas, with Santa Croce heading the list, that pilgrims to Rome should visit to gain full absolution, and it is "the first bull to guarantee indulgences to pilgrims who would look with devotion at some of the venerated images in Rome." [12]

It will be remembered that Israhel van Meckenem's print referred in its inscription to Pope Gregory's vision while he was celebrating mass. This vision is not mentioned in accounts of the life of the pope nor has it dogmatic roots, but the legend seems to have developed from folk belief around 1400. None of the early representations of the Mass of St. Gregory indicates Santa Croce as the

Image of Pity. *Mosaic, with silver frame.*
Byzantine, early fourteenth century. At
Rome, Sta. Croce in Gerualemme. Courtesy
Instituto centrale del restauro, Archivio
fotografico, Rome.

Image of Pity. *English, fifteenth century. In Carthusian manuscript. Courtesy British Museum.*

place of the vision; it is, in fact, mentioned for the first time on the other Meckenem print (Lehrs, No. 107). There is, however, sufficient evidence that the Carthusian order, anxious to help its new charterhouse in Rome, was busily engaged in spreading the belief that Santa Croce was, indeed, the scene of the vision, implying that the portable mosaic was the visual rendering of St. Gregory's vision.[13] One of the great masterpieces of French fifteenth-century painting, Enguerrand Charonton's *Crowning of the Virgin,* commissioned in 1453 by the Carthusian monks of Villeneuve-lès-Avignon, depicts the vision of St. Gregory while he was celebrating mass in the church of Santa Croce.[14]

Further evidence of Carthusian efforts to propagate their claims is found in England. According to Campbell Dodgson, the Man of Sorrows is the most frequently recurring subject among the English woodcuts of the later fifteenth century.[15] Dodgson already noticed the connection of several of them with the Carthusian Order, and Bertelli found more examples, the most important being an English fifteenth-century Carthusian manuscript [16] containing an extremely accurate rendering of the Santa Croce mosaic obviously intended to serve as a model for artists. At least one of the woodcuts reproduced by Dodgson, although technically quite awkward, shows how closely the model was followed.

Since Israhel van Meckenem's print is an equally faithful rendering of the Roman original, we must assume that he, too, had a similar drawing at his disposal, and that the Carthusian network was as active in Germany as it was in England.

The Gregorian Man of Sorrows was closely connected with the granting—and abuse—of indulgences, one of the major causes of the rift between Protestants and Catholics. Rutger de Venlo died eight years after Martin Luther nailed his famous proclamation to the doors of the *Schlosskirche* at Wittenberg. Although Cologne remained loyal to the Catholic cause, it is likely that the inscription beneath the print was eliminated because in view of the changing times, the connection with the pope's vision no longer seemed appropriate. The extraordinary benefits claimed for indulgences associated with the Gregorian Man of Sorrows—14,000 years for five *Pater Nosters* and five *Ave Marias* recited kneeling—were common knowledge and were obviously the reason why the subject was chosen by Rutger.[17]

The records kept by the *Stift* St. Gereon during the time Rutger served as a canon do not in the least reflect the great religious and social upheavals of the period. Life in St. Gereon evidently went on quite unchanged. Thus it is not surprising that a print that is essentially medieval would have appealed to Rutger.

The third state of Israhel van Meckenem's Man of Sorrows, though rare and possibly unique, is merely a shadow of what the artist had intended. Its value lies not in its esthetic merits but in the documentary evidence it provides.

NOTES

1. The print is described in *U.S. Library of Congress, Prints and Photographs Division ... Catalog of the Gardiner Greene Hubbard collection of engravings . . .* compiled by Arthur Jeffrey Parsons (Washington: Government Printing Office, 1905), p. 368, as an anonymous fifteenth-century Italian engraving, and its inscription was misread in the key words.

2. *Die Matrikel der Universität,* ed. Hermann Keussen, 3 vols. (Bonn: P. Hanstein, 1919–31), 1:54, 99; 2:99, 293, 815; 3:62.

3. Compare Gertrud Wegener, *Geschichte des Stiftes St. Ursula in Köln* (Cologne: H. Wamper, 1971).

4. Compare Johannes Christian Nattermann, *Die goldenen Heiligen, Geschichte des Stiftes St. Gereon zu Köln* (Cologne: Verlag Der Löwe, 1960). (Veröffentlichungen des Kölner Geschichtsvereins, 22). The author gives excerpts from the will of Canon Leonhard Maess, a contemporary of Rutger. It stipulated that immediately upon his death thirty masses be read, that during his obsequies sixty more be celebrated, and that memorial services be held in other Cologne churches; finally, that memorial masses be read once a month for a whole year at St. Gereon. The proliferation of memorial masses, requiring an inordinate number of priests, became such a serious problem that the Municipal Council of Cologne tried to impose a limitation on them, but without success. Compare pp. 355–6; for a similar case, compare p. 276.

5. The most recent and most complete bibliography on the subject can be found in Carlo Bertelli, "The Image of Pity in Santa Croce in Gerusalemme" in *Essays in the History of Art Presented to Rudolf Wittkower* (London: Phaidon, 1967), pp. 40–55. I want to thank Prof. Tilmann Buddensieg of the Freie Universität, Berlin, for having brought this essay to my attention.

6. Max Lehrs, *Geschichte und Kritischer Katalog des deutschen, niederländischen und französischen Kupferstichs im XV Jahrhundert,* 9 vols. (Vienna: Gesellschaft für vervielfältigende Kunst, 1908–34), 9.

7. I wish to thank Jean Adhémar, conservateur en chef of the Cabinet des Estampes, Bibliothèque nationale, Paris, for having supplied a photograph of this print and for his permission to publish it.

8. I wish to thank Fritz Koreny of the Graphische Sammlung Albertina in Vienna for his assistance. Dr. Koreny, who wrote his doctoral dissertation on Israhel van Meckenem, is preparing a book on the artist.

9. The prize he carried away on this visit was the finger of St. Catherine with the ring, which, according to legend, Christ himself had placed there. If some sources are to be believed, he bit off the finger from the hand. The relic can still be seen in the church of Santa Caterina which Raimondello built at Galatina, where he lived.

10. Bertelli, p. 51.

11. The interval was further reduced in 1389 to thirty-three years, the assumed length of the earthly life of Christ, until in 1470 Pope Paul II fixed the intervals at twenty-five years, as it has been ever since.

12. On the subject of Gregorian indulgences, compare Bertelli, p. 51, and Nikolaus Paulus, *Geschichte des Ablasses im Mittelalter*, 3 vols. (Paderborn: F. Schöningh, 1922–23), 3:294.

13. Bertelli, p. 41, refers to "the superstitious belief that the mosaic itself had been composed by Pope Gregory with his own hands, using fragments of bones of the martyrs (a tale which I myself heard related by a sacristan of our own days)."

14. Bertelli, p. 47.

15. Campbell Dodgson, "English Devotional Woodcuts of the late fifteenth Century, With Special Reference to Those in the Bodleian Library" in *The Walpole Society* 17 (1928–29): 95–100.

16. British Museum MS., Add 37049; Bertelli, p. 48.

17. The number of years allegedly granted varies between 14,000 years in Rome and 32,755 years in England. Compare P. Romuald Bauerreiss, "Der 'gregorianische' Schmerzensmann und das 'Sacramentum S. Gregorii' in Andechs" in *Studien und Mitteilungen zur Geschichte des Benediktiner Ordens*, N.F. 13, 1926, p. 61; Dodgson, p. 99; Paulus, *Geschichte des Ablasses*, 3:294. The careless handling of indulgences in the decades preceding the Reformation is particularly evident on two other Meckenem prints, both showing the Mass of St. Gregory: one promises 20,000 years of indulgences for seven *Pater Nosters* and seven *Aves* (Lehrs, No. 354); the other (Lehrs, No. 353) offers double the number of years for the same number of prayers.

The "Pembroke" Album of Chiaroscuros

BY ALAN M. FERN AND KAREN F. BEALL

Fifty years ago the Library of Congress purchased an album of color prints from a London dealer. On its golden anniversary in the Library, this album has become the object of considerable scholarly interest since a few of the prints it contains have turned out to be both scarce and important. Moreover, the album is associated with a distinguished and fascinating group of collectors. This would seem amply to justify our taking this occasion to publish a few notes about it and its contents in order to make this collection better known to scholars of printmaking.

It is not surprising that so little attention was paid to the album when it first arrived in the Library of Congress. Most of the woodcuts it contains were made in the first half of the sixteenth century in Italy, a period until recently out of fashion among art historians; today, Italian "Mannerist" artists are seen with new eyes, so that the work of the followers of Raphael and Michelangelo, Parmigianino and Beccafumi, is regarded as a powerful and fascinating development in late Renaissance art. Furthermore, half a century ago the woodcut was as little appreciated as a medium for original printmaking as were the Italian Mannerists as original artists. Photography had but recently supplanted wood engraving as the primary means for the reproduction of pictures in printed books and magazines, and the tremendous achievements of printmakers like Edvard Munch and Paul Gauguin in woodcut were barely recognized by writers on the graphic arts, who preferred the etchings of Charles Meryon or the drypoints of Anders Zorn.

Facing page: Chiaroscuro woodcut in three blocks by Girolamo Bolsi, depicting Bartolommeo Neroni's stage set for L'Ortensio, designed for a festival in Siena in 1560. Published by Andrea Andreani in 1589.

The History of Chiaroscuro Woodblock Prints

From the very beginning, the woodcut seems to have been condemned to play the double role of reproductive medium and original printmaking technique. When it first made its appearance in Europe, probably in the late fourteenth century, the woodcut was used for such utilitarian purposes as the production of patterned textiles and the illustration of broadsheets.[1] In the fifteenth century, Albrecht Dürer was one of the earliest artists to produce both intaglio and woodblock prints, and he seems to have had no scruple about turning the execution of his woodcuts over to professional engravers in contrast to his practice with etchings and engravings. As an adjunct to book production the profession of wood engraving enjoyed its own guild organization in the fifteenth century, and for 150 years rivaled engraving on metal as a lucrative occupation for the craftsman.

Printing in color[2] had been known since at least 1457, when the printers Fust and Schöffer produced two-color initials in the Mainz Psalter by a complex process. By the end of the century, several German artists had introduced color into their prints, sometimes through such simple devices as the use of colored papers or—like Erhard Ratdolt in the 1490s—through the use of several blocks successively printed in different colors. Hand coloring was a common way of enlivening printed pictures in the fifteenth century, and much of the earliest color printing imitated the "local color" of the hand-painted print.

Shortly after the beginning of the sixteenth century, however, a different approach was taken by a few German printmakers. The design was cut in wood to be printed in black, but a second block was also used, to be printed in a neutral or background color behind the key (or outline) block; highlights were cut away on this tint block so that the white of the paper served as a third color in the finished print. This process, which effectively imitated the appearance of the drawing on toned paper heightened with white paint, came to be called the chiaroscuro (or light-and-dark) print.

The new technique was almost immediately utilized for the reproduction of drawings by a few printmakers in Italy. Drawings were treasured as works of art, and the desire to possess reproductions of the works of great masters was as strong then as it is now; the chiaroscuro print was the Skira or Jaffe reproduction of the sixteenth century, and these prints were treasured by collectors who could not actually acquire drawings by all the artists they admired.

In 1516 the Venetian Senate received from Ugo da Carpi (ca. 1480–1523 or –1532) a petition for the grant of exclusive rights to the production of chiaroscuro prints.[3] In his petition, Ugo claimed that he had invented the

The chairoscuro woodcut of Pan, upper left on the facing page, and the drawing by Parmigianini, right on facing page, illustrate the way Italian artists adapted the original motifs of drawings to the medium of the woodcut. The print, probably by Ugo da Carpi, is no. 22 in the Pembroke Album, and the drawing is int he Caginet des dessins of the Louvre, Paris.

process, and although this was not strictly true he had in fact used the technique in a different fashion than had his German predecessors. Ugo da Carpi and the Italian chiaroscurists who followed him relied far less on a key block to define the composition of their prints. Instead, they built their pictures out of three or four successive tone blocks, achieving an effect closer to the subtle tonal modulation of a wash drawing than was the practice in Germany. Usually the blocks were printed in related colors (several shades of green, brown, or grey, for example), but occasionally, a striking effect was achieved through the use of startling contrasts of hue. As in the German prints, the tone of the paper shows through the background block, to serve as highlights.

Ugo da Carpi is the earliest, and possibly the most accomplished, of the artists represented in the Library's album, but the others are just as interesting. Domenico Beccafumi (1486–1551) was renowned as a painter and draftsman. Antonio da Trento (1508–50) was a brilliant craftsman and possibly a rogue.[4] Bartolommeo Coriolano (1599–1676) and Andrea Andreani (1540?–1623) were both important figures in the history of calligraphy as well as printmaking; Andreani republished prints made by a number of his predecessors after somehow acquiring their blocks (which he altered by inserting his own initials as a signature).[5]

All that has been said about the reproductive function of the chiaroscuro print should not be taken to imply that these were merely mindless copies. On the contrary, even though the original motifs of these prints—the composition, general distribution of light and dark, and the postures of the figures—were taken from the drawings of other artists, the printmakers were actually concerned with making an equivalent for the drawing rather than a facsimile. There was a conscious accommodation of the quality of the medium to the print being produced, and as a result many characteristics of the original drawing were altered in order to produce a handsome and eloquent print.

As the chiaroscuro print became more popular some artists even designed drawings expressly for production in this medium. Parmigianino, for example, is known to have organized a workshop devoted to the production of prints after his drawings; the drawings he intended for publication as chiaroscuros were made in broad areas of wash, while his pen and ink drawings were published as etchings and engravings.[6] In other instances, such direct supervision by the artist was not possible; the prints after Raphael's cartoons for the tapestries in the Sistine Chapel, for example, were published after Raphael's death and are so different from the drawings in scale, color, and dramatic impact that it is obvious the original artist never had this adaptation in mind. But the prints themselves are handsome and effective works of art, bearing testimony to the artistry of the printmaker.

Before turning to the album itself, it might be of interest to note that the technique of chiaroscuro printmaking continued to be practiced well into the eighteenth century, after which it was supplanted by the color aquatint, prints in the "crayon manner," and—finally—by photoengravings as a reproductive medium. Chiaroscuro has been revived as a medium for original printmaking in this century, by such artists as Charles Shannon and William Nicholson at the beginning of the century, and by Leonard Baskin today.

The technique of creating a chiaroscuro wood-cut, using several blocks printed in different colors, is illustrated by the individual proofs of each block and the final print shown below. Reproduced from J. M. Papillon's Traité historique et pratique de la gravure en bois *(volume 2, between pages 154 and 155). published in Paris in 1786 by P.-G. Simon.*

The "Pembroke" Album

In June 1918 the Library of Congress purchased item 148 in Maggs Brothers' catalog 364. This was described as "ENGRAVING IN CHIAROSCURO. A Remarkable Collection of 90 Original Engravings . . . by the Early Masters of the Art, comprising examples by Hugo de Carpi . . . Andreani . . . Coriolano . . . and others; the whole mounted in a large folio scrap book, *bound in old English red morocco gilt.* A most unusual collection of exceedingly rare and interesting engravings from the famous collection of the Earl of Pembroke." After a few more sentences of general description, the prints are listed except for "several which are not identified." [7]

This is almost accurate, but a number of other observations about the physi-

cal characteristics of the book might have been included. It is a collection of leaves 44.5 by 35 centimeters in size, in a binding about 2 centimeters larger in each dimension. On the spine is lettered: "CUT IN WOOD / THE 5 CHIE [evidently "Chief"; see below] MASTERS / VOL: VIII." On the lower left corner of the front of the binding is a sticker with the number 306 (a sales label, as we shall show in a moment). The end sheets are marbled paper, awkwardly pieced together (in keeping with the unsophisticated workmanship of the binding), and on the first leaf is written: "Vol. 8th. 32 Double prints taken out—1773—." In support of this are twenty-eight blank leaves from which prints have evidently been cut away, and a number of stubs of pages which were completely removed, virtually all of these at the end of the album. Actually, ninety one prints are in the album.

The paper used in the album carries a watermark consisting of a fleur-de-lis in a cartouche, surmounted by a crown, with the cipher "WR" beneath. C. M. Briquet associates the cipher with the successors to the firm of Wendelin Riehel of Strasbourg,[8] and the Baron del Marmol, who reproduces a similar watermark on plate 56 of his *Dictionnaire des Filigranes*,[9] dates it as following 1690. On the other side of each folio sheet is the watermark "VI" in open capitals.

Moreover, two of the prints (see list below) carry the collector's mark of Prosper Henry Lankrink (Lugt 2090);[10] otherwise, none of the prints bears an ownership mark of any kind.

The Puzzle of Provenance

The collection of the Earls of Pembroke was sold at auction at Sotheby's in London on July 5 and 6, 1917, and the album just described was lot 306 of the second day's sale.[11] It seems likely that Maggs acquired the book at that time, but how the prints came into the Pembroke collection—or how long they had been there—remains a matter for conjecture.

In the Pembroke sale were eighteen volumes of prints, in addition to a number of separate items, and fifteen of these albums were numbered (from I to XIV, with vol. XIII in two parts); three other albums were miscellaneous groups of engravings. Lot 306 is volume VIII; it remains for us to discover the present locations of the other albums. All the albums were described by Sotheby as "Mounted in old Folio Volumes (early part of the eighteenth century), whole-bound smooth red morocco, gilt back and sides."[12]

Spine of Pembroke Album.

The Pembroke family were statesmen and soldiers, patrons of the arts and collectors, and enjoyed connections with painters like Prosper Henry Lankrink and Sir Peter Lely, with Shakespeare, and with Oxford University.[13] At Wilton, the family seat near Salisbury, a distinguished collection had been amassed over the years, but portions of it seem to have been imperfectly inventoried. Part of the difficulty in tracing the lineage of the Library's album is that none of the works of graphic art at Wilton was cataloged up to the time of the sale (the remaining prints and drawings have been), and since the fifteenth Earl disapproved of the practice of marking prints, none of the items was imprinted with the Wilton Library stamp.[14]

One turns to earlier collections hoping for a clue to the presence of a large group of chiaroscuro prints that an earlier Lord Pembroke might have acquired, but here again records are inadequate for the purpose.

We know, for example, that at least two of the prints in the Library's album had been in the possession of Prosper Henry Lankrink (1628–92). Lankrink was a painter of German extraction and Netherlandish training who came to England as a young man.[15]

He was an assistant to Sir Peter Lely and an associate of Horace Walpole, who epitomized him as a good collector who "bought much at Lely's sale, for which he borrowed money of Mr. Austen; to discharge which debt Lankrink's collection was seized after his death, and sold. He went deep into the pleasures of that age, grew idle, and died in 1692, in Covent Garden, and was buried at his own request under the porch of that church."[16] Lankrink was not only a buyer at the Lely sale, he was one of the organizers of it in 1688. Although scarce, copies of the catalogs of the sales of Lely and Lankrink have survived and have been reprinted;[17] the paintings are listed by artist and title, but the prints and drawings possessed by these artist-collectors are not enumerated. Thus, it is impossible to say precisely where Lankrink acquired his chiaroscuro prints, whether Lely was the source (although his enthusiasm for Italian art makes this likely), and who purchased the prints at the Lankrink sales in 1693 and 1694. It is interesting to note in this connection that a number of the separate Italian engravings in the Pembroke sale are listed as coming from the Lely collection, evidently because these prints bore Lely's mark.

One of the later buyers of objects from the Lely and Lankrink sales was Hugh Howard (1675–1737), a painter of Irish origin who came to England in 1688, just at the time of the Lely auction, joined the party of the Earl of Pembroke who was then Minister Plenipotentiary to the Peace Conference in

Above, a drawing by Domenico Beccafumi in crayon and ink, heightened with white, depicting three figures variously described as river gods and as Old Testament personages, and above right, an engraved early state of the print based upon the drawing. Both are reproduced from the Delia E. Holden Collection in the Cleveland Museum of Art.

Rijswijk, Holland, and traveled on the Continent until 1700.[18] After his return to England he became a noted portrait painter who counted Pembroke among his patrons, enjoyed several royal posts, and became wealthy enough to amass a collection guided, as Frits Lugt says, by his excellent taste.

Lugt writes that in the Sotheby sale of December 12, 1873, and the week following, of the collection assembled by Howard and retained by his family for more than a century and a half, there were (among other prints) "une série presque complète des clairs-obscurs de da Carpi, Andreani, etc., une pièce non décrite par Bartsch." [19] Considering that in the Library's album, just before the pages bearing the prints, is written in an eighteenth-century hand: "Vol: VIII. The 5 Chief who Cut in Wood, and only after Great Italian Painters, all that they did both single and as Intire Books," it might be inferred that this inscription was the source for the claim by the describer of the Howard collection that it contained an "almost complete series" of the chiaroscurists. Actually, the group is anything but complete, although it is extensive; at least one of the prints, however, is in fact not described in Bartsch's catalog.

The date of the paper makes it almost impossible for Lankrink to have assembled the album, and the binding is clearly of early eighteenth-century manufacture. The album might have been assembled by Hugh Howard, but if this is true then Howard must have also put together the fourteen other albums in the Pembroke series, since these are numbered in sequence. One fact suggests that Howard did not do this.

Shown below is the final state of the print, in which tones have been added to the engraving by the chiaroscuro block. It is no. 49 in the Library's Pembroke Album.

Lugt writes of the albums of drawings sold in the 1917 Pembroke sale that they were "toujours conservés dans quatre albums reliés en maroquin, datés novembre 1772. Une inscription sur le quatrième dit que les dessins qu'il contient proviennent des trois autres 'to prevent injury by their being too crowded.'" [20] This sounds remarkably like the note (dated 1773) in the Library's album and would seem to suggest that, like the albums of drawings, this volume of prints was assembled according to normal procedure in the library at Wilton by the eighth, ninth, or tenth Earl of Pembroke. This is as far as we can go with certainty, given the evidence in our hands at this time.

The Prints

At the end of this article is appended a list that will at least provide tentative titles and attributions for the ninety one prints in the Pembroke Album. Although several scholars have recently published detailed research into the work of some of the artists and engravers who produced chiaroscuro prints, the entire field demands more thorough investigation. Some of the prints in the album have not been reconsidered since Adam Bartsch published his catalog in the early nineteenth century.

The list will show that Parmigianino is associated with more than a third of the prints in the collection, trailed by Guido Reni, Beccafumi, and Raphael among the "inventors" or original artists of the prints. Ugo da Carpi is the printmaker most fully represented, with more than twenty of his chiaroscuros in the album, followed by Coriolano with sixteen prints, mostly after Guido Reni.

The problem of attribution is not simplified by the presence of a number of prints bearing Andreani's monogram but which are known to exist in other states, bearing the signatures of other artists. These are identified in our list as "monogram of Andreani," but we have endeavored to locate the original printmaker as well. Prints in the album which also exist in a state bearing Andreani's monogram are described as "republished by Andreani."

The greater portion of the prints are explicitly religious or mythological in subject, but there are a number of intriguing exceptions—among them some of the scarcest prints in the album.

A group of figures by Beccafumi, for instance, is known in only one other example (in Siena) in this state. The drawing upon which the print is based and an early state of the print, without the tone block, are in the Cleveland Art Museum and have been published by Louise S. Richards.[21] The figures have been described as river gods and as Old Testament personages. There appears to be a relationship between these and Beccfumi's designs for the pavement of the Cathedral in Siena.

Another fascinating print in the album depicts the stage setting of *L'Ortensio,* designed for a ducal wedding festivity in 1560 (also in Siena) by Bartolommeo Neroni (called "Li Riccio"), and cut on wood by Girolamo Bolsi in 1589. We have located copies of this print only in the British Museum and in the Bertarelli Collection (Sforzesco Palace) in Milan; both of these copies carry a long inscription by Andreani, the publisher of the print, describing the subject and crediting the designer and engraver.

We have already mentioned the fact that these chiaroscuro woodcuts were adapted from a variety of sources. The Library's album includes three prints after Raphael's tapestries for the Sistine Chapel (or their designs, now in the Victoria and Albert Museum, London), and they provide a striking example of the broadening and simplification inherent in the translation from drawing to chiaroscuro print. Mary Pittaluga [22] has identified several of the drawings for other chiaroscuro prints, and has compared the prints derived from them in a critical article; even if one cannot agree with her that the prints are without merit in comparison with the drawings—perhaps the loss of subtlety is offset by a gain in robustness—it is valuable to be able to study the process of translation at first hand.

The Pembroke Album also contains several proofs of "key blocks," showing the design in black before the addition of the colored tint blocks to the finished print. These, too, are valuable tools to the student of printmaking, as are the several versions of the same subject (album numbers 46 and 47, for example), the reversed copies, and other variations on the same motif that can tell us much about how these prints were conceived.

The Miraculous Draught of Fishes, shown first as a cartoon in gouache over charcoal, done by Raphael for a tapestry in the Sistine Chapel, about 1516, and second as a chiaroscuro woodcut in three blocks by Ugo da Carpi. Measuring 10 feet 3½ inches by 13 feet 1 inch, the cartoon was too large to reverse by tracing it directly on the woodblock, as in the case of the Parmigianino drawing shown in this article. The cartoon is in the Victoria and Albert Museum in London, and the woodcut, which bears the monogram (1609) of Andrea Andreani, is no. 55 in the Pembroke Album.

This is a glimpse at a very rich collection of comparatively uncommon sixteenth-century prints. We are just beginning to learn more about them, and to be guided by our colleagues who have already studied this area more thoroughly than we. It is our hope that this listing of the prints in the Library's "Pembroke" Album may help to advance the study of chiaroscuro printmaking.

NOTES

1. *The First Century of Printmaking, 1400–1500* (Chicago: Art Institute of Chicago, 1941). *Les Plus Belles Gravures du Monde Occidental* (Munich, Paris, Amsterdam, Vienna: 1965–66), p. 5. Arthur M. Hind, *An Introduction to a History of the Woodcut* (London: Constable and Co., 1935); Pierre Gusman, *La Gravure sur Bois . . .*, 2 vols. (Paris: R. Roger et F. Chernoviz, 1916).

2. *Color in Prints*, edited by E. Haverkamp-Begemann [New Haven, Conn.: Yale University Art Gallery 1962; *Yale Art Gallery Bulletin* 27, no. 3, and 28, no. 1 (1962).] See also the many articles cited in the bibliographic notes to this catalog, and Jacob Kainen, *John Baptist Jackson* (Washington, D.C.: Smithsonian Institution, 1962; United States National Museum Bulletin no. 222), especially pp. 7–12.

3. Institut néerlandais, Paris, *Clairs-Obscurs*, exhibit catalog (Paris: 1965). See also *Color in Prints*, p. 13, and works cited in the bibliographic entry in this catalog above no. 10.

4. The drawings of Parmigianino were evidently so desirable that Antonio da Trento, who was then working under Parmigianino's direction in Bologna, disappeared about 1530 (according to Vasari) with a number of drawings as well as engraved copper plates and woodblocks; the printmaking materials were recovered, but the drawings—and Antonio—never reappeared. Giorgio Vasari, *Lives of the Most Eminent Painters*, vol. 5, (London: Philip Lee Warner for the Medici Society, 1913–14), pp. 249–50. See also S. J. Freedberg, *Parmigianino: His Works in Painting* (Cambridge, Mass.: Harvard University Press, 1950), p. 181. A. E. Popham, *The Drawings of Parmigianino* (London: Faber and Faber, 1953), pp. 35 and 47; and Konrad Oberhuber, *Parmigianino und sein Kreis* (Vienna: Albertina, 1963).

5. *Color in Prints*, p. 17, and Giovanni Copertini, *Il Parmigianino*, vol. 2, (Parma: Mario Fresching Editore, 1933–39), p. 45, n. 4.

6. Ibid., n. 11; Popham, p. 29.

7. Maggs Bros., *Incunabula . . . Manuscripts . . . Woodcut Illustrated Books of the XVth and XVIth Centuries*, catalog no. 364 (London: 1918), pp. 36–38.

8. C. M. Briquet, *Les Filigranes*, vol. 2, (Paris: Alphonse Picard et Fils [et al.], 1907), p. 395.

9. Baron F. del Marmol, *Dictionnaire des Filigranes* (Paris: Marchal et Billard, 1900).

10. Frits Lugt, *Les Marques des collections* (Amsterdam; Vereenigde Drukerijen, 1921), p. 386.

11 .Sotheby, Wilkinson, and Hodge, London, sale of July 5–6, 9–10, 1917; second day, p. 32.

12. Ibid., p. 21.

13. Frits Lugt *Les Marques des collections . . . Supplément* (The Hague: Martinus Nijhoff, 1956), pp. 377–378.

14. Ibid., p. 378.

15. Lugt, *Marques*, pp. 386–87.

16. Horace Walpole, *Anecdotes of Painting in England* (London: Ward, Lock and Co., [1879?], pp. 229–30.

17. "Sir Peter Lely's Collection," *The Burlington Magazine* 83 (August 1943) ; 185–91. Prints are only mentioned on page 188: "As also a great Quantity of Prints of *Mark Anthony,* and others the most Curious." Note by Henry and Margaret Ogden in *The Burlington Magazine* 84 (June 1944) :154. "P. H. Lankrink's Collection," *The Burlington Magazine* 86 (February 1945) :29–35. See also Lugt, *Repertoire des catalogues des ventes,* vol. 1, (The Hague: Martinus Nijhoff 1936), entry 142, and Lugt, *Marques*, pp. 388–89.

18. Lugt, *Marques*, p. 550.

19. Ibid.

20. Lugt, *Marques . . . Supplément*, p. 378.

21. Louise S. Richards, "River Gods' by Domenico Beccafumi," *The Bulletin of the Cleveland Museum of Art* 46 (February 1959) :24–29.

22. Mary Pittaluga, "Disegni del Parmigianino e Corrispondenti Chiaroscuri Cinquecenteschi," *Dedalo* (Milan and Rome) 9 (June 1928) :30–40.

Prints in the "Pembroke" Album

A Revised List by Alan M. Fern and Karen F. Beall

One of the purposes of a scholarly journal is to increase man's knowledge. In its silver anniversary issue of January 1969, the *Quarterly Journal of the Library of Congress* published an article on the "Pembroke" album of chiaroscuro woodcuts by Alan M. Fern and Karen F. Beall. The purpose of such articles frequently is to provoke responses in the hope of bringing additional information to light. Thus, the list below is a revised version of the one that accompanied the original article. Most of the corrections and additions have been suggested by Dr. Bertha H. Wiles, and we are grateful to her for allowing them to be incorporated in this republication.

ABBREVIATIONS

B	Bartsch, Adam. Le Peintre-Graveur. . . . Leipzig, 1886, vol. 12 is intended unless otherwise noted.
Coll. mark:	Collector's mark.
M.	Meyer, Julius. Allgemeines Künstler-Lexikon. . . . Leipzig, 1872, vol. 1 (Andrea Andreani) ; vol. 3 (Domenico Beccafumi) .
O.	Oberhuber, Konrad. Parmigianino und sein Kreis. [Exhibition catalog] Vienna, Graphische Sammlung Albertina, 1963.
P.	Passavant, J. D. Le Peintre-Graveur. Leipzig, 1964, vol. 6.
Paris	Paris, Institut Néerlandais. Clairsobscurs, gravures sur bois imprimées en couleurs de 1500 à 1800. . . . [Exhibition catalog] Paris, Rotterdam, 1965–1966.
S.	Servolini, Luigi. Ugo da Carpi. In Rivista d'Arte, July–September 1929, p. [297]–319.
Sanminiatelli	Sanminiatelli, Donato. Domenico Beccafumi. Milan, 1967.

PRINTS

1. *The death of Ananias*. Ugo da Carpi, after Raphael Sanzio. B. II, 27 (second state) ; S., p. 300, no. 10.

2. *Christ healing the paralytic man*. Attributed to Nicolà Vicentino, after Perino del Vaga (earlier said to have been after Francesco Mazzola, called il Parmigianino) . Coll. mark: Lankrink (Lugt 2090). B. II, 14; P., p. 220, no. 15; Paris, 151. See J. A. Gere in *The Burlington Magazine*, 102: 9ff. (January 1960) , where this is identified with frescoes, now lost, on the lower walls of the Massimi Chapel, Sta. Trinitá dei Monti, Rome.

3. *The flight into Egypt*. Anonymous, after Raphael. Coll. mark: Lankrink (Lugt 2090). B. II, 9.

4. *Martha and Mary Magdalene before Christ*. Anonymous, after G. F. Penni (earlier attributed to Raphael) . B. II, 12; P., p. 220, no. 12. This design was used for a lunette on the upper walls of the Massimi Chapel (see no. 2 above) ; mentioned in H. Voss, *Die Malerei der Spätrenaissance in Rom und Florenz* (Berlin, 1920) I, p. 63.

5. *Diogenes with the featherless cock*. Ugo, probably after Parmigianino. B. VI, 10 (without inscription) ; Paris, 86; S., p. 310, no. 21; O., 91 (Oberhuber mentions Vasari's unreliable attribution of the print to Parmigianino) .

6. *Venus and cupids*. Ugo, after Baldassare Peruzzi (earlier attributed to Raphael) . B. VII, 3. See Sidney Freedberg, *Painting of the High Renaissance in Rome and Florence* (Cambridge,

Mass., 1961) I, p. 566; II, fig. 685 on p. 502, where this is identified with one of the decorations in the Villa Madama, Rome.

7. *The cardinal and the doctor.* Ugo, after Raphael. B. X, 6; p. 309, no. 1.

8. *Temperance.* Attributed to Vicentino, republished by Andreani. B. VIII, 5; Paris, 156; M. vol. 1, 726, no. 17 (first state) ; O., 109.

9. *Hope.* Attributed to Vicentino, after Parmigianino, published by Andreani. B. VIII, 2; M. vol. 1, p. 726, no. 15 (first state) ; O., 106.

10. *Sibyl reading a book.* Ugo, after Raphael. B. V, 6; S., p. 298, no. 5.

11. *Raphael and his beloved.* Ugo, after Raphael. B. IX, 3.

12. *Man seated, seen from behind.* Antonio da Trento, after Parmigianino. B. X, 13. Werner Schade in *Italienische Farbenholzschitte des 16 bis 18 Jahrhunderts* (Weimar, Schlossmuseum, 1957) , p. 16, nos. 31 and 32, identifies the theme of this print as Narcissus gazing at his reflection while Echo is turned to stone. A. E. Popham has rejected this

13. *The Virgin, Child and St. John.* Anonymous, after Parmigianino. B. III, 12; Paris, 43.

14. *The adoration of the Magi.* Attributed to Vicentino, after Parmigianino. B. II, 2 (first state) .

15. *The Virgin, St. Sebastian and a holy bishop.* Ugo, after Parmigianino (not mentioned by Servolini) . B. III, 26 (first state) ; O., 90.

16. *The entombment.* Andreani, after Raffaelino de Reggio. LC impression from single block and carries no inscription; although derived from the same source as no. 58 in the album, this is a different print and may not have been intended as a chiaroscuro key-block.

17. *Saints Peter and John curing the sick.* Anonymous, after Raphael. B. IV, 27.

18. *The marriage of St. Catherine.* Anonymous, after Correggio. B. III, 19. This is not precisely a chiaroscuro print. The color suggests that it may come from the workshop of the Remondini in Bassano and may not be the print cited by Bartsch.

19. *The resurrection.* Ugo, after Raphael. B. II, 26; Paris, 75; S., p. 304, no. 18.

20. *St. Peter preaching the gospel.* Ugo, after Polidoro da Caravaggio. B. IV, 25; Paris, 80; S., p. 309, no. 4; O., 0.80.

21. *Apollo and Marsyas.* Probably Ugo, after Parmigianino. B. VII, 24 (second subject, first state) ; Paris 94; S., p. 313, no. 25; O., 95. This print and no. 22 were evidently prints from the same block, and proofs exist with both subjects on the same sheet. Although always given this title, the print is actually the contest of Apollo and Pan, according to Emmanuel Winternitz (in conversation with Morgan Library curator) .

22. *Pan.* Probably Ugo, after Parmigianino. B. VII, 24 (first subject, first state) .

23. *Charity.* Perhaps Vicentino, after Parmigianino, republished by Andreani. B. VIII, 3; Paris, 152; M. vol. 1, p. 726, no. 14 (first state) ; O., 107.

24. *Fortitude.* Vicentino or Antonio da Trento, after Parmigianino. B. VIII, 7 (probably Antonio da Trento) ; O., 108 (Vicentino?) . Ascribed to Ugo by Pittaluga.

25. *The Virgin in an oval.* Anonymous, after Parmigianino. B. III, 4; Paris, 42.

26. *The rest on the flight into Egypt.* Anonymous, after Antonio Campi da Cremona (or his circle) . B. II, 10; O., 188.

27. *The sacrifice of Abraham.* Anonymous, after Parmigianino. B. I, 3; Paris, 39.

28. *Saints Peter and John.* Probably Ugo, after Parmigianino, republished by Andreani. B. IV, 26; M. vol. 1, p. 725, no. 8 (first state) ; S., p. 309, no. 5.

29. *Diana hunting the stag*. Antonio da Trento or Vicentino, after Parmigianino. B. VII, 10; O., 131.

30. *The sacrifice*. Anonymous, after Parmigianino. B. X, 21. The actual subject is Mutius Scaevola's ordeal by fire. Meyer (vol. 3, p. 158, no. 28) gives this print to Antonio da Trento.

31. *Faith*. Attributed variously to Ugo and Vicentino, after Parmigianino, republished by Andreani. B. VIII, 1; M. vol. 1, p. 726, no. 13 (first state) ; O., 105.

32. *Prudence*. Attributed variously to Ugo and Vicentino, after Parmigianino, republished by Andreani. B. VII, 6; Paris, 152; M. vol. 1, p. 726, no. 18 (first state) ; O., 110.

33. *Fortitude*. Attributed variously to Ugo and Vicentino, after Parmigianino, republished by Andreani. B. VIII, 4; Paris, 152; M. vol. 1, p. 726, no. 16 (first state) .

34. *The philosopher*. Antonio da Trento, after Parmigianino. B. X, 1; O., 139.

35. *The philosopher Diogenes and the allegory of astronomy*. Probably Antonio da Trento, after Parmigianino. B. VIII, 16; O., 138.

36. *The marriage of St. Catherine*. Not in Bartsch.

37. *The Holy Family with St. Margaret and a bishop*. Possibly Antonio da Trento, after Parmigianino, republished by Andreani. B. III, 24 (first state) ; Paris, 136; M. vol. 1, p. 725, no. 9, (first state) ; O., 140.

38. *St. John*. Probably Antonio da Trento, after Parmigianino. B. IV, 4; O., 123.

39. *Pallas*. Probably Antonio da Trento, after Parmigianino. B. VII, 23; O., 132.

40. *An apostle (Paul?)*. Domenico Beccafumi. B. IV, 22; P., p. 151, no. 8; M. vol. 3, p. 258, no. 16; Sanminiatelli, 12.

41. *St. Philip (or Andrew?)*. Beccafumi. B. IV, 13; P., p. 151, no. 6; M. vol. 3, p. 258, no. 13 (St. Andrew) ; Sanminiatelli, 9.

42. *An apostle*. Beccafumi. B. IV, 15; P., p. 151, no. 7; M. vol. 3, 258, no. 15; San-miniatelli, 11.

43. *St. Peter*. Beccafumi. B. IV, 14; P., p. 150, no. 5; M. vol. 3, p. 258, no. 12; San-miniatelli, 10.

44. *St. Philip*. Beccafumi. B. IV, 23; M. vol. 3, p. 258, no. 14; Sanminiatelli, 6.

45. *A philosopher*. Beccafumi,, B. X, 16; M. vol. 3, p. 258, no. 19; Sanminiatelli, 7.

46. *Two nude men: one standing, one reclining*. Engraving. Beccafumi. Not in Bartsch. P., p. 149–150, no. 4; M. vol. 3, p. 257, no. 4; Sanminiatelli, 2.

47. Same as above. Engraving and 1 chiaroscuro woodblock.

48. *Four doctors of the church(?)*. Attributed to Baccafumi. B. IV, 35; Paris, 45; M. vol. 3, p. 258, no. 21; Sanminiatelli, 3.

49. *Three male figures*. Engraving and chiaroscuro woodblock. Beccafumi. Not in Bartsch. M. vol. 3, p. 257, no. 5; Sanminiatelli, 4. Only one other copy of this print in this state is known; the drawing and an impression of the engraved key-plate are in the Cleveland Museum of Art. Sometimes called "River Gods," the design appears related to the pavements in the Cathedral of Siena.

50. *The Virgin, Child, and saints*. Andreani, after Ligozzi. B. III, 27, (first state) ; M. vol. 1, p. 720, no. 24 (first state) .

51. *Christ at the table of Simon the Pharisee*. Ugo, after G. F. Penni (earlier attributed to Raphael) , monogram of Andreani. B. II, 17; Paris, 73; M. vol. 1, p. 725, no. 6 (second state) ; S., p. 304, no. 16. See note for no. 4 in the album.

52. *Christ curing the lepers.* Vicentino, after Parmigianino, monogram of Andreani. B. II, 15; M. vol. 1, p. 725, no. 5 (second state); O., 101.

53. *Eve after the fall.* Andreani, after Beccafumi. B. I, 1; P., p. 220, no. 1; Paris, 46; M. vol. 1, p. 716, no. 1.

54. *The Virgin and Child surrounded by saints and kneeling donor.* Alessandro Gandini, after Parmigianino (sometimes attributed to Girolamo da Carpi rather than Parmigianino), monogram of Andreani. B. III, 25; Paris, 122; M. vol. 1, p. 725, no. 10 (second state); O., 142.

55. *The miraculous draught of fishes.* Ugo, after Raphael, monogram of Andreani. B. II, 13 (second state); Paris, 71; M. vol. 1, p. 725, no. 7.

56. *Surprise.* Probably Ugo (possibly Vicentino), after Parmigianino, monogram of Andreani. B. X, 10 (third state); P., p. 222, no. 10; Paris, 98; S., p. 304, no. 20; O., 94. The subject of the print is possibly Achaemenides surrendering to the Trojans on Aeneas' ship. See Bertha H. Wiles in *Museum Studies I* (Chicago, Art Institute of Chicago, 1966), p. 96 ff.

57. *The adoration of the Magi.* Ugo or Vicentino, after Parmigianino, monogram of Andreani. B. II, 2; M. vol. 1, p. 724, no. 3 (second state); O., 98.

58. *The entombment.* Andreani, after Raffaelino de Reggio. B. II, 24; Paris, 49; M. vol. 1, p. 718, no. 16. (See no. 16 in the album.)

59. *Circe.* Ugo after Parmigianino, republished by Andreani. B. VIII, 6; M. vol. 1, p. 726, no. 24.

60. *Circe.* Ugo, after Parmigianino, monogram of Andreani. B. VII, 8; M. vol. 1, p. 726, no. 25.

61. *Nymphs bathing.* Ugo, after Parmigianino, monogram of Andreani. B. VII, 22; Paris, 89; M. vol. 1, p. 726, no. 22 (second state); S., p. 304, no. 19; O., 93.

62. *Mutius Scaevola.* Andreani, after Balthasar Peruzzi. B. VI, 7; Paris, 58; M. vol. 1, p. 727, no. 27.

63. *St. Cecilia,* Antonio da Trento, after Parmigianino, monogram of Andreani. B. IV, 37; M. vol. 1, p. 725, no. 12 (second state); O., 120.

64. *Temperance.* Possibly Vicentino, after Parmigianino, monogram of Andreani. B. VIII, 5; M. vol. 1, p. 726, no. 12 (second state); O., 109.

65. *Ritual in honor of Psyche.* Probably by Nicolà Vicentino, after Francesco Salviati, monogram of Andreani. B. VII, 26 (second state); P., p. 222, no. 26; Paris, 141; M. vol. 1, p. 726, no. 21 (second state). This is related to a famous painting (now lost) on the ceiling of the Palazzo Grimani, Venice. See Iris H. Cheney in *Art Bulletin,* 45: 341 (1963).

66. *Jason returning with the golden fleece.* Possibly Ugo, after Parmigianino, monogram of Andreani. B. VII, 19; Paris, 88; M. vol. 1, p. 726, no. 26.

67. *Virtue.* Andreani, after Jacopo Ligozzi. B. VIII, 9; M. vol. 1, p. 720, no. 25 (LC without inscription in lower right corner).

68. *Stage design for L'Ortensio, 1589.* Girolamo Bolsi, after Bartolomeo Neroni. B. X, 29; M. vol. 1, p. 724, no. 38. This impression lacks the long inscription, which connects the print with Andreani, present in the copies in the British Museum and in the Raccolta Bertarelli, Milan.

69. *The Tiburtine Sibyl and the Emperor Augustus.* Antonio da Trento, after Parmigianino. B. V, 7; Paris, 133; O., 111.

70. *Ceiling with three angels.* Ugo, after Giulio Romano. B. X, 25; S., p. 309, no. 2.

71. *The Blessed Virgin.* Anonymous (possibly by Andreani), after Francesco Vanni. B. III, 11; M. vol. 1, p. 718, no. 9.

72. *Herodiade.* Bartolomeo Coriolano, after Guido Reni. B. II, 29 (third state).

73. *Christ carrying the cross.* Andreani, after Alessandro Casolani. B. II, 21; Paris 48; M. p. 718, no. 12.

74. *The Virgin, Child, and a bishop.* Andreani, after Alessandro Casolani. B. III, 22; Paris, 51; M. vol. 1, p. 718, no. 12.

75. *St. Jerome.* Bartolomeo Coriolano, after Guido Reni. B. IV, 33.

76. *Study of a giant.* Bartolomeo Coriolano, after Guido Reni, B. VII, 13.

77. *Sibyl holding a tablet.* Bartolomeo Coriolano, after Guido Reni. B. V, 5; Paris, 112.

78. *Sibyl.* Bartolomeo Coriolano, after Guido Reni. B. V, 3; Paris, 110.

79. *Sibyl.* Bartolomeo Coriolano, after Guido Reni. B. V, 4; Paris, 111.

80. *Sibyl.* Bartolomeo Coriolano, after Guido Reni. B. V, 2; Paris, 109.

81. *The Virgin and Child.* Bartolomeo Coriolano, after Guido Reni. B. III, 5 (third state).

82. *The poet Aretino.* Anonymous, after Titian. B. X, 5. See Fabio Mauroner, *Le incisioni di Tiziano* (Padua, 1943), p. 44, no. 10, pl. 25; engraved as a book frontispiece in Venice in 1537, the woodcut is attributed by Mauroner to Francesco Marcolini. It appeared in later books and also as a chiaroscuro.

83. *The Virgin, Child, and St. John the Baptist.* Bartolomeo Coriolano, Guido Reni. B. III, 20 (third state).

84. *The Virgin and Child.* Bartolomeo Coriolano, after Guido Reni. Reverse of previous print.

85. *S. Carlo Borromeo.* Giovanni Battista Coriolano. Single block. B. vol. 19, p. 67, no. 2, with letters not described in Bartsch.

86. *The Virgin and Child.* Bartolomeo Coriolano, after Guido Reni. Same as no 84, with minor changes including inscriptions.

87. *Head of the Virgin.* Bartolomeo Coriolano, after Guido Reni. B. III, 3.

88. *The Virgin and Child.* Bartolomeo Coriolano, after Guido Reni.

89. *Landscape (with hermit or saint in prayer).* Bartolomeo Coriolano. (Reverse adaptation of print by Hendrik Goltzius; Paris, 243 and 245; Hollstein, 381.)

90. *The Infant Christ prefiguring the Passion.* B. X, 23, anonymous, after Guido Reni (unsigned in Bartsch). This is apparently an unpublished state with signatures at left and right. Bartsch describes the cross on which the infant lies as a "cushion." Dr. B. H. Wiles suggests that the letters at lower left might be "BFC" intertwined, for "Bartolomeo Coriolano fecit," but remains uncertain about the meaning of the letters at the right.

91. *Head of cupid.* Bartolomeo Coriolano, after Guido Reni. B. VII, 2.

Old Master Prints: Elias Holl the Younger

BY EDGAR BREITENBACH

So many of the artist prints acquired by the Library are of recent origin that it is sometimes forgotten how rich are the collections of old master prints. Indeed, the Library of Congress began its serious acquisition of prints with the excellent Rembrandts, Dürers, and other works from the fifteenth through the eighteenth century given by Mrs. Gardiner Greene Hubbard.

This year one of our major print acquisitions was a group of twelve etchings of the greatest rarity done in 1638 by Elias Holl the Younger (1611–57), which were found in the stock of an important New York dealer.

Today photography has taken over the task of describing the world and its activities, leaving to the other art forms a more imaginative, aesthetic role; but before photography came into general use in the 1840s, the print had both a documentary and an aesthetic function. These little etchings by Holl, showing as they do the use of tools, the appearance of costumes, plants, and animals and the everyday activities of people, nicely exemplify this dual function.

Holl's prints show the twelve months of the year, each plate being devoted to a single month and showing a peasant performing some task appropriate to that month. Only in the month of May is the activity frivolous; here the lute player seems to embody the relaxation and courtliness of spring in full bloom. Otherwise, the activities are all connected with farming or husbandry.

On all twelve prints the horizon is low, and the empty space above is filled with an engraved ornament. Some ornaments bear a vague resemblance to plants, fruits, or flowers, while others are abstract decorative motifs that defy

Following 5 pages: Designs for the last twelve months of the year by Elias Holl the Younger.

identification. The stiff, controlled engraving technique (similar to that used in making niello plates, in which metal is incised with a design and the incisions filled with a rich black compound) contrasts strikingly with the free drawing of the etched scenes in the lower part of the prints.

That this group of prints is exceedingly rare is demonstrated by the fact that Holl's biographer, Albert Hämmerle, was able to see only two sets of the prints when he wrote his article on Holl in 1930.[1] One set was found in the Germanisches National Museum in Nürnberg, the other in the Museum für Kunst und Industrie in Vienna. Hämmerle mentioned the existence of a third set of prints, which had been described to him but which he had never seen.

This set differed from the others in one respect only: the name of the publisher, Paulus Fürst, did not appear in its usual place under the word "Ianuarious" on the first print, and therefore Hämmerle assumed these prints to be proofs taken before the publisher's name was engraved. The description of this "proof" set perfectly fits the set of prints just acquired by the Library of Congress, and these prints bear the stamp of the famous collection of the Princes of Waldburg-Wolfegg (Lugt 2542), which was assembled in the seventeenth century and from which prints were sold in 1901. Possibly, the prints we have just acquired were released in the 1901 sale, but the more recent owners of the prints are not recorded.[2]

From the title page, which is not included in our proofs but is present in the complete copies in Nürnberg and Vienna, we can learn the date of the prints (1638) and the purpose of publication: to provide models for "goldsmiths, painters and other devotees of the arts." [3] Our series, therefore, belongs to the vast body of ornament prints, a type of publication in which Paulus Fürst specialized. Goldsmiths and other craftsmen such as those who decorated firearms with silver inlay and cabinetmakers were invited to use the floral ornaments, while painters and printmakers might derive inspiration from the representation of the months.

The title page reveals another interesting fact. Crowning the German text

and within the floral cartouche which surrounds it are two large capital letters CR. These are the initials of Christian Richter of Altenburg, whose identical series, in reverse, was published by Peter Isselburgk seven years earlier, in 1631. Such piracy was common in the baroque age, but one wonders whether Elias Holl and his publisher realized the significance of the initials CR, which could so easily have been replaced by Holl's own.

On both Richter's and Holl's title pages the cartouche is surmounted by a device in French. Written in cursive letters, it reads: "Tout avec le temps." This leaves open the possibility that even Richter might not be the inventor, but might in turn have copied from a French or Flemish source.

Elias Holl the Younger is only a minor artist. Hämmerle in 1930 was unable to cite a single painting by Holl. All Hämmerle knew of his work, apart from his Twelve Months, was a drawing, a not too significant landscape reminiscent of Dutch models. Yet Holl deserves some attention by virtue of the fact that he was the son of a famous father. Elias Holl the Elder was one of the outstanding German architects during the first half of the seventeenth century. Official architect for the municipal government of Augsburg, he designed many public buildings in the style of the Late Renaissance which are landmarks of the city to this day.

Life in Augsburg was precarious during the period of religious strife. Al-

though the city government was in Protestant hands, there was also a powerful Catholic bishop within the walls who held one of the oldest sees in Germany. When the Catholic League was temporarily successful in 1630, the older Elias Holl suffered many indignities, the greatest of which was his removal from office. Five years later the situation was even more critical. With the death of Gustaf Adolf at the battle of Lützen (1632) the Protestants had lost their leader. In April of 1635 the Swedish defenders of beleaguered Augsburg were ready to withdraw and to turn the city over to the emperor. The elder Holl may have thought of emigration but decided against it because of his age and of his heavy family responsibilities. Fearing for the safety of his three grown sons, who

Old Master Prints: Elias Holl the Younger | 35

might have been seized as hostages or pressed into military service for the emperor, however, he arranged for their escape. In the year 1635 he entered the following passage in the family record, which is our main source of information concerning his son Elias:

> Anno 1635, as the city [Augsburg] surrendered and went back to the Emperor, my three sons, Elias the painter, Jeronimus the goldsmith and Hans, the journeyman-cabinetmaker, left on Wednesday, 28th of May, together with the Swedish Commander of the Old Blue Finnish Regiment, Hans Jorg aus dem Winckhel. All three sons were well provided with equipment and food . . . the commander has promised me that he will provide sleeping quarters for my three sons in the same lodgings as the Lieutenant Captain, until they have reached Erfurt safely. After which they can seek to carry on their trades wherever they please. To this end they would be given a pass and safe-conduct. Although they suffered great hardship owing to the inclemency of the weather, they reached Leipzig in safety, but all suffered sore feet.

Little is known of Holl's life during the years he spent as a refugee from his native city. Hämmerle assumes that he lived for some time in Leipzig, perhaps working for Hans Jacob Gabler, another refugee from Augsburg. In 1638, and probably for several years, he was in the employ of the publisher Paulus Fürst in Nürnberg. Apart from ornament prints, the first published numerous illustrated pamphlets on political and cultural topics. None of the illustrations bears the signature of an artist, but some may well be the work of Elias Holl. In 1646 the elder Holl died, leaving two houses to his family. This inheritance, together with a new climate of religious tolerance after the peace treaty of Münster in 1648, may have persuaded Holl to return to his home town around 1650. He married in the following year and died in 1657, in the forty-sixth year of his life.

NOTES

1. *Zeitschrift für das Schwäbische Museum,* 1930, p. 11–17.

2. Since these lines were written, two more sets became known to us, one lacking the title page, but with the publisher's line on the representation for January, in the print collection of the British Museum in London; the other is in the Graphische Sammlung in Munich. This copy, acquired in 1959 at a Karl & Faber auction, is identical with ours in that it lacks the title page and the publisher's name.

3. XII Monatsbüchlein Vor die Goltschmidt, Mahler, vnd dergleichen Liebhaber. Nürnberg, Paulus Fürst excudit 1638.

Joueur de Marionnettes. Plate 63 from Carle Vernet's *Cris de Paris* (ca. 1820–22).

Street Cries in Pictures

BY KAREN F. BEALL

From Tutchland I come with my light wares all laden,
To happy Columbia in summer's gay bloom,
Then listen fair lady and pretty young maiden,
Oh buy of the wand'ring Bavarian a broom.
Buy a broom, buy a broom,
Oh buy fo' the wand'ring Bavarian a broom.
To brush away insects that sometimes annoy you,
You'll find it quite handy to use night and day,
And what better exercise pray can employ you,
Than to sweep all vexatious intruders away.
Buy a broom, buy a broom,
And sweep all vexatious intruders away.

This charming song lithographed and published in 1828 or 1829 to the tune of the familiar *Ach du lieber Augustin* stands as evidence of the appeal the street crier had for the people. Although later in the century the ambulatory tradesmen largely disappear, the tradition is one of many centuries' duration.

The street cry has never really been studied as a pictorial art from, although histories of the cries of Paris and London were written in the last century. The single figures of the criers looming large in simplified settings are very much like the popular costume prints dating from the fifteenth and sixteenth centuries.

The street cry has never really been studied as a pictorial art form, although who earns his living by walking the streets selling his wares or providing a service necessary to the community. Pictorial representations of these people enjoyed a universal popularity. In this brief essay only a glimpse into the nature of these pictures in Europe and the United States will be attempted, although Latin American and Far Eastern examples are also known. At the end is a list of pertinent material in the Library.

Street names on a map of central Paris in the year 1292 revealed at once the influence and localization of the trades in city life. Streets named for the ironmonger, the saddler, and the butcher tell of the importance of the markets.[1] The same could be said for other medieval cities, for as soon as people began to live together in large numbers each man began advertising his goods or the service he rendered. With the growth of the cities and the increasing influence of the guilds toward the end of the fifteenth century a greater interest in secular subjects and their representation developed.

Sometime before illustrations were feasible, street cries themselves made their appearance in literature. A little poem *Crieries de Paris* by Guillaume de la Villeneuve appeared at the end of the thirteenth century, and *Le livre des mestiers* by Etienne Boileau contains examples from the same period.[2] In England in the following century William Langland introduced the cry of the "cokes and here knaves" in his prologue to *Piers Plowman:* [3]

Hote pyes, hote!
Goode gees and grys, ga we dyne, ga we!

This cry was heard with slight variation for four centuries.

Hawkers and vendors also appear in another poem of about the same period, formerly attributed to John Lydgate. Entitled *London Lickpenny,* it records the journey of a poor Kentishman through the streets of London.[4]

In to london I gan me hy
Of al the lond it bearethe the prise
Hot pescods, one gan cry

The broom girl from the sheet music Buy a Broom, in the Prints and Photographs Division.

Strabery rype, and chery in the ryse
One bad me come nere and by some spice
Pepar and saffron they gan me bede
Clove, grayns, and flowre of rise
For lacke of money I might not spede

Ballads often included the cries and occasionally the broadsheets carried representations of the criers. *The Famous Rat-Catcher* of about 1615 is a surviving example in the Pepysian Library, Cambridge. At one time the ballad singers were the carriers of news, but after the newspaper came into existence about 1600 the ballad took on a new and more romantic flavor. The importance of music in the street noises, however, cannot be overemphasized. In London, it has been said that the vendors were recognized by the sounds rather than the words uttered, and this may well have been true elsewhere. Yet the words provide a curious glance into language and changing customs. The cry of the seller of rushes, which the poor bought to strew on the floor in lieu of carpets, suggests the origin of the phrase "not worth a rush," used to describe something without value.[5]

During the sixteenth century the theater—the commedia dell'arte, and somewhat later the antimasques—offered opportunities for the appearance of the street tradesmen. Winifred Smith in her thesis tells us that "The Italian street scene seems to have been a norm for improvisd comedies from the latter part of the sixteenth to at least the middle of the seventeenth century." [6] It is not surprising therefore to find mongers in some of the designs for the plays. The so-called *Recueil de Fossard,* from the sixteenth century, contains a print of a milkmaid; Inigo Jones made drawings, including the well-known sketch of a seller of mouse traps, in connection with a performance in 1683 of Sir William Davenant's *Britannia Triumphans.*

The appearance of criers in theatrical productions remained popular for centuries—le Théâtre des Variétés in Paris performed *Les Cris de Paris* in 1822; more than a century later George Gershwin included street sellers in his opera *Porgy and Bess.*

The earliest pictorial representations occurred almost simultaneously in Italy and France. Giovanni Antonio da Brescia engraved a milkman, about 1475, which bears the inscription "late done late frescha" (milk, ladies, fresh milk). There is an anonymous set of Paris cries dating from the late fifteenth or early sixteenth century in the Bibliothèque de l'Arsenal, Paris. These examples con-

The famous Ratketcher, with his trauels into France, and of his returne to London.

To the tune of *the iouiall Tinker*.

I   THere was a rare Rat-catcher,
      Did about the Country wander,
  The soundest blade of all his trade,
  Or I should him deeply slaunder:
      For still would he cry, a Ratt tat tat ,
      tara rat, euer:
      To catch a Mouse, or to carouse,
      such a Ratter I saw neuer.

A page from a volume edited by Hyder E. Rollins, A Pepysian Garland; Black-Letter Broadside Ballads of the Years 1595–1639, Chiefly from the Collection of Samuel Pepys, *published by Cambridge University Press in 1922.*

Above: The milkman, engraved about 1475 by Giovanni Antonio da Brescia. Reproduced from Arthur M. Hind's Early Italian Engraving; a Critical Catalogue, *volume 6, published for the National Gallery of Art, Washington, by Bernard Quaritch Ltd., London, 1948.*

stitute the beginning of an unbroken tradition of pictorial cries in the two countries lasting well into the nineteenth century. Even as late as 1954 a little book, *Paris des Rues,* was published in France. During the seventeenth the *London Cries* were illustrated for the first time.

In the eighteenth century when people were travelling more and thereby developing a curiosity about the costumes and customs of other countries, prints of the cries enjoyed their greatest popularity. This is attested to by the great number of sets and subsequent editions of many of them. Publishers, realizing their market, translated the verses or captions into other languages.

The subject was confined to France, Italy, and England until the middle of the eighteenth century when series began cropping up elsewhere. First came Switzerland, Austria, Russia, Germany, and the United States, followed after the turn of the century by Denmark, Belgium, Holland, Spain, and Portugal.

Aside from England, France, and Italy, the earliest known literary references are to be found in Germany where the street vendors, particularly in Hamburg, were well known. In 1725 Johann Philipp Präetorius introduced a chorus of cries at the beginning and end of his musicals *Der Hamburger Jahrmarkt* and *Die Hamburger Schlachtzeit*—but the prints came later.[7] One of the largest sets known is from Hamburg consisting of 120 plates by Christoffer Suhr first published in 1808. This set is prefaced by an essay by the Lutheran clergyman K. J. H. Hübbe, on the literary and musical background of the city's cries. This antiquarian viewpoint is apparently a unique one of the time.

New sets appeared well into the nineteenth century until the industrial revolution so changed society that the colorful hawker was no longer a necessary member of society.

The earliest series owned by the Library of Congress may well be the most famous one ever produced. It is Annibale Carracci's *Diverse Figure,* later called *Le Arti di Bologna.* Before leaving his native Bologna for Rome in 1595, Carracci made seventy-five drawings of the street trades, which were bound into a book. The story of these cries is related by Giovanni Atanasio Mosini in his preface to the 1646 edition of Simon Guillain's engravings of them. Before they left the Carracci workshop they were used as samples by the students for their exercises in draftsmanship. The book passed into the hands of an unknown person, from whom it went to the Cardinal Lodovico Ludovisi and then to Lelio Guidiccioni. From Guidiccioni it went to Leonardo Agostino, from whom Mosini got it. It was Mosini's friends who urged him to have the drawings etched. The young French artist Simon Guillain was commissioned to do the

Left: The seller of fagots, from a Cris de Paris *of the late fifteenth or early sixteenth century, reproduced from Victor Fournel's* Cris de Paris *published in 1887.*

The book seller, from Annibale Carracci's Diverse Figure, *published in Rome in 1646.*

Costui, che d'angue, e uipere pungenti
Tuol far de l'Anatomico·facondo,

Sol mostra su l'autentiche patenti
Il priuilegio d'ingannare il Mondo.

De notte, ora ai teatri, ora al Redutto
Son quel che col feral serve de lume;
E pur che i paga mi so andar per tutto.

7

I 'tend the playhouses at nights;
I am the man that lanterns lights;
At gaming-houses too:
Go any where about the town,
Contented travel up and down,
If I but get my due.

Above: The quack doctor, as depicted by Guiseppe Maria Mitelli and engraved by Francesco Curti.

Right: The lantern man, from the 1785 edition of Gaetano Zompini's Le Arti che vanno per via nella Cittá de Venezia.

46 | Prints and Drawings from the Fifteenth Century to 1800

plates with the advice of the architect-sculptor Alessandro Algardi, who had at one time studied with Lodovico Carracci, probably a cousin of Annibale, although authorities differ on the relationship between the Carracci. Five additional drawings by Annibale, belonging to a friend of Mosini, were added to the seventy-five in his book although they do not depict vendors.[8] Each sheet contains one figure, or occasionally two, a casually clad heroic type generally in motion in an abbreviated setting of Italian character, although not clearly Bolognese.

The Prints and Photographs Division has two editions of the Guillain prints, one with title page, table of contents, and portrait of Annibale by Algardi in addition to the eighty illustrations. The title page fits the description of the 1646 edition. Unfortunately the introduction by Mosini is lacking and on many of the prints one can see that the numbering has been altered. The clearer numbers correspond to those in the contents. The other volume was published in 1740. Its title has been changed to *Le Arti di Bologna,* and captions as well as new, bolder numbers have been added on each print but the same plates have been used. In this album there is a four-page preface on the life of Annibale.

The Guillain prints were widely known and they inspired, among others, Giuseppe Maria Mitelli (1634–1718), who created his own set of forty, which were published in 1660. Two editions exist, one engraved by Mitelli, the other by Francesco Curti. The latter is the volume owned by the Library (missing the title page) and the plates are in many cases reversed from Mitelli's own set. This reversal is a common occurrence in the copying of prints as the second engraver often forgets that his image will be reversed in printing and that he must therefore reverse the picture as he etches it.

Mitelli romantically dedicated his cries to the statue of Neptune in the main square of Bologna before whom all the people must pass. Neptune gives good water to them all, Mitelli says; he hears everything and is therefore the wisest judge of this many-faceted life.[9] The images have much of the spirit of Carracci and for the most part adopt his motifs but they are nonetheless Mitelli's own, no figure being close enough to his model's to be called a copy. A newly introduced character—often of central importance in the commedia dell'arte— is the quack doctor, a fat, comic figure.

A third important Italian series in the Library's collections is an eighteenth-century Venetian set by Gaetano Zompini. It is not only one of the most important works of the artist but is important in the context of eighteenth-century book illustration. The drawings for *Le Arti che vanno per via nella Città di*

Venezia were made about mid-century. The two editions in the Library were published in Venice in 1785 and in London in 1803. A sheet of English verses is inserted in the front of the 1803 album; in the earlier volume they are cut and pasted underneath the Italian ones. Obviously the publisher was aiming at the English market, which was actively interested in things Italian at this time. This set also drew inspiration from the Carracci characters although now several figures often appear together and the backgrounds are more fully developed. The theater was an important part of Venetian life at the time and Zompini gives us several scenes relating to it including the man handing out keys to the loges and the lantern man offering to show a couple home after a performance lest one should fall in the darkness, perhaps into a canal.

After more than two centuries of having the words recorded in literature, visual cries also achieved popularity in England during the seventeenth century. Much of the broadsheet material is now lost but a few pieces, including a rare set of half-length figures, remain from the first half of the century in British collections. These designs also appear on a series of silver counters for use in a game.[10]

The drawings for two interesting English albums in the Library dating from the 1680s are the work of the Dutch-born artist Marcellus Laroon (also called Lauron and Mauron). Laroon left Holland when very young and was living in London by 1674. Published editions of one of the albums date from 1687, but the largest and the first in which the prints are numbered and inscribed is the edition of 1711, which contains seventy-four prints. The captions, except for two in English and two in Latin, are in English, French, and Italian. Pierce Tempest, the publisher, was clearly aware of the already existing market in France and Italy. The plates were probably engraved by several hands. John Savage is responsible for at least two of them and very likely Tempest himself engraved some of the others. No direct connection can be made between these and any other *London Cries* but there is an affinity between the Laroon drawings and a French set by Jean-Baptiste Bonnart dating one or two years earlier. In both sets there is a strong sense of movement as in the seventeenth-century Italian ones. With the characters exaggerated, the prints border on satire (as does the quack doctor in the Italian set) and seem almost to anticipate the work of William Hogarth. In fact a drawing by Laroon reproduced in Robert Raines's recent monograph on the artist is startlingly like the famous Hogarth *Shrimp Girl.* The prints in this album alternate between men and women. Apparently there was an awareness of a greater market for pairs of etchings

Two versions of a print from a drawing by Marcellus Laroon of a girl selling Dutch biscuits, both of them from albums entitled The Cries of the City of London Drawne After the Life. *The upper one is from a 1711 edition. The upper right one was made from the reworked place reflecting changes in style. It is part of an album not assembled until the 19th century.*

than for the entire set of seventy-four.

The second Laroon album contains the same title page and many of the same prints but there are curious differences. As all of the prints are cut and mounted on sheets many of which are watermarked 1813 one may assume that the prints came from more than one source. With one exception the same plates appear to have been used but they have obviously been strengthened and the printing must have been some years later as the hats, collars, and shoes of a number of the figures have been changed to accord with a later fashion. The long blunt-toed shoes are replaced by slender pointed-toed ones and the floppy ties have disappeared. Small fitted caps replace broad-brimmed ones. It is known that Louis Philippe Boitard reworked some of Laroon's plates; perhaps these are his. One plate, the milkmaid, was copied in reverse by the Dutchman Jacob Gole and carries the caption in Dutch as well as in the original three languages.[11]

During the years 1973 97 the *Cries of London* after Francis Wreatley were printed—a set of thirteen prints (fourteen if one counts two versions of one of the plates) engraved by four artists. The delicate charm of these pictures has given them a lasting popularity.

The Library has British political cartoons of the period such as James Gillray's *Sandwich Carrots* of 1796, which satirizes the unpopular Lord Sandwich, a politician whose administration was as disastrous as his personal life was immoral. The composition is reminiscent of Wheatley's *Hot Spice Gingerbread* dating half a year earlier. Another major cartoonist, Thomas Rowlandson, is responsible for numerous representations of street hawkers, some of which are in the Library's collections.

A cartoon drawn by Isaac Cruikshank in 1799, entitled *The Enraged Politician, or the Sunday Reformer, or a Noble Bellman Crying Stinking Fish,* depicts numerous shouting vendors after the law was changed to permit highly perishable mackerel to be sold on Sundays. Although this cartoon appeared eighty-eight years afterward, it reflects the clamor and congestion described by Ralph Crotchett in a letter to the *Spectator* on December 18, 1711. In it he offers his services (for compensation, as he is without employment) as Comptroller General for the Cries of London, which he feels lack discipline. He refers to both vocal and instrumental cries—the "twanking" of pots and pans and the sow gelder's horn—and says they are full of "incongruities and barbarisms," that London appears "a distracted city." He offers to "sweeten and mellow the voices . . . and to take care that those may not make the most noise who have the least to sell." He then cites the match seller who was so raucous that a potential customer paid him to stay off his street. What a surprise when the next day all of the match sellers in the neighborhood came by his house in the hopes that they too would be paid off! But worst of all, says Crotchett, is "that idle accomplishment which they all of them aim at of crying so as not to be understood."

Mentioned previously was the set of 120 Hamburg cries (Christoffer Suhr's *Der Ausruf in Hamburg*) published in 1808 and reissued in 1908 in facsimile. The hand-colored aquatints of the original edition with their titles in Low German have a clearly German character and reflect the customs of the city. A number of the prints are night scenes, which is rather unusual although Mitelli included one night scene in his Bolognese set. The costumes, particularly of the women, are neat, colorful, and most attractive—certainly not indicative of the poverty one might expect. Perhaps Suhr is idealizing a bit or perhaps he merely carries on the tradition of costume pictures. Compare these well-dressed, cheerful people with those in Carle Vernet's *Cris de Paris*, whose patched clothes and downcast faces present more the picture one expects. This set of 100 colored lithographs is one of the best known and most popular of the numerous French series and is an important, recent addition to the Library's collections. In the play *Les Cris de Paris* previously mentioned, an actor named Vernet appeared.[12] Whether this is pure coincidence or whether the artist actually took part remains a matter of conjecture, but it is likely that he at least knew the production. One of the most charming of the prints shows a long outmoded method of extermination: a young man carries branches to attract June bugs, which he then catches and puts into his sack. At the same time he calls to the children and offers to pay for each dozen they bring him. A law enacted in France in 1791 had provided for paying a bounty on the destructive beetles.

To this point the series mentioned have all appeared in roughly the same form—one or two large figures overshadowing a sketchy background, each trade filling a page. Cries appear, however, in many forms. One sheet titled *Strassenbilder,* published in Stuttgart with German, Dutch, English, French, and Spanish captions, contains six scenes. Intended primarily for children, it is a sort of forerunner of today's comic strip. Two sets in a private California collection are attached to scrolls placed in boxes with spools at either end which one turns in viewing. In children's books of both British and American cries, the cuts are interspersed through the text.

The English editions for children were the chief factor in creating interest in the cries in the United States. Many American editions were published beginning in the last quarter of the eighteenth century and continuing well into the

The beetle exterminator, from Carle Vernet's Cris de Paris, *published about 1822.*

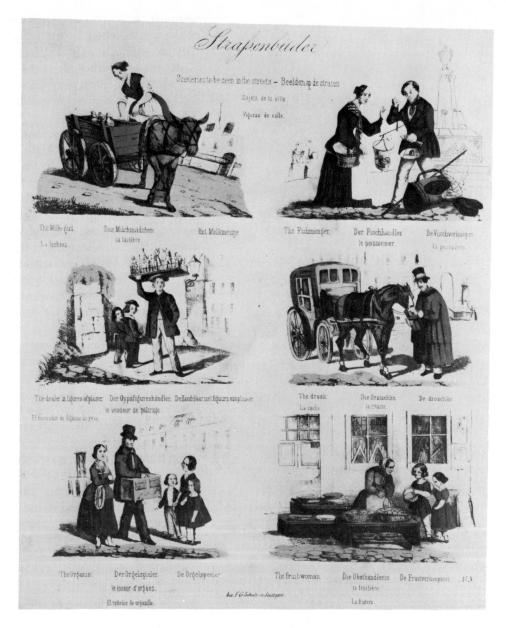

Street scenes, published in Stuttgart.

nineteenth. These little books not only acquaint the reader with the customs of the city but teach a moral lesson as well and sometimes even include a bit of propaganda for the parent. The wood engraving technique of Thomas Bewick replaced the more elegant copperplate engraving of the eighteenth century and was adopted for the American editions. It is likely that Alexander Anderson, the first wood engraver in America, and his students and followers were responsible for many of the images produced here. Anderson was a self-taught engraver who became interested in the work of Bewick and who is known to have worked for publishers of juvenile books. William Ralph, John Hall, and William Croome have initialed some of their works so these at least can be identified with certainty.

Many editions of the *London Cries* were printed in the United States. They prompted the *Cries of Philadelphia* first advertised in 1787 and those of New York dating from 1808. Although based on the English books the text has been altered so that it pertains only to American places. For example there are references to New Jersey watermelons and Long Island oysters. An 1810 edition of *Philadelphia Cries,* of which the Library has a copy, is an adaptation of the 1808 *New York Cries* with some of the same illustrations (or close copies) and the text only slightly altered. One of the changes is the inclusion of a Negro selling pepper-pot soup, a dish apparently not known in New York. In a book illustrated by William Croome, *City Cries: or a Peep at Scenes in Town,* are a number of Negroes—one selling hominy, who was said to be the most musical of all the city's criers, and another who offers to split wood.

An American alphabet table of twenty-four cries (letters J and U omitted) is in the Rare Book Division. This treatment was not uncommon both here and in England. One of the particularly attractive British examples is by the poster artist William Nicholson, who included two cries in his book *An Alphabet.*

These then are a few examples of the application of a subject popular for four centuries. One can also find cries in costume books, almanacs, playing cards, and china figurines. Figurines were made of Lucia Elizabeth Vestris, who popularized the song *Buy a Broom* quoted at the beginning of this article. Sigmund Krausz made and copyrighted in 1891 a set of photographs of people who frequented the streets of Chicago—among them a knife grinder and a bill poster. This set is in the Prints and Photographs Division.

The iconography of street life is probably the most fascinating aspect of these pictures, although stylistically it is interesting to see the great variation from crude drawings, to cartoons, to sophisticated sets. One is grateful that these

The flower girl, from An Alphabet *by William Nicholson, published in New York in 1898.*

once necessary and colorful figures have been preserved for us by artists with varying approaches, who give us pictorial documentation of the habits, tastes, dress, and even language of a dying order and of bygone times. If one feels momentarily relieved to think that our streets are no longer filled with hawkers outshouting one another, one must then ask if today's traffic is preferable or whether present-day singing commercials are better than those that inspired them. Surely all will agree that these prints are a delightful mirror of this humble genre.[13]

NOTES

1. George Unwin, *The Gilds and Companies of London* (New York: 1964), p. 33.
2. Victor Fournel, *Les Cris de Paris, types et physionomies d'autrefois* (Paris: 1887), p. 5.
3. William Langland, *Piers Plowman*, ed. Elizabeth Salter and Derek Pearsall (London: 1967), p. 66.
4. Eleanor Prescott Hammond, *English Verse Between Chaucer and Surrey* (New York: 1965), p. 239.
5. Charles Hindley, *History of the Cries of London, Ancient and Modern*, 2d ed. (London, 1884), p. 8.
6. Winifred Smith, *The commedia dell'arte* (New York: 1964), p. 117, n.
7. Christoffer Suhr, *Der Ausruf in Hamburg* (Hamburg: 1963), p. 5.
8. Denis Mahon, *Studies in seicento art and theory* (London: 1947), pp. 233–40.
9. Achille Bertarelli, *Le incisioni di Giuseppe Maria Mitelli* (Milan: 1940), p. 50.
11. Gole copied ten of the Laroon designs. See F. W. H. Holstein's *Dutch and Flemish*
11. Gole copied ten of the Laroon designs. See F. W. H. Folstein's *Dutch and Flemish Etchings, Engravings and Woodcuts ca. 1450–1700*, vol. VII, (Amsterdam: 1952), p. 206.
12. Fournel, *Les Cris de Paris*, p. 8.
13. Other works on the subject of this article include the following:
Sir Frederick Bridge, *The Old Cryes of London* (London: 1921).
A. Hyatt Mayor, "Alive, Alive O," in Metropolitan Museum of Art, *Bulletin* XI, no. 6 (February 1953).
William Roberts, *The Cries of London* (London: 1924).
Marguerite Fitsch, *Essai de catalogue sur l'iconographie de la vie populaire à Paris au XVIII° siecle* (Paris: 1952).
Hyder Edward Rollins, *A Pepysian Garland, Black-Letter Broadside Ballads of the Years 1595–1639* (Cambridge: 1922).

Abraham S. Wolf Rosenbach, *Early American Children's Books* (Portland: 1933).

Andrew W. Tuer, *London Cries: With Six Charming Children . . . and About Forty Other Illustrations* (London and New York: n.d.).

Andrew W. Tuer, *Old London Street Cries and the Cries of To-day With Heaps of Quaint Cuts Including Hand-Coloured Frontispiece by Andrew W. Tuer* (London and New York: 1885).

Rudolph Wittkower, *The Drawings of the Carracci in the Collection of Her Majesty the Queen at Windsor Castle* (London: 1952).

Pictorial Street Cries in the Library of Congress Collections

Busby, T. L. Costume of the lower orders of London painted and engraved from nature by T. L. Busby. London, published for T. L. Busby by Messrs Baldwin and Co., Paternoster-Row . . . [1820] 30.4 cm.   GT737.B8

Contents: frontispiece of sandwich man advertising the book in English and French; title page; two-page introduction; 23 hand-colored etchings of members of the lower orders alternating with pages of text. Each plate inscribed by artist and published with dates from November 1, 1819, to August 15, 1820.

Carracci, Annibale. Diverse figure al numero di ottanta, disegnate de penna nell' hore de Ricreatione, da Annibale Carracci intagliate in rame, E cavate, dagli Originali, da Simone Guilino Parigino per utile di tutti li virtuosi, et intendenti, Della Professione della Pittura, e del Disegno. In Roma, Nella Stamperia de Lodovico Grigniani . . . [1646] 41 cm   NC1155.C3

Contents: title page; table of contents; portrait of Carracci with inscriptions AL del (for Alessandro Algardi), sg (for Simon Guillain), Romae, MDCXLVI; 80 etchings numbered 1 to 80 (no no. 18; two no. 19). Most of the etchings had earlier numbers now burnished out in varying degrees and carry the signatures, initials, or monograms of artist and engraver; plates 14, 15, and 69 have only the artist, and plates 25, 53, 54, 56, 57, 61, 62, and 64 have neither.

Carracci, Annibale. Le arti di Bologna da Annibale Caracci ed intagliate da Simone Guilini coll' assistenza di Alessandro Algardi. Aggiuntavi la Vita del sudetto Anniballe Caracci . . . in Roma, MDCCXL (1740) Apresso Gregorio Roisecco Mercante de' Libri . . . . 38.1 cm.
NC1155.C28

Contents: hard cover with image of newsboy; first title page with heads of nine criers; imprimatur on verso; four-page life of Carracci; his portrait (AL del, sg, Romae MDCXLVI erased); 80 etchings with black line borders, new numbers, and titles. The signature of the engraver is gone on all of the plates and that of the artist is gone on plates, 25, 40, 48, 52, 53, 54, 56, 57, 61, 62, 64, 78, 79. There is a new signature for the artist on plate 11.

City cries or a peep at scenes in town. By an observor. Illustrated with twenty-four designs by [William] Croome. Philadelphia, George S. Appleton, 164 Chestnut St.; New York, D. Appleton & Co., 200 Broadway. 1851.14 cm. PZ6.C499

Contents: hard cover with image of newsboy; first title page with heads of none criers; title page with copyright inscription on verso; two-page introduction; two-page table of contents; text (p. 9–102) with 24 wood engravings interspersed; title page of publisher's catalog of juvenile works and 15 pages of advertising.

The cries of Banbury and London and celebrated stories. Banbury, printed by J. G. Rusher. n.d. 9.9 cm. Juv. Coll.

Contents: title page with wood engraving of market women numbered pages 2–16, each with wood engraving and text below.

Cries of London. Part first. New York, printed and sold by Mahlon Day at the New Juvenile Book Store, no. 376, Pearl Street. n.d. 16.6 cm. DA688.C88

Contents: dust cover with wood engraving of rabbit seller; eight pages of hand-colored wood engravings with text below; advertisements for juvenile books and toys on back cover.

The cries of London. New York, printed and sold by S[amuel] Wood at the Juvenile Book Store, no. 357 Pearl Street, 1811.10 cm. 1911 Juv. Coll.

Contents: title page with wood engraving of St. Paul's Cathedral and on verso a description of London; poetical description of the British metropolis on recto and verso; second title page with dust man; numbered pages 6–29.

The cries of London. Cooperstown, stereotyped, printed and sold by H. & E. Phinney, 1834. 9.2 cm. 1834 Juv. Coll.

Contents: dust cover dated 1836 with wood engraving of crier and with Phinney misspelled Plinney; first title page with alphabet on verso; title page with St. Paul's Cathedral, and dated 1834, and with description of London on verso; poetical description of the British metropolis on recto and verso; second title page with dust man; 31 numbered pages, each with a wood engraving of a crier; two wood engravings of boys on verso of dust cover. Pages 8, 11, 14, 20, 23, 26, and 27 signed or initialed by John Hall. The wood engravings are, in the main, copies in reverse of 1811 edition published by S. Wood.

Four other editions of the Cooperstown *Cries* may be described as follows:

1824. Lacks outer cover; first title page with alphabet on verso; lacks pages 29–31.

1824 Juv. Coll.

1834. Lacks first title page and page 31. Dust cover misspells Phinney as Plinney.

1834 Juv. Coll.

1839. Lacks dust cover, first title page, poetical description, and page 31.

DA 688.C86. 1839 Min. Case

1849. Lacks dust cover, first title page, and page 31. 1849 Juv. Coll.

The cries of London, as they are daily exhibited in the streets with an epigram in verse, adapted to each. Embellished with elegant characteristic engravings. "Let none despise, the merry cries of famous London Town." Philadelphia, published by Johnson & Warner, no. 147, Market Street. 1813 Part IV. 16.4 cm.

DA688.C7

Contents: dust cover with title; title page with addition: printed for Benjamin Johnson, no. 22 North Second Street . . . ; 12 hand-colored engravings of cries alternating with numbered pages of text.

The cries of Philadelphia: ornamented with elegant woodcuts. Philadelphia, published by Johnson and Warner, no. 147 Market Street. John Bouvier, printer. 1810. 12.6 cm. 1810 Juv. Coll.

Contents: title page with woodengraving of the Battery in New York and description of Philadelphia on verso; pages 4–36 with 24 hand-colored wood engravings interspersed throughout the text. Although four illustrations are new, most of them are imitations of the *New York Cries* of 1808 and the text is altered only slightly.

[Laroon, Marcellus] The cryes of the City of London drawne after the life; in 74 copper plates. Les cris de la Ville de Londres dessignez apres la nature. L'arti comuni che vanno p[er] Londra fatta dal naturale. P. Tempest excudit cum privilegie. London, printed & sold by Henry Overton at the White Horse without Newgate . . . 1711.

NC1115.L3

Contents: title page with etching of man resting numbered 1; plates 2–74 numbered and captioned in English, French, and Italian and inscribed "MLauron delin; P. Tempest ex. (exc. or excud.) cum privilegio." Second title page, plate 37, lacking date. Plates 24 and 71 carry inscription of the engraver, J. Savage; plates 13, 25, 49, and 62 carry inscription of Overton; plates 53 and 71 carry English titles only; plate 67 carries a corrupted Latin caption; plate 74 carries a Latin caption.

An album with the same title contains 80 etchings cut and mounted onto other leaves, many of which are watermarked 1813. Some plates are unchanged but most are strengthened and many have the inscriptions, numbers, and/or captions omitted. Alterations in costume occur in plates 5, 11, 20, 21, 25, 26, 28, 32, 36, 40, 42, 44, 46, and 59. Plate 23 is by Jacob Gole and reverses the original image. Following plate 74 are six extraneous ones: (1) A title page of the Cries of London in six parts, being a collection of seventy-two humorous prints, drawn from the life by that celebrated artist, Laroon, with additions & improvements by L. P. Boitard (with illustration). Boitard delint.; Ravenet sculpt. (2) Plate no. 1, part 2nd of the London Cries in 12 prints, plate 13. F. Boucher del.; P. Angier sculp. Dainty Sweet Nosegay. (3) Plate no, 1, part 3rd . . . no. 25, Tiddy Diddy Doll, loll, loll, loll. (4) Plate has only the caption buy my curds and whey. (5) No. 12:72 with the caption Buy my right Yorkshire cakes, buy my muffins. (6) No. 3:15, the celebrated Miss Wilkinson the female wire dancer (slightly changed from plate in Laroon) .

[Loire, Leon Henri Antoine. Russian cries] Published by Daziaro, Moscow and St. Petersburg. [18–] 12.8 cm.

Prints and Photographs Division, lot 9887

Contents: Twenty-four numbered lithographs with publisher's name on nos. 5, 11, 17, 23. Signature L. Loire on stone of nos. 13–24.

London cries and public edifices from sketches on the spot by Luke Limner. London, Griffith and Farran, corner of St. Paul's Churchyard. [1847] 14.1 cm.   DA688.L37

Contents: hard cover with title and illustration; title page; 24 pen lithographs interspersed through 24 pages of text. Each plate has the place name inscribed above the image and the cry below it.

[Mitelli, Giuseppe Maria. L'arti per via disegnate . . . dal Sig Giuseppe Ma. Mittelli . . . Franco Curti intaglio. Gioseppe Longhi forma in Bologna. n.d.] 33.4 cm.

Prints and Photographs Division

Contents: lacks title page; 40 unnumbered plates with Italian quatrain, signed by Mittelli (spelled Mitelli on two plates) and Curti except 3 plates signed only by Curti.

[Modern London, being the history and present state of the British metropolis . . . London, R. Phillips, 1804] 26.2 cm.   DA683.P54.1804a

Contents: lacks title page; description of the plates representing the itinerant traders of London in their ordinary costume with notices of the remarkable places given in the background. Thirty-one hand-colored engravings alternating with appropriate pages of text. Each plate gives place name above image and cry below it; Craig del.; published April 25, July 7, and August 7 and 25, 1804, by Richard Phillips, 71 St. Paul's Church Yard.

[More, Gottlob] Dresden types. 1895. Dresden, copyright Carl Tittmann. 43 cm.

DD901.D745.M8

Contents: dedication page; table of contents; 12 colored collotype reproductions of contemporary street characters.

The new cries of London. New York, printed and sold by Mahlon Day, at the New Juvenile Book Store, no. 376 Pearl Street. 1832. 14.1 cm.   1832 Juv. Coll.

Contents: dust cover with title and wood engraving of pineapple seller; frontispiece with milkmaid; title page with wood engraving of pineapple seller; London anomalies pages [5]–6; 23 pages each with wood engraving and poem below.

An 1834 edition of the same work has a title page with wood engraving of an orange seller inserted between pages 22 and 23.   1834 Juv. Coll.

Orlowski, G. Russian cries in correct portraiture from drawings done on the spot by G. Orlowski; and now in the possession of the Rt. Honorable Lord Kinnaird, 1809. Pubd. March 25 & sold by Edw. Orme, printseller to the king, engraver & publisher, Bond Street, Corner of Brook St., London. 35.6 cm.   Prints and Photographs Division

Contents: paper cover with title; title page with hand-colored etching by J. Swaine; eight hand-colored etchings and engravings, six with Russian and English titles, publishers note, and the signatures Orlowski del and J. Godby sculpt. 2 sheets cut inside inscriptions.

Smith, John Thomas. The cries of London; exhibiting several of the itinerant traders of ancient and modern times. Copied from rare engravings, or drawn from the life by John

Thomas Smith, late keeper of the prints in the British Museum, with a memoir and portrait of the author. London, John Bowyer Nichols and Son. 25 Parliament Street, 1839. 28.2 cm.

DA688.S654

Contents: frontispiece, engraved portrait of Smith; title page with printer on verso; advertisement; table of contents and list of plates; biographical memoirs of the author (p. ix–xv) ; introduction (p. 1–11) ; 30 numbered and titled etchings each filling a page; and 95 numbered pages of text. Postscript by the editor (p. [96]–99) ; final page with advertisement on verso. Numbers on plates 19 and 29 interchanged. Plates 14, 16, and 18–30 signed with Smith's monogram; plates 15, 16, 18, 23, 25, 28, and 29 dated 1819.

Smith, John Thomas. Etchings of remarkable beggars, itinerant traders and other persons of notoriety in London and its environs, by John Thomas Smith. London, published . . . by John Thomas Smith, December 1st, 1815, No. 4 Chandos Street, Covent Garden. 36.5 cm.   NE2195.57

Contents: engraved title page with coat of arms of Westminster and London; 20 unnumbered etchings of the lower orders with Smith's monogram and the inscription of the publisher.

[Suhr, Christoffer] Der Ausruf in Hamburg, vorgestellt in Ein hundert und Zwanzig colorirten Blättern gezeichnet und geätzt von Professor [Christoffer] Suhr. Mit Erklärungen begleitet. [A facsimile edition bearing the imprint Hamburg, 1808, issued with an introduction by Dr. J. Heckscher. Berlin, Hermann Barsdorf, 1908] 23.6 cm.   GT3450.S8

Contents: colophon; preliminary title page; title page; four-page introduction; four-page index of plates; 22-page introduction by Heckscher; 146-page description of the plates; page of errata with instructions for bookbinder on verso; 120 plates.

Ticklecheek, Timothy. The cries of London displaying the manners, customs and characters of various people who traverse London streets with articles to sell to which is added some pretty poetry intended to amuse and instruct all good children with London and the country contrasted, written by Timothy Ticklecheek. Embellished with thirteen elegant copper plate prints, Youth's Pocket Library, entered at Stationers Hall, London published by J. Fairburn, 146 Minories, 1797. 10.7 cm.   GT 3450.T5

Contents: frontispiece with engraving of flower seller; title page; preface (p. 3–8) ; text (p. 9–54) with engravings interspersed facing pages 13, 16, 19, 22, 25, 28, 31, 34, 37, 40, 45, 46.

The uncle's present, a new battledore. Published by Jacob Johnson, 147 Market Street, Philadelphia. n.d. 18 cm.   PE1119.A1.U5

Contents: alphabet table with 24 letters accompanied by an appropriate crier in wood engraving; letters U and J omitted.

[Vernet, Carle] Cris de Paris dessinés d'après nature par C. Vernet. A Paris, chez Delpech quai Voltaire N° 3. [1822?] 36 cm.   Rosenwald Coll.

Contents: title page; 100 numbered, colored lithographs (plate 25 missing) signed on stone by the artist and with the inscription of the lithographer; French titles with cry below.

Zompini, Gaetano. Le arti che vanno per via nella citta di Venezia inventate, ed incise da Gaetano Zompini. Agiuntavi una memoria di detto Autore . . . Venezia MDCCLXXXV (1785). 33 cm. [Second edition]   NE1713.Z7 1785

Contents: title page; frontispiece with title; table of contents; 60 numbered but unsigned plates, each with a triplet in Italian and English translation pasted below. According to René Colas, *Bibliographie Générale du costume et de la mode* (Paris, 1933), item 3120, the first edition of this work was published in 1753.

Zompini, Gaetano. Le arti che vanno per via nella citta di Venezia inventate, ed incise da Gaetano Zompini. Published by Lackington Allen and Co. Temple of the Muses. Finsbury Square. 1803. 43.4 cm.   NE1713.Z7 1803

Contents: frontispiece becomes title page with publisher's entry; two pages of English verses; 60 numbered (but unsigned) plates with Italian triplet.

Single Sheets in the *Prints and Photographs Division*

Adam, Victor. Cris de Paris et moeurs populaire dessinés par Victor Adam: Cries of Paris and plebian customs drawn by Victor Adam. Lith. de Lemercier. London, 1st February 1832 published by Ch. Tilt, 86 Fleet Street; [Paris] publié le 1er Fevrier 1832 par H. Jeannin rue du Croissant, no. 20; New York, 1st Fevrier [sic] published by Bailly et [sic] Ward, no. 96 W. St.

Sheet no. 1 with 15 lithographs of criers, captioned in French and English.

Adam, Victor. Cris de Paris et moeurs populaire dessinés par Victor Adam: Cries of Paris and plebian customs drawn by Victor Adam. Lith. de Lemercier. London, 1st March 1832, published by Ch. Tilt, 86 Fleet Street; publié a Paris 1er Mars 1832 par Jeannin, rue du Croissant, no. 20; New York, 1st March 1832 published by Bailly et [sic] Ward, no. 96 Wm. St.

Sheet no. 2 with 15 lithographs of criers, captioned in French and English.

Duplessi-Bertaux, Jean. Suite des cris des marchands ambulants de Paris par J. D. Bertaux.

Set of 12 numbered etchings signed with the initials of the artist except for nos. 2 and 3. Each image to outer border 8.5 x 5.8 cm.

Le Prince, Jean Baptiste. Premiere suite de cris et divers marchands de Petersbourg et de Moscou, dessines d'apres nature.

Six numbered etchings signed and dated either 1764 or 1765.

Le Prince, Jean Baptiste. 2me suitte [sic] de divers cris de marchands de Russie.

Six numbered etchings, three of which are signed and dated 1765.

Le Prince, Jean Baptiste. IIIe suitte de divers cris de marchands de Russie.

Six numbered etchings signed and dated either 1767 or 1768.

All of the above reprinted in *Oeuvres de Jean-Baptiste le Prince* . . . Paris, chez . . . Basan & Poignant . . . F. Chereau . . . MDCCLXXXII (1782).

Rowlandson, Thomas. Cries of London. Rowlandson delin.; Merke sculp. London, pub Jan 1t, 1799 at R. Ackermann's 101 Strand.

Nos. 1, 2, 3, 5, 6, and 8 of a set of eight hand-colored etchings, each image including border approximately 33.7 x 26.4 cm.

Strassenbilder; sceneries to be seen in the streets; beeldenop de straten; sujets de la ville; figuras de calle. Bei F. G. Schulz in Stuttgart.

Sheet no. 3, containing six scenes with captions in English, German, French, Dutch, Spanish. Hand-colored lithographs. 42.1 cm. (sheet).

A British political cartoon by James Gillray, satirizing the unpopular Lord Sandwich. Published by H. Humphrey of New Bond Street, London, on December 3, 1796. In the Prints and Photographs Division.

Guild Days in Norwich

BY EDGAR BREITENBACH

Nearly fifty years ago, the Library of Congress acquired an intriguing volume from Maggs Brothers in London. Offered as "A most interesting and valuable book for designs used on the banners carried in the processions on the annual guild days 1683–1718. 186 drawings on 52 folio leaves," it was priced at 27/10/0. As sometimes happens in large collections, no attempt was made at the time to identify the acquisition further.

The book is bound in cardboard covers, with a leather strip along the spine. Clippings from two British sales catalogs of the late nineteenth or early twentieth century pasted on the front cover describe the book as a collection of "designs to be exhibited on houses on Guild Days about the time of Queen Anne." The descriptions are nearly identical, but one of them carries the heading "London." Although Maggs Brothers gives the correct total of leaves, they actually bear an old pagination running from 183 to 236.[1] The festival drawings occupy folio 184[r] to 211[r]. The remainder of the leaves are blank, except for two sanguine drawings on fol. 221[v] and fol. 232[r], both studies from the nude, and an entry on fol. 236[v] listing heraldic designs which the compiler was commissioned to make.[2]

The records covering the annual festivals between the years 1683 and 1719 [3] follow a consistent pattern: there is the name of an elected official, which changes annually; mottoes, in Latin, English, or both languages, numbering between five and eleven,[4] and an equal number of pen and wash drawings illustrating these mottoes. The uniformity of the style leads us to believe that the

Above: Peasant couples riding through Norwich during Guild Days festival. Folio 201ᵛ.

Left: Folio 210ᵛ shows mottoes and shield illustrations for the 1718 Guild Days. The subjects included a fortune-teller, Dick Fool, a lawyer being bribed, and a boy presenting verses to a lady.

drawings were made by one person and at one time, most likely soon after 1719. The fact that in two instances the artist makes changes or corrections [5] seems to indicate that they are copies of earlier models. The net impression one gains from surveying the whole is that the volume was assembled by someone with strong antiquarian interests.

The Guild Days mentioned in all three bookdealers' descriptions actually took place in Norwich, not in London as one of them claimed.[6] The annual Guild Days of Norwich, celebrating the installation of the new mayor, rivaled those of London in their sumptuousness and represented one of the most costly public spectacles of its kind in England. By 1731 the financial burden on the leading citizens of Norwich had become so unbearable, and the debts so high, that a thorough reform was necessary.[7] The celebrations continued as a civic pageant, although on a much reduced scale, until 1835, when the Municipal Corporations Act took effect, thus putting an end to what had once been one of the chief glories of Norwich.

The Guild Days derive their name from the St. George's Guild, which organized the event annually from the late fourteenth century onward until its dissolution in 1731. The Guild was originally a religious fraternity, and each year it sponsored a procession in honor of St. George, the patron saint of England. After Henry VIII broke his ties with Rome and established the Church of England, the celebration became more and more secular. By the seventeenth century, the religious elements were all but forgotten; what survived was a splendid folk festival, which drew numerous spectators from far and wide.

Benjamin Mackerell,[8] a local historian of the period, gives us an eyewitness account of the events during the last years of the Guild's existence:

A speech boy on horseback addressing a magistrate. Folio 193ʳ.

> *About VIII. o-clock in the morning the whole body of the Court, Sᵗ George's Company, and the Livery, met at the house of the New-Elect, where they were entertained with Sugar-Rolls and Sack; from thence they all proceeded, with the new elected Mayor along with them, to the Old Mayor's, in the following manner: The Court first, Sᵗ George's Company next, and the Livery last. At the Mayor's they had a Breakfast provided for them, of Pasties, Roasted Beef, and boiled Legs of Mutton. From whence, in an inverted order to the last viz. the Livery first, Sᵗ George's Company next, and the Court last, they proceeded to the Cathedral Church, where a*

Sermon was preached, always by the Minister of the Parish in which the Mayor lived, and was his Chaplain during his Mayoralty. When the Sermon was ended, the Court had their horses brought, finely caparisoned, which they mounted; and at the Entrance into the Royal Free-School, which was curiously adorned with Greens and Flowers, in a Bower stood one of the Lads thereto belonging, who stood ready against the New Mayor should come up, to address himself to him in an Oration in Latin, as did several others in different places, on horseback, as the Court proceeded with their Robes of Justice, the Aldermen in their Scarlet, and the Sheriffs in their Violet Gowns, with each a white Wand in his hand, with Trumpets sounding, the City Music playing them along the streets, with the Standard of England carried before them. Then followed St George's Standard and Company, supported by very tall stout men, who had dresses suitable and proper for them. In this manner they proceeded, though but slowly, occasioned by

A Norwich girl representing a muse addressing the mayor and his entourage. Folio 201^r.

their stopping several times in different places to hear the Speeches that were then repeated by the Free-School Boys before mentioned. Being arrived at the Guild-Hall in the Market, the New Elected Mayor had his Robe of Justice put on to him, the Gold Chain put about his neck, the Keys of the Gates delivered to him, according to custom. He was then sworn, after which he generally made a speech to the Citizens to this purpose: "That since the Inhabitants of the City had conferred so great an honour upon him, he would endeavour to discharge this high Trust now reposed in him with the utmost fidelity and impartiality," & c.

After his Charge and Proclamation be read, the whole Body again remounted their Horses, and proceeded to the New-Hall, in the same manner they went to the Guild-Hall. After the whole Company were come into the Hall, and every one had placed himself to his own liking, or if at any time any dispute arose about precedency, that matter was always adjusted by the Alderman of the Feast. As soon as the Court and their Ladies, with the rest of the Company were seated, the Dinner was served up: first at the Mayor's table; next at St George's; and then, as fast as they could, all the rest of the tables were plentifully filled with great variety of all kinds of eatables, but little or no Butchers' meat; but as to Pasties, Tarts, Pickles, Lobsters, Salmon, Sturgeon, Hams, Chickens, Turkies, Ducks, and Pigeons, in great plenty even to profusion. And these all served up in good order, and besides what Beer every one chose to drink, either small or strong, a bottle of Wine was delivered to every Man to drink after dinner. . . .

After the choice of the four Feast-Makers[9] for the next year be over, that the Banquets be given to the Ladies, and it grows towards Evening, the whole Body arose from their seats, and put themselves into order, and waited upon the New Mayor home, where all of them were again entertained with Sugar-Rolls and Sack; and then concluded the day with waiting upon the Old Mayor home; the Court first, St George's Company next, and the Livery last, as in the Morning; where they stayed and drank as long as it was proper.

The great Guns were many times discharged in the day; as betimes in the Morning, when the Mayor went and came from Church, and several times besides.

The Dragon carried in the procession.

Dick-Fool with flags hanging out from the houses.

The whole Street, formerly the whole Parish that the Mayor lived in, was made as handsome as could be: the Streets were all strewn with green rushes, and planted with Trees, variety of Garlands, Ship Antients and Streamers in abundance; besides the outsides of the Houses were all covered with Tapestry Cloaths, and adorned with many curious Pictures, especially the New-Elect's house. But as great damages have been done to many Pictures, and Tapestry Cloaths grown old and out of fashion, except such as are in panels, it may well be supposed that there will be no more of this for the future.

The Dragon, carried by a Man in the body of it, gave great diversion to the common People: they always seemed very much to fear it when it was near them, but always looked upon it with pleasure when it was any little distance from them. The last Dragon was made but a few years ago, and was so contrived as to spread and clap his wings, distend or contract its head: it was made of basket-work, and painted Cloath over it.

As there was always a multitude of people to see the Procession, it was necessary to have several Persons to keep them from coming too near, or break the Procession. For this purpose there were six Whifflers, somewhat like the Roman Gladiators, who were neatly dressed, and had the art of brandishing their very sharp Swords in the greatest Crowds with such dexterity as to do harm to none; and of a sudden they would dart them up many yards into the air, and never failed catching them by their Hilts.

To this purpose also a man or two in painted canvass coats, and rediculous red and yellow Cloth Caps, adorned with Cats' Tails and small Bells, went up and down to clear the way, whose weapons were only small wands. These were called or known by the name of Dick-Fools; even these had their admirers, but it was amongst the Children and the Mobility.

Our book of drawings is a record of what the "Royal Free-School" contributed to the Guild Days for the period of about four decades, between the years 1683 and 1719, to which we have already alluded. It gives the name of the newly elected mayor, the year of his tenure, the mottoes on which the boys elaborated in their speeches, and the pictures serving to illustrate the mottoes. We shall explain later how these pictures were used.

The Royal Grammar School, known today as the Norwich School, is one of the oldest institutions of secondary education in England. Established by the bishops of Norwich as a monastic school, it was in existence as early as 1240. In 1540, after the dissolution of the monasteries, the City of Norwich acquired the buildings of what had been a Dominican monastery and soon afterwards renamed its school the "Royal Grammar School." Among its famous pupils were Admiral Lord Nelson and Rajah Brooke of Sarawak. The special role assigned to the school at the mayor's inauguration was documented for the first time in an ordinance of 1566. It stipulates that an orator, usually a schoolboy from the top form, should greet the mayor upon his arrival at the cathedral with a short speech in Latin "comending Justice and Obedyence or souche like matter," while "every Scholler . . . that can make verses shall . . . have in readynes syxe verses . . . subscribed with his name, wch shall be affixed upon the West dore of the cathedrall." [10]

At first, the connection between the schoolboy orations and the city pageant was a loose one. In the early seventeenth century, however, the orations became an integral and rather formalized part of the celebrations. There was always an orator, an older boy, who addressed the mayor from a bower erected at the school's entrance,[11] and ten to twelve younger students who, splendidly attired, made their short speeches stationed on horseback along the route of the procession.[12] We may assume that the theme of these speeches was derived from the mottoes. Although the boys practiced for many hours beforehand, as an added precaution should their memories fail, the text was inscribed on the inside of a small pasteboard shield. The front side of the shield bore the motto and a painting illustrating its meaning, so that the bystanders ignorant of Latin should have at least some clue as to what was going on.

None of the orations or the short speeches seem to have been preserved verbatim. By reading the mottoes, however, one forms a fairly good idea of what sentiments were expressed. They followed a certain formula, as is customary for speeches of this kind. There were the standard references to classical mythology and history and, less frequently, to biblical stories, literature (Don Quixote), and

Peter Seaman Esq: 1707

1: ———— *Tenet insanabile multos*
    Scribendi Cacoethes.

2: *Gratum est quod civem patriæ, populoqz dedisti,*
    Si facis ut patriæ fit idoneus.

3: *Egimus Do Socij,* ~~nadigeni noa diverdien~~ *umbon* in

4: *Pros Byriusqz mihi nullo discrimine agitur.*

5: *O Fortunatos nimium fua fi bona norint*
    Indigenas.

6: *Sæpe premente Deo, fert Deus alter opem*

1: three or four Hawkers crying news
2: a Master teaching boyes in a Schoole
3: Country fellows & their Mates riding through yᵉ Guild.
4: yᵉ Queen upon her Throne, two Men before her shaking hands, one in a Scotch habitt, yᵉ other an English one
5: Justice blinded holding a pair of Scales in her hand equally balanced.
6: Storm of Thunder raine &c at one end yᵉ Sky clearing up & the Sun peeping out at the other end

The mayor's name and mottoes for 1707 are shown. The illustration, "three or four Hawkers crying news," was to accompany the first motto. Folio 201ʳ.

contemporary events and personages (the Duke of Marlborough). All of the subjects were no doubt intended to illustrate civic and personal virtues and, by implication, to demonstrate the students' broad range of knowledge. Naturally, allusions were made to the festival events of the day, to Snap the Dragon and to Dick Fool, and to the huge crowds that the Guild Day attracted. As a grand finale, there was a salute to "His Worship the Mayor," as well as a tribute to the might and glory of the city of Norwich.

The documents do not make it clear whether the boys wrote their own speeches or were given a prepared text; possibly the masters supervised their efforts. It seems that different approaches were taken at various times. Occasionally, the speeches met with criticism. In 1723 the usher of the school was ordered to bring before the Court the speeches delivered on the previous Guild Day; thereafter he was commanded to submit them to the mayor in advance.[13] It may have been a youth's greatest ambition to be chosen as orator, yet only those with wealthy parents could afford it. It meant new clothes, with laces and gold- and silver-thread embroidery, and the availability of a horse, "the best . . . that could be procured in the whole county . . . richly adorned and dressed up with ribbons wherever they could be fastened." Although Mackerell does not say so, one may assume that the artist who painted the shields had also to be paid. We can only guess at the amount of social pressure that may sometimes have been applied to win the cooperation of the parents; the same techniques may have been used, too, in the selection of the feastmakers. At any rate, the reforms of 1731 also affected the tradition of the speech boys.

No works of art are so ephemeral as those made for festivals. Over the years, countless paintings must have been produced to decorate the houses of the mayor's parish, not to mention the pictures that adorned the shields of the schoolboys. Almost nothing has been preserved and the names of the artists have long been forgotten, although some may lie hidden in unpublished documents. This very fact lends special importance to the Library's compendium of drawings, which is quite likely the most comprehensive pictorial record of the Norwich Guild Days in existence. Since these are copies, we can only guess how the originals looked. Some of the scenes suggest that their creators were well versed in stage design.[14] The artists were familiar with classical and biblical iconography transmitted through prints, and they made much use of emblem books. What fascinates us most today, however, are the numerous scenes from contemporary life. There are drawings of orator and speech boys, and of the mayor's procession, with careful attention paid to the hat, mace, and sword, the symbols of his office.

Dutch merchant ships. Folio 192^r*.*

Left: Boys rehearsing speeches before their master. Folio 201^v*.*

We are introduced to Snap the Dragon, a last vestige of an earlier time when the image of St. George slaying the dragon was carried in the procession, and to a town girl posing as a muse who addresses the mayor unaware that her medieval predecessor represented the princess rescued by St. George from the monster. Some of the spectators are shown, simple peasants riding into town with their wives. We notice a cobbler's shop, boys selling newspapers, a peep show, a lady at a palmist's, and a funeral procession. Coffeehouse scenes showing the smoking of long clay pipes occur quite often; in one of these drawings a young man lights his pipe by letting a sunbeam pass through a lens. There are also scenes of moneylenders and lawyers in their offices and of a lawyer being offered a bribe. Drawings showing cargo vessels flying the British, French, and Dutch flags serve to emphasize the city's wide trade connections and proximity to the sea. The final picture in the collection shows "A Wherry with passengers going down to Yarmouth."

What one is apt to overlook is the fact that all of these glimpses of contemporary life in Norwich around 1700 actually serve to illustrate mottoes taken from classics. We have not attempted to trace the literary sources, yet most likely they are taken from school texts of Vergil, Ovid, Cicero, and a few others. To illustrate an abstract idea, the authors of emblem books frequently made use of pictures of commonplace events. The gulf between the thought expressed in a motto and its pictorial equivalent is often so wide that one can sympathize with Mr. Ewing, who at times despaired of understanding the pictures in terms of the mottoes.[15] Ewing's remarks show clearly how far removed he already was from the baroque way of thinking. The moment one ignores the literary-pictorial equation, the pictures, taken by themselves, become intelligible, the more so when expressed in purely vernacular terms. As we look at them, we become one in spirit with the happy festival crowds of Norwich.

A funeral procession in Norwich.

NOTES

1. Two watermarks occur, a shield surmounted by a fleur-de-lis, and the capital letters LA.
2. On p. 236 ᵛ the following entry: "An account of what I have Given to S ʳ Henry Sᵗ George concerning Heraldry. Since I received a Pattant from him.
first of Mr. William Cory his Funerall
   of Mr. Richard Haight his Wife's Funerall
   of Mr. Thomas Hoggans (or Hoogans) Funerall
   of Sʳ William Cooks Mother an Hatchment
   of William de Grey of Marton Esqr his Funerall."
3. The records for the years 1695–99 are omitted; those for 1702 were evidently left out by mistake and then entered on the first page, fol. 184.ʳ
4. A few of them are in Greek. There are no mottoes listed in 1686 and 1711.
5. In copying the pictures for 1709 he drew in reverse the figure of Tomyris holding the severed head of Cyrus over a bowl and then drew the same figure correctly next to it. Under the attendant figure of an old man he wrote: "place this figure lower by the table." For the year 1718 he separates the charging Don Quixote from the windmill, which in his version is being attacked by a man on foot. He corrected his mistake by writing "not this" next to the foot soldier, and "the windmill here" next to Don Quixote. It is not clear if some mechanical device was used.
6. We are greatly indebted to James L. Howgego, director of the Guildhall Library in London, and to his deputy librarian John Bromley, who referred us to a publication entitled *Notices and Illustrations of the Costumes, Processions, Pageantry, etc., formerly displayed by the Corporation of Norwich* (Norwich: Charles Muskett, 1850). The book, published anony-

mously, was written by William C. Ewing, a local historian, who states in the preface that he has been "considerably assisted by a Book of Drawings, made nearly a century and a half ago, in the possession of the Editor" (i.e., Ewing himself). The illustrations in his book leave no doubt that our book is identical to the one once owned by Ewing. We were unable to establish when and where his estate was sold. Miss Rachel Young, assistant director of the Castle Museum in Norwich, informed us that Ewing left Norwich in 1854 or shortly thereafter and that he died sometime before August 1864. We want to express our gratitude to Miss Young for patiently answering our numerous questions. The only copy of Ewing's book that could be located in the United States is owned by the library of the University of Illinois; we are grateful to the librarian for making it available to us though interlibrary loan.

7. See A. D. Bayne, *A Comprehensive History of Norwich* (London: 1869), p. 182.

8. Quoted in Ewing's *Notices and Illustrations* . . ., pp. 20–21.

9. To be chosen to serve as a feast-maker was an honor, but it also entailed a heavy financial burden, as the feast-makers had to pay the bills for these lavish banquets. Absenteeism was high among potential candidates who could not afford the expense, but it did not help them in the least. The garland, symbol of the election, was sent to their house; if they refused to serve they had to pay a stiff fine. Social pressure of this kind finally led to the downfall of the Guild. To quote again from Mackerell's text: "Thus fell this honourable tyrannical company, who had lorded it over the rest of the citizens, by laws of their own making, for an hundred and fourscore years; had made all ranks of men submit to them; neither had they any regard to the meanness of persons' circumstances, by which they had been the ruin of many families, and had occasioned much rancour and uneasiness every annual election of common-councilmen, when the conquerors always put the vanquished on to the livery; thereby delivering them over to the mercy of St. George, who was sure to have a pluck at them as they assembled and met together; until this gentleman alderman Clarke had the courage to oppose and withstand them; and having taken a great deal of pains and time, at last effected this great work, and brought this insolent company to a final period; for which good deed he ought to have his name transmitted to the latest posterity." Quoted from Susan S. Madders' *Rambles in an Old City* (London: 1853), pp. 219–20.

10. H. W. Saunders, *A History of the Norwich Grammar School* (London: 1932), p. 151.

11. The bower was considered to be the classic surrounding for a poet and scholar.

12. If our codex lists fewer than ten mottoes in a given year, it does not necessarily mean that there was a smaller contingent of boys, but that presumably the remaining mottoes were no longer available to the compiler of the drawings.

13. Saunders, p. 301. One wonders whether the illustration of motto 6 for 1691 is not a case in point. The motto reads, harmlessly enough, *"Dux faemina facti,"* which is rendered into English simply as "Ye riding." The picture shows a peasant couple riding on horseback, yet instead of the husband sitting in the saddle with the wife behind (as portrayed in another drawing), she sits in the saddle, while the husband in back of her has horns on his forehead.

14. We want to thank James G. McManaway of the Folger Shakespeare Library, Washington, D.C., and Martin Holmes, Castle Bank, Appleby, Westmoreland, England, for their interest in the Norwich compendium. Both scholars looked for possible connections between our drawings and stage designs.

15. Ewing, *Notices and Illustrations* . . ., preface.

Peasant couple riding on horseback.

Three Italian Drawings

BY EDGAR BREITENBACH

Three Italian drawings of the mid-eighteenth century that have been in the Library for a long time have somehow never received the attention they deserve. All three are very large, one being a kind of poster, and the other two being architectural drawings.[1]

The poster is a pen-and-wash drawing measuring 76 by 52.1 centimeters. It is, strictly speaking, a poster within a poster, the inner one being a broadsheet surrounded by a rococo frame consisting of figurative scenes, rocaille, entwined trees and plants, and at the top, three coats of arms. The inner poster is rendered in trompe l'oeil fashion, pretending to be a printed broadsheet, curled at the corners with dragonflies flitting across it.

Although it lacks a signature, there are certain clues as to the type of artist likely to have made this drawing. The figurative elements of the framework reveal a man of quite modest achievement. He is much better equipped to render plants, rocaille ornaments, and above all, lettering. At the end of the inscription underneath the frame of the outer poster one sees the hand of a man holding a pen. The motif of a writing hand at the end of a text was occasionally used by writing masters.[2] One may thus assume that the creator of this drawing was a writing master by profession and, like many of his colleagues, a schoolmaster as well. No doubt he was active in Modena, since the subject matter of his design is closely tied to this city.[3]

The inner poster, the "printed" broadsheet, lists the towns and hamlets which compose the district of Modena. As the inscription in the lower margin

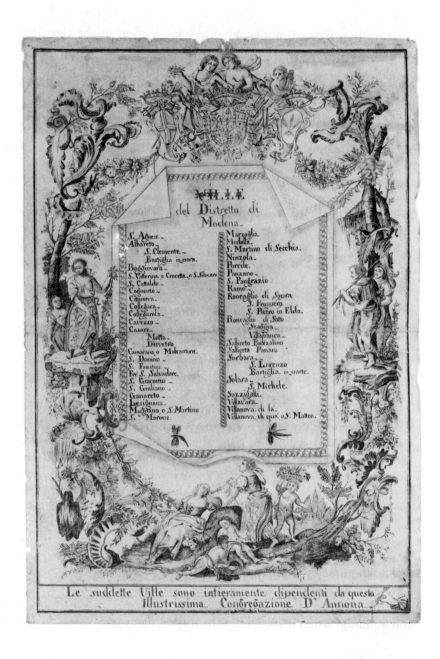

An anonymous writing master's poster of Modena listing the communities administered by the Modenese grain administration, the Congregazione d'Annona. LC–USZ62–55865.

explains, they were all under the direct supervision of the Congregazione d'Annona,[4] a government agency which regulated the production and sale of grain products; hence the allusions to tilling the land and reaping the harvest, and the coat of arms of the Congregazione, displaying three spikes of wheat. The jurisdiction of the agency was limited to the district of Modena.

The communities mentioned in the drawing are also listed in a rare and, for its time (1750), quite unusual guidebook outlining the new administrative organization of the duchy of Modena.[5] Following the example of England and France, the Stato Estense, as the duchy was called, received a modern administrative structure during the long reign (1737–80) of Duke Francesco III while a similar change occurred in Austria. It was a gradual process finally completed in 1754, when the duke moved to Milan as governor of Austrian Lombardy, whose ruler, Archduke Pietro Leopoldo, was a minor. The poster reflects a section of this governmental reorganization. We can only surmise as to its purpose; quite likely, it was made in the 1750s to publicize the functions of the Congregazione d'Annona.

The two architectural drawings, measuring 51 by 75 centimeters, are the work of Francisco La Vega, an architect who played a very important part in the rediscovery of Herculaneum and Pompeii. From 1764 he worked in Herculaneum under the guidance of Roque Joaquín de Alcubierre, a Spanish military engineer whose death in 1780 left La Vega in sole charge of the excavations. For the map he drew of Herculaneum, a modern archeologist has praised La Vega as the "best of the eighteenth-century excavators." [6]

The two drawings concern a theater and a ballroom which were to be built as an extension to the residence of the Spanish minister to Naples, Don Alphonso Clemente de Arostegui, by order of the king of Spain. One of the drawings shows the ground plan and exterior view, and the other, longitudinal and transversal cuts of the interior walls. The extension was to be built on a quite unusual site; on the roofs of a row of two-story buildings, which contained shops at ground level and living quarters or storage rooms on the upper floor.[7] Since these shops did not have sufficient depth to accommodate a ballroom and theater over them, the planned extension had to be made wider, forming a colonnade over the front of the shops. This new facade had to harmonize with the adjacent palace of the Spanish minister. The moldings around the windows were made to resemble those of the older building, and the spandrils of the arches were decorated with the royal insignia, the Bourbon lily, and the tower of Castile. Needless to say, the building material used for this project was wood, made to look like stone through the ingenuity of the stucco artisans. Thus, in its temporary character it is related to festival architecture, together with triumphal arches and modern fairground buildings.

The second sheet, showing the interior walls and ceiling decorations as well as the stage, is exquisitely drawn, with numerous minute details. Like the Modena drawing, it too pays tribute to the trompe l'oeil fashion of the time by suggesting paper crumpled at the edges. The system of decoration is remarkable in showing an overwhelming influence of the recently discovered wall paintings in Herculaneum. Instead of rococo ornamental exuberance, one notices here the restraint of incipient classicism. There is a rhythm of windows and delicately decorated wall sections, with mirrors to which candlesticks are attached. The middle of the center section is marked by a niche containing a statue, evidently one excavated in Herculaneum. For a contemporary visitor, expecting a vast, illusionistic painting on the ceiling, as he would see in other places, whether castle or church, this ceiling, subdivided as it is into small compartments, each with its own decorative theme, must have come as a surprise. This system, too, is derived from the excavations, as are the many small, figurative scenes. The only allusion to contemporary power is found in the center section, where one notices heraldic emblems—the bars of Aragon and the pomegranate of Granada—and the insignia of the great knightly orders.

La Vega further subdivided the vast sweep of space into three sections. On leaving the minister's residence, one entered a room whose ceiling suggests the roof of a tent, with floral ornaments and a few classical scenes. Between this room and the larger center section was a gallery for the musicians. Both of these sections served as a ballroom. At the far end was the stage with its machinery, and behind this, an exit passage leading to a stairway permitting descent toward the city.

The occasion for which this unusual building was created was the wedding in May 1768 of a boy of seventeen, Ferdinand IV, king of the Two Sicilies (that is Naples and Sicily), and his fifteen-year-old bride, Maria Carolina of Austria. Ferdinand was the son of Charles III, king of Spain, who as a young man had wrested the Sicilian kingdom from the Austrians, and thus in 1734 became the first Bourbon king to rule over the Two Sicilies. He was considered a good ruler and there was much regret when in 1759, after the death of his older brother, King Ferdinand VI of Spain, he was called to Spain to succeed the latter and left his young son, the future Ferdinand IV, in Naples under a regency.

Charles took a keen interest in the excavation of Herculaneum from its

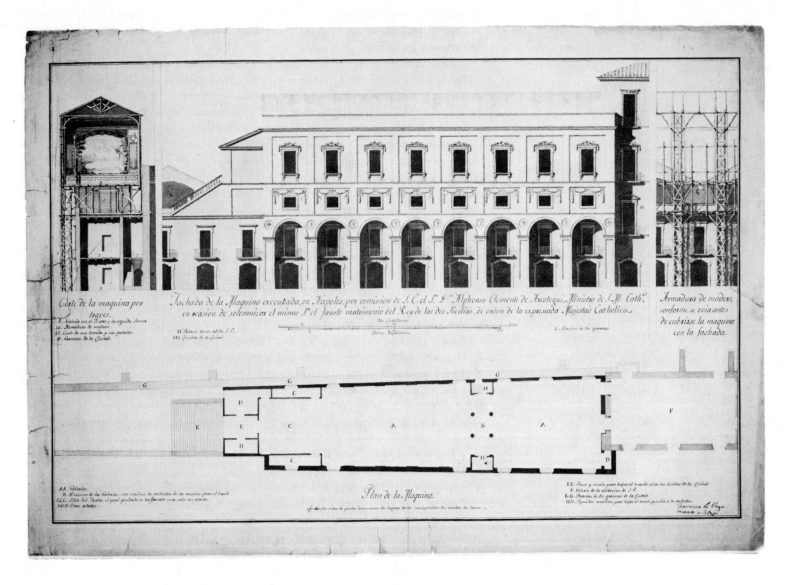

Elevation of Francisco La Vega's projected annex to the Spanish Legation in Naples, ca. 1765. LC–USZ62–51672.

Transversal cut of the projected annex. LC–USZ62–51671.

inception in 1738, and it was he who in 1755 created the Accademia Ercolanese, of which La Vega became a member.[8] The king also paid for an expensive publication to describe and illustrate his collection of artifacts, thereby spreading knowledge of the excavated objects over the rest of Europe.[9] One should keep these facts in mind, as it is quite possible that the unusual decoration of the ballroom actually reflected the king's taste. The choice of an architect who played a leading role in the excavations seems to support this assumption.

Ferdinand's young bride, Maria Carolina, was not the king's first choice. He had been betrothed to her older sister, Maria Josepha, who died suddenly of smallpox on October 15, 1767, the eve of the day she was due to depart for Naples. This fact is important for the dating of La Vega's drawings. All preparations were completed by May 1767; consequently the two sketches must have been made at some time after the formal betrothal in 1764, probably in 1765. Even the serenata to be performed on the stage of the ballroom, *Il Giudizio d'Apollo,* must have been completed at that time. It consisted of two parts, apparently corresponding to the two stage settings drawn by La Vega: the first represents a stately, vaulted hall, flanked by rows of garlanded columns, the second, an idyllic seashore, reminiscent of the Bay of Naples.[10]

The arrangements for sending Maria Carolina as a substitute for her sister were made as speedily as circumstances would permit. In an age when monarchs held absolute power, the lot of princesses and, to a lesser extent, of princes, was not altogether to be envied. Since alliances between nations were based on family relationships, princesses frequently were pawns in the game of power politics. The marriage of Maria Carolina and that of her sister had both been arranged by Charles III of Spain and the princesses' mother, the Empress Maria Theresa, archduchess of Austria and queen of Hungary and Bohemia, who was anxious to regain a political foothold in Naples through this marriage. The young princess accepted the arrangement without demur, but we know from her own letters and those of her brother, Leopold, who accompanied her to Naples and who later became emperor, that she left Austria with a heavy heart. We know, too, that she nearly had a nervous breakdown when her German entourage had to leave her at the Neapolitan border where she met her unprepossessing husband, whose uncouth manners shocked her.[11] The wedding celebration in Naples went on for a whole month. For the nobility it was a succession of banquets, balls, theatrical performances, and outings; for the common people it was a long-remembered folk festival with two Cockaigne towers offering free food and wine.[12]

Maria Theresa had, upon her daughter's departure, given her a long treatise on how the young queen should behave in order to succeed in her new country. It is a moving document, inspired by wisdom and common sense. Two of her precepts were: never interfere in government affairs, and never choose a favorite. Nevertheless, since the king was a weak playboy who had little interest in ruling the country, the queen took the reins into her own hands, soon choosing a favorite, Sir John Acton, to be prime minister. Acton, a British officer, steered the country on an anti-French course. Naples was briefly occupied by French forces in 1799 and by Napoleon's armies in 1805. The royal couple twice fled to Sicily. Maria Carolina died in 1814 in Hetzendorf, Austria, where she had lived in exile. Her husband returned to Naples after Napoleon's downfall in 1815. His remaining ten years were a reign of ruthless tyranny.

We have as yet no documentary evidence that La Vega's building was executed as planned. Such evidence may well be contained in Neapolitan or Spanish archives, in reports of foreign diplomats attending the wedding, or among the correspondence of the queen, who, like her mother, was an untiring letter writer.

Although the main facts of his career have now been uncovered, Francisco La Vega remains a somewhat shadowy figure. Being primarily an architect engaged in underground excavations (it is interesting to note that the contemporary buildings of Herculaneum were left standing above the excavations), he is not listed in any contemporary artists' encyclopedias. As a Spaniard, he is not included in the biographical dictionaries of prominent Neapolitans. Most likely born in the 1730s, he may have developed his considerable skill as a designer at Portici, among the artists and scholars brought together by the king to describe, restore, and reproduce his amazing collection. His mentors may have been Luigi Vanvitelli and Camillo Paderni, both of whom were architects and designers. After completion of the work on the reproductions for the king's catalog, La Vega seems to have been employed as an excavating architect. The only early encyclopedia to mention his is Pietro Zani's *Enciclopedia Metodica Critico-Ragionata delle Belle Arti*.[13] There he is listed as Francesco de Vega, Spanish painter, active between 1736 and 1760; in the column under "merito" he gets the top epithet "bravissimo."

NOTES

1. The Modena drawing was presented to the Library in 1915 by Mrs. Ridgely Hunt. There is no record of how the two architectural drawings were acquired. I suspect that they were transferred to the Library after 1945 with Nazi material which contains a number of pictures on the subject of theater architecture.

2. *Swiss Folk Art* (Washington: Smithsonian Institution, 1968), exhibition catalog, no. 215. This drawing, dating from about 1800, was made by a retired school teacher and writing master. In both instances the lettering is good but the figures are weak.

3. I want to express my indebtedness to Angelo Spaggioli of the Archivio di Stato in Modena for answering many questions, and to Michael A. Abelson, Nyack, N.Y., for lending me a copy of his very informative essay, "Le strutture amministrative nel ducato di Modena e l'ideale del buon governo (1737–1755)," *Rivista Storica Italiana* 81 (1969) : 501–26.

4. Annona is a Roman goddess of agriculture. The agency's earlier name was "Congregazione dell'Abbondanza."

5. *Catalogo delle città e luoghi principali dello stato di Modena diviso in tre partimenti secondo l'uso della ducale cancelleria con una breve notizia de' tribunali e magistrati residenti nella città capitale*, Modena, 1750. The publication is described by Luigi Amorth in *Modena Capitale* (Milan: Aldo Martello editore, 1967), p. 195.

6. Sir Charles Waldstein (Walston) and Leonard Shoobridge, *Herculaneum, Past, Present, and Future* (London: Macmillan & Co., 1908), pp. 61, 80, 128–29.

7. The minister's residence and the adjacent shops were located in back of a long row of Naples granaries. A city map of 1775 shows these granaries at the Piazza della Conservazione de' Grani Pubblici, now called Piazza Dante. See Cesare De Seta, *Cartografia della Città di Napoli* (Naples: 1969), v. 3.

8. Michelangelo Schipa, *Nel Regno di Ferdinando IV Borbone* (Florence: Vallecchi editore, 1938), pp. 132–33.

9. This monumental publication started in 1755 with an unillustrated catalog by Ottavio Antonio Bayardi, *Catalogo degli Antichi Monumenti . . . di Ercolano* (Naples: 1755), followed by two volumes illustrating the paintings (*Le Pitture Antiche d'Ercolano e Contorni Incise con Qualche Spiegazione* (Naples: vol. 1, 1757; vol. 2, 1760), and later, seven more, which do not concern us here. The vast numbers of plates included in these volumes were designed and engraved by a group of artists working in the king's palace at Portici. La Vega designed more than thirty plates, almost all of which are in volume one. He proudly signs himself as a Spaniard and Royal Designer in Portici. If he were young at that time, as I assume, he must have learned a great deal from his older colleagues who likewise contributed to the king's publication. Among them was Luigi Vanvitelli (1700–1773), the architect of the splendid royal castle in Caserta which included a theater, and the father of Carlo Vanvitelli (1739–1821), who in 1767 or 1768 built the pavilion at the Neapolitan border town of Portella for the reception of the young queen, another instance of a temporary building connected with the wedding.

10. Schipa, *Regno di Ferdinando*, pp. 27–28. The title reads: *Il giudizio d'Apollo Serenata— In occasione di festeggiarsi le augustissime nozze di Ferdinando IV di Borbone—e—Maria Giuseppa d'Austria—Re e Regina delle Due Sicilie etc. etc.—Per ordine di S.M.C. Carlo III—Re delle Spagne e dell'India—Solennizzata da S.E.—D. Alfonso Clemente de Arostegui—Ministro Plenipotenziario e Consigliere di Stato della prefata Maestrà divisa in due Parti con inter-*

locutori Giunone, Pallade Venere, Apollo e coro di Muse. It is followed by a page of handwritten notes.

11. Rules of protocol demanded that Maria Carolina travel to her new country as queen. Thus the wedding ceremony was performed in Vienna with her brother taking the place of the absent groom. As an example of Ferdinand's oafish manners it may be mentioned that on his wedding night he rose at daybreak to go hunting.

12. V. Florio, "Memorie Storiche Ossiano Annali Napolitani dal 1759 In Avanti," *Archivio Storico per le Province Napoletane* 30 (1905): 532. The erection of Cockaigne towers on special occasions was an old Neapolitan custom. In appearance, they suggested a fortress covered with food. When the king gave the signal, the people were asked to take the "fortress" by storm and help themselves to whatever food and drink they could get. There were similar "cuccagnas" at the celebration of the wedding of King Charles to Maria Amalia of Saxony (see Harold Acton, *The Bourbons of Naples, 1734–1825* (London: Methuen & Co., 1956), pp. 42–45.

13. Pietro Zani, *Enciclopedia Metodica Critico-Ragionata delle Belle Arti,* vol. 19 (Parma: Dalla Tipografia Ducale, 1817–24), p. 87.

Some Architectural Designs of Latrobe

BY FISKE KIMBALL

Benjamin Henry Latrobe, founder of the professional practice of architecture in America and designer of many of the finest buildings of the early Republic, landed at Norfolk, aged thirty-one, on March 20, 1796 (1795 as they still counted a date before the Spring solstice). Remotely of French descent on his father's side, American on his mother's, he was born in England, schooled in Germany, and had a sound professional training in architecture under Samuel Pepys Cockerell, and in engineering under Smeaton. He wrote and drew with facility; his mind and hands were never idle. A great mass of his diaries, letters and drawings survives, chiefly in the hands of his descendants. It is from one of these, Cap. William Claiborne Latrobe, that three volumes of his architectural drawings have lately come by gift to the Library of Congress. They are drawings hitherto unpublished, throwing light particularly on his early works in America, some of these wholly unknown to us.

I. "DESIGNS
OF BUILDINGS ERECTED OR PROPOSED TO BE
BUILT
IN VIRGINIA, BY
B. Henry Latrobe Boneval.
From 1795 to 1799."

Ten days after landing, Latrobe wrote in his diary, "idly engaged since my arrival . . . designing a staircase for Mr. A's new house, a house and offices for

View in Perspective of Mr. Pennock's Hall & Staircase.

Staircase of Capt. William Pennock's House,
Norfolk, 1796.

Captain P—— . . ." In the "Explanation of the Vignette in the Titlepage" of the album before us, he began: "During my residence in Virginia from 1795 to 1799, the applications to me for designs were very numerous, & my fancy was kept employed in building castles in the air, the plans of which are contained in this Volume. The only two buildings which were executed from the drawings were Captn Pennocks house at Norfolk, and Colonel Harvies at Richmond. . . ."

The album has thirty-four pages of drawings and writing, covering twelve distinct projects, all for domestic buildings with the exception of one unidentified church. We see that Capt. William Pennock's house ("Captain P's") was the first of all Latrobe's designs in Virginia. He gives an amusing account of its genesis:

> This design was made in consequence of a trifling Wager . . . that I could not design a house . . . which should have only 41 feet front; which should contain on the Ground floor, 3 Rooms, a principal Staircase, & back stairs; and, — which was the essential requisite, — the front door of which should be in the Center.

Latrobe won the wager, gave Pennock the ingenious plan at small scale, and learning later in Richmond that Pennock was having difficulty in erecting the house with local builders, returned to Norfolk to accommodate the design to their mistakes. The staircase, of unusual form, he drew in perspective with a skill then novel in America. The house stood on Main Street in Norfolk—the Geography and Map Division of the Library of Congress places it between Concord and Granby Streets—in the heart of the present city, and has long ago vanished.

One of the more ambitious of the schemes was that for the seat of Colonel John Harvie. The main house had a drawing room with a projecting circular bay at the center of the garden front, behind a hall with semicircular ends. Wings were to contain the kitchen and an office. The external treatment shown was prophetic of that of the Wickham-Valentine house in Richmond, erected by Latrobe's pupil Robert Mills a score of years later. Latrobe states that the wings were not executed.

Apparently the house built by Harvie was erected shortly before Latrobe left Virginia (December 1, 1799) for it was first taxed in 1800, having meanwhile, on July 1, 1799, been conveyed to Robert Gamble. The deed mentions the brick mansion house and brick stable (Richmond Land Books, 1799 and 1800, Henrico Deed Book V, 609), according to Miss Mary Wingfield Scott, the great authority on Richmond houses, who has also supplied me with tracings of the drawings on the insurance declarations of 1802 and 1815 to the Mutual Assurance Society. These show that the house is indeed the very one, with the bow projecting at the rear, although the facade was considerably garbled in execution. This is evident also in the drawing of the front included in Lancaster's *Historic Virginia Homes and Churches*. The house, which gave the name to Gamble Hill where it stood, and which long ago disappeared, was called "Grey Castle," doubtless from the novelty, at that time, of its being plastered externally.

The other house designs—including one for "Millhill" which I am unable to trace, and one on the bluff above Shockoe Creek at Richmond—show a related architectural character. Plans are full of spatial variety; frequently there are projecting rooms with octagonal or curved bays. There is more than one small central Roman dome. Grouped triple windows are not uncommon. The few columns used are of Grecian cast. In the designs are one or two small outbuildings which are given the form of garden temples with Greek Doric porticoes. Some perspective drawings show an informal parklike landscape treatment of the grounds.

Except for Monticello (never seen by Latrobe), which Jefferson was remodelling at the moment in somewhat similar vein, and for which he proposed a similar park and temples, there was then nothing at all in America like these houses. They represent very much the same style, under the general influence of Soane, as some of the houses in the English books of the same time, such as John Plaw's *Sketches for Country Houses,* 1800, or Laing's *Hints for Dwellings,* 1800, but freely invented without dependence on specific examples.

II. "DESIGNS
of a BUILDING
proposed to be erected at
RICHMOND in VIRGINIA,
to contain
A THEATRE, ASSEMBLY-ROOMS, AND AN
HOTEL
by
B. HENRY LATROBE BONEVAL, Architect &
Engineer.
Begun Decr 2^d 1797. finished Jany 8th
1798."

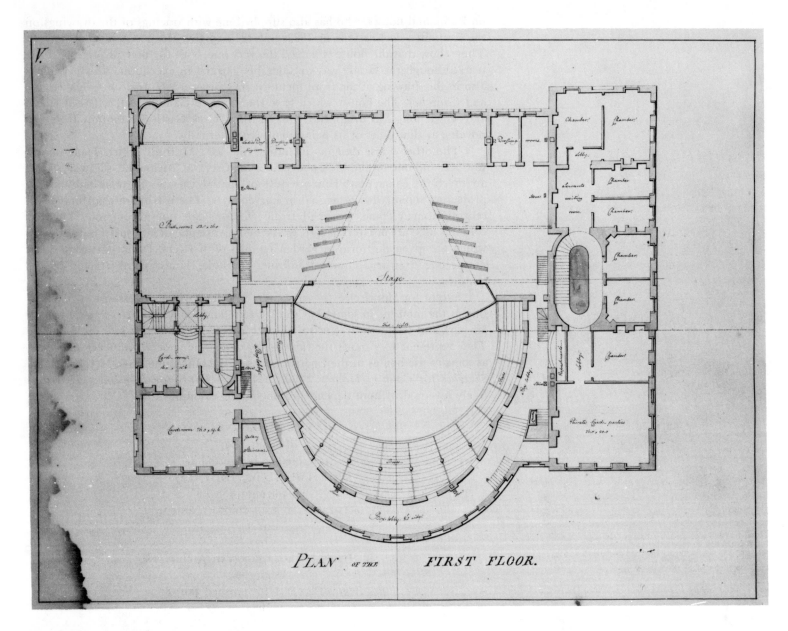

PLAN OF THE FIRST FLOOR.

Left: Proposed Theatre, Assembly Rooms, and Hotel, Richmond, 1797–98.

This project, mentioned briefly also in Latrobe's diary under these dates, is one of which we know little further. The standard histories of Richmond and the historical journals are silent regarding it.

The building was to stand just north of Broad Street, facing west on Twelfth, with the assembly rooms along the north side, the hotel along the south. This was the "Academy Square" where stood the modest building of Quesnay's short-lived Academy, used as a theatre until it burned in 1803. We may surmise that John Harvie, who was a prime mover in the Academy project, was concerned also in this new one of Latrobe's. The theatre was to be an ambitious one, with two main tiers of boxes—thirty-one boxes in all—a pit sixty feet in diameter and a wide deep stage. Most interesting is the projection of the auditorium in a semicircular facade, anticipating in that regard Semper's scheme for the Dresden court theatre of 1838. So far as I recall, nothing of the sort had been proposed so early. In George Saunders's *Treatise on Theatres* (London: 1790), which illustrates the principal examples, there is nothing of the kind, and the whole combination of the plan, extremely ingenious, was entirely Latrobe's own. His exterior treatment, in stucco, was of sober functional character, not unrelated to the style of Soane, with arcades blind and open, instead of any academic membering.

The enterprise was far too grandiose for the means of Richmond and Virginia at the end of the century, when the new state capital was still a straggling town. The short-lived Boston Theatre, built in 1793–94 by Bulfinch was valued at £12,500; the Park Theatre in New York, built by Marc Isambard Brunel in 1793–96 cost $179,000. It was these handsome structures, doubtless, which inspired Richmond to an emulation beyond its power. The brick theatre built on Academy Square in 1806 and destroyed in the fatal theatre fire of 1811, which is commemorated by the Monumental Church on the site, was of comparatively slight pretensions.

III. "DESIGN
OF A
CITY HALL
proposed to be built in New York.
by B. H LATROBE F.A.P.S.
Philadelphia 1802."

The handsome set of drawings with this inscription on the title page reveals to us something hitherto not widely known: that Latrobe submitted plans for the building which represented the greatest new opportunity offered to designers in America in the first years of the new century—plans now first shown to the public.

The basic documents regarding the project have been published most fully in I. N. Phelps Stokes, *Iconography of Manhattan Island* (vol. I, 1915, pp. 462–464, plate 75 and vol. V, 1926, pp. 1393–94). Latrobe's participation, however, was wholly unknown to Stokes, as to other writers who have previously discussed the City Hall.

As early as March 24, 1800, the Common Council of the city of New York had appointed a committee "to consider the expediency of erecting a New City Hall . . . as also a proper Place, a Plan of the Building, an Estimate of the expense . . . ."

On February 20, 1802, the following advertisement appeared in the *New York Daily Advertiser and in the American Citizen and General Advertiser:*

> The Corporation of the City of New York having it in contemplation to build a new Court House and City Hall, the undersigned, a Committee appointed for the purpose, hereby offer a premium of 350 dollars for such plan to be presented to either of the subscribers, prior to the first day of April next, as may afterwards be adopted by the board. The scite on which it is to be erected is insulated, covering an area of three hundred by two hundred feet. The plan must shew the elevation of the four facades. The interior arrangement of the building must comprize four court rooms, two large and two small, six rooms for jurors, eight for public offices, and for the common council, and appropriate rooms for the city-watch, the housekeeper in the vestibule or wings. Occasional purposes may require other apartments, which may also be designated. A calculation of the expense requisite for its construction, must accompany the plan.

> J. B. PREVOST   SELAH STRONG
> J. B. COLES   PHILIP BRASHER.
> ROBT. LENOX

"Out of twenty-six plans delivered in," said a writer in the *Daily Advertiser,* October 2, 1802, "five or six are pre-eminently distinguished." The names of only four competitors have hitherto been known to us. Joseph F. Mangin and John McComb, Jr., signed the winning design. Besides theirs, a design was "delivered

Project for New York City Hall, 1802.

by Dr. Smith"; another, according to William Dunlap's *History of the Rise and Progress of the Arts of Design,* 1834, was presented by Archibald Robertson, the miniature painter, who also offered plans for public buildings on other occasions.

Latrobe's concern with the matter has but lately become known by an incidental reference to it in a letter regarding another competition, that for designs for the College of South Carolina. It was addressed to John Ewing Calhoun, kinsman of the younger and more famous John C. Calhoun. Preserved among the Calhoun papers in the South Caroliniana Library of the University of South Carolina, it was published by Mrs. Margaret B. Meriwether in *The State,* Columbia, January 4, 1943, which Mrs. Meriwether kindly called to my attention. The letter is long, but its statement of Latrobe's principles of participation—or more frequently nonparticipation—in public competitions is highly relevant to the New York instance. His discussion of prevailing conditions and probabilities, his prescient fear of the outcome, make it worthy of wider publication in the excerpts presented here:

PHILADELPHIA *April 17, 1802*

Sir, I am highly flattered by your polite letter of the fourteenth currt. and if anything could induce me to enter into such a competition as is proposed by the advertisement of the trustees of the South Carolina college, it would be the letter you have written me. But there are reasons—which your politeness renders it proper for me to state to you—which have long prevented men who have a reputation to lose, and who do not absolutely depend upon a chance of business for support, from encountering the sort of rivalry which a public notice calls forth. The merit of the design of a professional man of experience and integrity is, that nothing is proposed but what is practicable; permanent; economical, with a view to ultimate expenditure and in point of taste—capable of encountering the severest criticism. But these are merits of which it is not easy for unprofessional men to judge in a plan drawing; and on that account the decision is not always according to merits . . .

Having determined never to submit a plan to any public body which should not be so digested in its minutest arrangements as to satisfy my own mind of its practicability, and eligibility; and which, in case of my death or absence, should not be sufficient to guide my successor to its perfect completion, I find it extremely inconvenient and humiliating to devote a month's time to making a complete set of drawings and calculations and to collecting such information respecting the materials to be had, the contracts to be procured, and the expense attending them, as would authorize a risk of reputation, and this only for the chance of being preferred to the amateur, and workman who may enter the lists against me. It is the misfortune of our country, that in most instances men of natural genius, who have had little instruction and less opportunity of improvement are preferred to men, who have expended the best part of their lives in endeavoring to acquire that knowledge which a good architect and engineer ought to possess. I have in all those instances, in which I have taken my chance with others, been thrown out by some such genius, and I have an habitual dread of them. They have, either as possessing the confidence of building committees, or holding a seat in the committee often made me repent that I have cultivated my profession in preference to my farm. And it is because I have no means of preventing the inroads of these gentlemen upon the steadiness, the consistency, and energy of my system of operations unless I were on the spot, that I feel particularly reluctant to offer a plan for a work to be erected at so great a distance.

But should even my plan be adopted, the sum of 350 dollars (which is the reward offered by the South Carolina Trustees) is a very inadequate reward only for the labor it would cost me, deducting the actual expense of my office. For before the fair and decisive drawings can leave the office a voluminous map of drawings of the whole detail must be made, first in the rough and then in two fair copies, one for myself, the other for my employer.

In one late instance, however, similar to the present flattering request of a gentleman high in the public, as well in my private respect has induced me to give a design for the city hall in New York. I have done so under the express stipulation, that I shall not be considered as a candidate, if even my design shall be preferred, unless I have the sole direction of the work, appointing my own superintendent, and at the same time rendering myself fully responsible for the success of my plans, and for the conduct of the superintendent. On these terms I have executed the two great works which have been committed to my care here. They have secured to the public a consistency, and uniformity and a promptness of operation, which cannot be expected from the measures of any committee; and to myself, the satisfaction of perfect success. . . .

Your obliged faithful hble. Servt.,
B. Henry Latrobe

We learn from this letter the following facts regarding the New York City Hall: Latrobe had, before April 17 (and presumably before the advertised date of April 1) submitted a set of plans; these had been specially solicited of him by "a gentleman high in the public, as well in my private respect."

Latrobe's two successful early undertakings in Philadelphia, the city water supply and the Bank of Pennsylvania, had both been completed early in 1801. That autumn was devoted to surveying and improving the navigation of the Susquehanna. In the spring of 1802 Latrobe was looking for new fields to conquer.

He had previously made three visits to New York. He was there in January and again in March of 1799, doubtless in connection with the engines for the waterworks built by Nicholas J. Roosevelt at his works in Passaic. He went again for a fortnight in June of 1800, when we find entries in his diaries at the Falls of Passaic, in New York itself, and at Morrisania, the seat of Gouverneur Morris.

The name of the respected public figure who had solicited Latrobe's presentation of a design for the City Hall we can only surmise, neither Latrobe's correspondence before 1803 nor his dairy for 1802 having been preserved. Of the principal public characters in New York at that time Gouverneur Morris is the only one with whom we know Latrobe to have had previous relations.

The designs which Latrobe sent form a most comprehensive set, comprising twenty-six sheets with forty-eight drawings in all. They cover every artistic and major structural aspect of the building, including many details at large—it being indeed, "so digested in its minutest arrangements as to satisfy my own mind of its practicability, and eligibility." The accommodations provided conform perfectly with those mentioned in the call for designs and their disposition is at once clear, ingenious, and convenient. The elements fall into a balanced plan grouped around a central rotunda, with the Council Room at the rear, the large court rooms to left and right—all within a simple cubical mass dominated by a Roman saucer dome. The principal story is raised above a high academic basement, with a monumental flight of steps leading up to a pedimented portico of eight columns of the Corinthian order of the Athenian Tower of the Winds. The stone wall surfaces are kept plain, the leading motifs being triple windows under arches.

On October 4, 1802, the City Council balloted to select a plan, and that of Joseph F. Mangin and John McComb, Jr., having a large majority of votes, was accordingly adopted. This accepted design, drawn entirely by the hand of Mangin, was put into execution in 1803 under the conduct of McComb, whose name alone appeared as architect on the cornerstone, and who proceeded to make the working drawings.

Joseph Mangin, the French author of the scheme, then city surveyor, was a man of whose origin and training we know practically nothing. From his drawings we see he was highly competent, although the plan is by no means so well digested as Latrobe's; from the style of the building (an accomplished version of the Louis XVI with no breath of more severely classical innovation), we may judge he had left Europe about the time of the French Revolution. By contrast with this, Latrobe's design belongs to a later era, well abreast of classical developments in England at the moment. It was, indeed, too advanced to be acceptable.

There can be little doubt Latrobe prophesied rightly that the decision, in such cases, would be swayed in favor of men "possessing the confidence of building committees," even though in this instance the victors were men of a competence then unusual in America, opponents by no means unworthy of his steel, whose building remains as one of the most admirable American monuments of the period.

His disappointment must have been short-lived. Before the end of November 1802, he was summoned to Washington. On the 29th he dined with President Jefferson, who created for him, March 6 of the following year, the post of Surveyor of the Public Buildings of the United States.

II PRINTS AND DRAWINGS IN THE NINETEENTH CENTURY

An Album of Rembrandt Restrikes

BY KAREN F. BEALL

Among the most sought-after prints today are those of Rembrandt van Rijn (1606–69). This has been consistently true since his death nearly three centuries ago. Technical proficiency, subtlety, and emotional power are among the outstanding qualities of his work.

It is no small task to produce prints of high quality from etched plates. In the case of Rembrandt, the artist himself pulled the finest impressions, but so great were the demands by collectors that further printings had to be made by other craftsmen. Rembrandt would have considered this an acceptable practice. He himself was a collector of plates and is known to have reworked and reprinted them. The best known example is a plate by Hercules Seghers, *Tobias and the Angel,* that Rembrandt reworked into *Flight Into Egypt.*

At least eighty out of approximately three hundred plates etched by Rembrandt (authorities differ greatly on the actual number of plates done by him) survived into the twentieth century. Of these many have been reworked and all have been reprinted in recorded editions. There is more than a casual interest, then, for both collector and curator in distinguishing originals and restrikes—not to mention the problem of copies.

Early in 1966 a fascinating album of restrikes was purchased through the Hubbard Fund for the collections of the Library of Congress. The following paragraphs are intended as descriptive instead of definitive, raising rather than solving questions of connoisseurship, since scholars have published little on this complex subject.

Samson Threatening His Father-in-Law. *Print from restrike album, after the Rembrandt painting.*

The album is a small folio, measuring approximately 49.6 × 32 centimeters, bound in marbleized paper over boards. It consists of 49 leaves, uniform in neither size nor make, bearing impressions from 120 plates. One of these carries three images, apparently originally separate but here copied together on one plate. The album has no title page, and the only marks of ownership are the blind stamp of one "G. Rames, notaire, à Aurillac (Cantal)" and a stamp in blue ink of "Seine colportage," suggesting that at some time the book was in the riverside bookstalls of Paris.

In trying to pinpoint the date of this particular album, it is essential to trace the ownership of the plates. When Arthur M. Hind published his catalog of Rembrandt's etchings in 1923, one plate was known to be in the hands of the Six family (descendants of Burgomaster Jan Six) and seventy-nine others in the hands of M. Alvin-Beaumont in Paris, who had acquired them from the son of Michel Bernard. Bernard in turn had purchased them from the widow of Auguste Jean in 1846. The plates had been in Jean's hands as early as 1810 but before that time they had been in the possession of the Basan family, who figure prominently in any discussion of Rembrandt restrikes. Pierre François Basan bought at least seventy-eight plates from the estate of Claude Henri Watelet in 1786 and at least fifty-three from the estate of Pieter de Haan around 1767. Watelet had acquired his group about 1760 in Holland.[1]

Basan published his first *Recueil de quatrevingt-cing estampes originales . . . gravées par Rembrandt . . . et trente-cing autres . . . in folio de cent-vingt pièces* after 1786. Dmitrii Rovinskii places it in 1785, but this seems impossible in light of the date of the Watelet sale. This and a later *Recueil* are as imperfectly described as they are rare, the only two known volumes being at the Hermitage Museum, where they were deposited by Rovinskii. Hind tells us that the fifty-three plates originally in the de Haan collection are reprinted in this folio. Two plates by J. J. de Claussin dated 1801 and 1807, not included in the first *Recueil,* appear in the second *Recueil* and also in the Library's album. Therefore, the album could not have been printed while the senior Basan, who died in 1797, was alive.

In 1906 a further edition was published to celebrate Rembrandt's tercentenary. Although it is believed that numerous impressions and *Recueils* were produced throughout the period 1786–1906, no information pertaining to them can be located in published sources. In all likelihood, the albums have been broken up and the individual items sold to collectors.

Hind lists by number the eighty plates reproduced in the 1906 edition, all

Page 1 of restrike album showing a bearded man (upper left) and three self-portraits of Rembrandt.

of which appear in the Library's album. A concordance following this article correlates information pertaining to the album with the entries in *Rembrandt's Etchings, True and False,* compiled by George Biörklund with the assistance of Osbert H. Barnard (Stockholm: 1955), and with the Hind catalog numbers.

Many, if not most, of the Rembrandt plates have been reworked, in some instances by artists whose identity is known. Some plates seem to be the original designs of other artists; some are copies after Rembrandt; some are eighteenth-century copies after other seventeenth-century Dutch artists; a few remain unidentified. The most helpful single source of information has been Biörklund and Barnard; in this and in *A Descriptive Catalogue of the Etched Work of Rembrandt,* by Charles H. Middleton-Wake (London, 1878), are described the greatest number of the works included in the Library's album.

A curious print is an unfinished landscape attributed by Biörklund to Pieter de With and by the Mariette sales catalog to Basan. Middleton-Wake lists two copies, one by Basan and one by François Vivares. (M. Mariette also had a vast collection which included some plates, three of which—not by Rembrandt—are represented in the album.) The impression in the album bears the inscription "dans aucun catalogue, oeuvre de Mariette." This leads one to reject Biörklund in this instance and to accept Middleton-Wake, who describes the Vivares plate as carrying this inscription.

One print, *The Pancake Woman* (BB 35–I), may help to date the Library's album. Hind lists six states of this plate and adds the note: "Modern, reworked (probably starting before [state] IV): Basan-Bernard."[2] The fourth state is the one included in the Library of Congress copy of Basan's *Dictionnaire des Graveurs* (Paris: 1789) and is inscribed "No. 122," but other 1789 copies read "Tome II, pag. 122." On the plate in the 1809 *Dictionnaire* the inscription has been erased and shading added across the top. A trace of the second 1789 inscription can be discerned on the print in the Library of Congress album, but the shading does not appear. Can it be assumed therefore that it must fall between 1789 and 1809? As we have already determined the 1807 date of the de Claussin plate, might this album then have been issued between 1807 and 1809? And what was its nature and purpose? Its appearance does not indicate an actual published volume but rather a record made for the owner of the plates. If the tentative dating should prove correct, this would place it in the hands of H. L. Basan shortly before the plates were sold to Jean. It is equally possible that the impressions were taken at different times and bound at a later date for safekeeping. The quality of the

The Pancake Woman *from Basan's Dictionnaire des Graveurs (1789) and from the restrike album, the second print bearing a trace of the inscription.*

De Claussin's Rembrandt, *and Rembrandt's* Jan Lutma, *both from the restrike album.*

impressions varies as many of the plates have been obviously reworked; other seem quite worn and have been less conspicuously altered.

It is hoped that others who know of similar albums or have further information relating to Rembrandt's restrikes will add to the meager published information so that in time a more thorough investigation may be made. In the meantime this album will serve the scholar as useful comparative material.

NOTES

1. Arthur M. Hind, *A Catalogue of Rembrandt's Etchings* (London [1923]), pp. 22, 23; and Dmitriĭ Rovinskiĭ, *L'Oeuvre gravé de Rembrandt* (Saint-Pétersbourg:: 1890), no. 17, col. 9.
2. Hind, p. 79.

CONCORDANCE

Key:
B–B—Biörklund and Barnard
H—Hind
MB—Modern Basan impression
R—Reject

Library of Congress Album		Artist	B–B	H	MB	Notes
No.	Subject					
1	Bearded old man in a fur cap.	Rembrandt	35–3	130	MB	
1	Rembrandt and his wife Saskia.	Rembrandt	36–A	144	MB	
1	Rembrandt in velvet cap and plume.	Rembrandt	38–8	156	MB	
1	Rembrandt in a cap and scarf, dark face.	Rembrandt	33–G	108	MB	Reworked.

Library of Congress Album		Artist	B–B	H	MB	Notes
No.	Subject					
2	Jakob Thomasz Haringh.	Rembrandt	55–E	288	MB	After plate reduced and some reworking.
2	Man in a high cap	Rembrandt	30–F	22	MB	After plate reduced.
2	Rembrandt's mother in widow's dress, black gloves.	Pupil/imitator ..	R–71	91	MB	
2	[Man with plumed hat] .	Unknown	....			Inscribed on plate: *Rembrandt f 1639.*
3	Joseph telling his dreams.	Rembrandt	38–E	160	MB	
3	Abraham caressing Isaac.	Rembrandt	37–2	148	MB	Basan printed from original plate. Basan copy also exists.
3	Three oriental figures (sometimes called Jacob and Laban).	Rembrandt	41–F	183	MB	Original plate used in 1868 "Etchers and Etchings."
3	The hour of death	Basan workshop, possibly James Hazard.	R–7	310	.....	After Ferdinand Bol. Inscription: *No. . . . du catalogue.*
4	Adam and Eve	Basan	38–D	159	.....	Inscription: *No. 29 du catalo (Middleton 206).*
4	David in prayer	Rembrandt	52–C	258	MB	Corroding of plate.
4	The strolling musicians .	Rembrandt	35–8	142	MB	Reworked.
5	Peasant family on the tramp.	Rembrandt	52–3	259	MB	

Library of Congress Album		Artist	B–B	H	MB	Notes
No.	Subject					
5	Titus	Basan workshop .	56–1	261	.....	Inscription: *Le fils de Rembrandt.*
5	The Spanish gypsy (Preciosa) .	Basan (?)	42–2	184	.....	Inscription: *No. 116 du cat.*
5	Christ and the woman of Samaria, among the ruins.	Rembrandt	34–L	122	MB	Reworked.
6	Jews in the synagogue ..	Rembrandt	48–D	234	MB	Somewhat reworked.
6	Bearded old man in a cap	Bol	R–48	350	MB	
6	Woman bathing her feet at a brook.	Rembrandt	58–D	298	MB	Reworked.
6	Rembrandt etching	Pupil/imitator ..	R–81	300A	.....	Inscription: *Rembrandt gravant une planche, oeuvre de M. Mariette.*
7	Virgin and Child with the snake.	Rembrandt	54–C	275	MB	
7	Circumcision in the stable	Rembrandt	54–B	274	MB	
7	Joseph and Potiphar's wife.	Rembrandt	34–G	118	MB	Reworked.
7	The adoration of the shepherds with the lamp.	Rembrandt	54–1	273	MB	
8	The pancake woman	Rembrandt	35–I	141	MB	Inscription: *Tome II, pag. 122* (barely visible) .

Library of Congress Album		Artist	B–B	H	MB	Notes
No.	Subject					
8	The Persian	Rembrandt	32–A	93	MB	
8	The stoning of St. Stephen.	Rembrandt	35–A	125	MB	Reworked.
8	St. Jerome kneeling in prayer.	Rembrandt	35–H	140	MB	
9	Christ returning from the temple with his parents.	Baron Vivant Denon.	54–F	278	.....	After Rembrandt. Denon used in *Recueil* de Basan. Inscription: *No. 54.*
9	The bathers	Rembrandt	51–B	250	MB	
9	Landscape with a cow drinking.	Rembrandt	50–1	240	MB	
10	Man in a cloak and a fur cap leaning against a bank.	Rembrandt	30–6	14	MB	Reworked (?)
10	Beggar with a wooden leg.	Rembrandt	30–4	12	MB	
10	Rembrandt with a flat cap and embroidered dress.	Rembrandt	38–1	157	MB	
10	[The blind Tobias with angel and dog.]	Unknown	....			Inscription on plate: *Rembrandt f 1633.*
11	Man drawing from a cast	Rembrandt	41–4	191	MB	Much reworked.
11	Christ disputing with the doctors (small plate).	Rembrandt	30–D	20	MB	After plate reduced.

Library of Congress Album		Artist	B–B	H	MB	Notes
No.	Subject					
11	Rembrandt's mother with hands on chest.	Rembrandt	31–G	50	MB	Watelet inscription erased, much reworked.
11	Beggarman and woman conversing.	Rembrandt	30–A	7	MB	
11	The tribute money	Rembrandt	35–2	124	MB	Reworked.
11	[Bearded man with arms folded, reading]	Unknown	....			
12	The raising of Lazarus (small plate).	Rembrandt	42–B	198	MB	
12	The flight into Egypt (night piece).	Rembrandt	51–E	253	MB	Reworked and corroded.
12	Beheading of John the Baptist.	Rembrandt	40–B	171	MB	
13	The flight into Egypt: Crossing a brook.	Rembrandt	54–D	276	MB	
13	Christ seated, disputing with the doctors.	Rembrandt	54–E	277	MB	
13	The golf player	Rembrandt	54–A	272	MB	Slightly reworked (?).
13	Angel departing from Tobit's family.	Rembrandt	41–G	185	MB	
14	Beggar woman leaning on a stick.	Rembrandt	46–A	219	MB	
14	Peasant in a high cap, leaning on a stick.	Rembrandt	39–B	164	MB	

Library of Congress Album		Artist	B–B	H	MB	Notes
No.	Subject					
14	Rest on the flight into Egypt (night piece).	Rembrandt	44–2	208	MB	Reworked.
14	The schoolmaster	Rembrandt	41–N	192	MB	Reworked.
14	The crucifixion	Rembrandt	35–1	123	MB	
14	The flight into Egypt (small plate).	Watelet	33–D	105	.....	Reverse copy (in *Recueil* de Basan).
15	Rembrandt in a fur cap (bust).	Watelet (?)	30–L	29	.....	Reverse copy. Poor printing. Date on plate, 1758.
15	[Young man wearing a hat].	Watelet	.....	.....	.....	Signed and dated in reverse on plate.
15	[Boy with upturned face]	Unknown	.....	.....		
15	The goldsmith	Rembrandt	55–B	285	MB	
15	Old beggarwoman with a gourd.	Rembrandt	30–16	80	MB	Reworked.
15	The monk in the cornfield.	Rembrandt	46–2	224	.....	
16	The cardplayer	Rembrandt	41–M	190	MB	Reworked.
16	The painter	Watelet	R–62	355	.....	After Willem Drost. Inscription: *Portrait de W. Drost . . . M. Mariette. . . .*
16	The star of the Kings (night piece).	Rembrandt	51–1	254	MB	Much reworked.

Library of Congress Album		Artist	B–B	H	MB	Notes
No.	Subject					
16	Nude men seated on the ground.	Rembrandt	46–C	221	MB	
17	Rembrandt drawing at a window.	Rembrandt	48–A	229	MB	Worn plate reworked.
17	Lieven van Coppenol (large plate).	Rembrandt	58–F	300	MB	After plate reduced to head only. Copy of original full size in *Recueil.* Worn and reworked.
18	Rembrandt in a soft hat and an embroidered cloak.	de Claussin	31–K	54	.....	Reverse of original by Rembrandt. Signed and dated 1801 on plate.
18	Jan Lutma, goldsmith ..	Rembrandt	56–C	290	MB	Reworked.
19	Beggars receiving alms at a door.	Rembrandt	48–C	233	MB	Reworked.
19	Christ and the woman of Samaria (arched).	Rembrandt	57–B	294	MB	
20	Abraham and Isaac	Unknown	45–D	214	MB	(MB copy same direction) Reverse possibly by Gérard Dou or Francesco Novelli.
20	Christ driving the money-changers away.	Rembrandt	35–B	126	MB	
21	Bust of a bearded old man.	Constantino Cumano (?).	31–E?	47?	.....	Reverse copy possibly by Cumano.

Library of Congress Album		Artist	B–B	H	MB	Notes
No.	Subject					
21	The adoration of the shepherds (night piece).	Rembrandt	52–1	25	MB	Much reworked.
22	Abraham and Isaac	Rembrandt	45–D	214	MB	
22	Peter and John at the gate of the temple.	Rembrandt	59–A	301	MB	Reworked.
23	Negress lying down	Rembrandt	58–E	299	MB	Corroded and reworked.
23	Ledekant	Basan workshop?.	46–D	223	.....	Inscription: *No. 178.* Copy possibly by Denon
24	A. Young man in a cap .	Unknown	R–59	65	.....	Copy in *Recueil.*
	B. Rembrandt with a broad nose.	Unknown	....	....	....	Inscription: *No. 5.* Copy from Basan's workshop in *Recueil.*
	C. Cupid resting	Unknown	R–10	313	.....	Reverse copy of Rembrandt painting of 1634. Copy in *Recueil.*
24	Nude standing, another seated.	Rembrandt	46–1	222	MB	
25	[Night piece with two figures].	Unknown	....	....		
25	St. Jerome in a dark chamber.	Rembrandt	42–E	201	MB	Much reworked.
26	Jan Asselyn ("Crabbetje"), painter.	Rembrandt	47–1	227	MB	Much reworked.

Library of Congress Album		Artist	B–B	H	MB	Notes
No.	Subject					
26	Arnold Tholinx, inspector	Basan	56–2	289	.....	
27	Return of the prodigal son.	Rembrandt	36–D	147	MB	
27	Head of Saskia and others	Rembrandt	36–B	145	MB	
27	Heads of three women, one asleep.	Rembrandt	37–D	152	MB	
28	Faust	Rembrandt	52–4	260	MB	
29	Christ at Emmaus	Rembrandt	54–H	269	MB	Copy of final state with triptych removed.
30	Lieven van Coppenol (small plate) .	Basan (?)	58–1	269	.....	Monogram of Basan on plate and inscription: *Copenol, No. 262 du catalogue.*
31	The descent from the cross: By torchlight.	Rembrandt	54–G	280	MB	Corroded and reworked.
32	Jan Uytenbogaert, Armenian preacher.	Rembrandt	35–D	128	MB	Much reworked.
33	Abraham Francen, art dealer.	Rembrandt	57–2	291	MB	From last state, much reworked.
34	Baptism of the eunuch ..	Rembrandt	41–E	182	MB	
35	Clement de Jonghe	Rembrandt	51–C	251	MB	Reworked.

Library of Congress Album		Artist	B–B	H	MB	Notes
No.	Subject					
36	[Hunter seated before a table in a farmyard].	Unknown				
37	The artist drawing from a model.	Rembrandt	39–2	231	MB	
38	Presentation in the temple (oblong).	Rembrandt	40–1	162	MB	Worn; reworked (?).
39	Jan Six	Basan (?)	47–B	228		Inscription: *F. Six Bourguemestre de Hollande*. Believed to be Basan copy rather than late printing from original plate, inscribed *Jan Six, AE 29*. Reversal of numbers not corrected.
40	The angel appearing to the shepherds.	Rembrandt	34–1	120	MB	Reworked.
41	Samson threatening his father-in-law.	Unknown				After Rembrandt painting in the Staatliche Museen, Berlin.
42	The raising of Lazarus (large plate).	Rembrandt	32–4	96		Probably after reworking for *Recueil*.
43	Landscape with a coach.	Philip de Koninck.	R–23	325		Middleton R. 1. Inscription: *201 du catalogue*.
43	Landscape with a coach.	Watelet (?)	R–23	325		Reverse. Copy by Watelet in Basan *Recueil*.

Library of Congress Album		Artist	B–B	H	MB	Notes
No.	Subject					
43	Unfinished landscape ...	Vivares (?)	R–43	345	.....	Middleton R. 12. B–B attributes to Pieter de With; copied by Basan workshop for *Recueil.* Inscription: *Dans aucun catalogue, oeuvre de M. Mariette.*
43	House with three chimneys.	Vivares	R–39	341	.....	Middleton R. 25. Inscription: *No. 88 du suppl. du cat.* B–B attributes to P. de With; copy by Basan shop.
44	Haybarn and a flock of sheep.	Unknown	52–A	241	.....	Reverse copy but not found listed after Rembrandt.
44	Landscape with canal and palisade.	Basan workshop .	R–36	338	.....	Copy after Pieter de With by Basan's shop. Inscription: *No. 84 du supple- ment du catalogue.*
44	The wooden bridge	Basan workshop .	R–35	337	.....	Inscription: *No. 83 du supplement du cat.* In *Recueil.*
45	[Three figures by a table]	de Claussin	.....	....		Signed and dated 1807 on the plate.
45	Six's bridge	de Claussin	45–A	209	.....	Copy by de Claussin Basan's *Recueil.*
46	[Landscape, buildings at left].	Unknown	.....	....		Plate in poor condi- tion.

Library of Congress Album		Artist	B–B	H	MB	Notes
No.	Subject					
46	[Landscape with man fishing].	Unknown	....			
46	[Landscape with two cows, town in background].	Watelet	....			Signed on plate which is corroded.
47	Lieven van Coppenol (large plate) .	Basan(?)	58–F	300	MB	Copies by both Basan and Denon.
48	The death of the Virgin.	Rembrandt	39–A	161	MB	Reworked.
49	Descent from the cross (second plate) .	Rembrandt	33–C	103	MB	Possibly original plate, much reworked; 18th-century inscription burnished off bottom margin but still barely visible; 19th- or early 20th-century printer's mark lower right.

The Capitol of Jefferson and Latrobe

BY VIRGINIA DAIKER

"In presenting to you this perspective of the Capitol, which I herewith leave at the President's House, I have no object but to gratify my desire, as an individual citizen to give you a testimony of the truest respect and attachment." [1]

The handsome watercolor rendering illustrated here is a gift to the Library of Congress from William Morrow Roosevelt of Whitemarsh, Pennsylvania. His grandfather Nicholas Latrobe Roosevelt found this national treasure in an old printshop in New York some years ago and acquired it for the family. It now becomes part of the Latrobe collection of more than two-hundred architectural drawings in the Prints and Photographs Division.

When Thomas Jefferson was inaugurated as President in 1801, he was at last in a position to press the Congress for adequate funds for the Capitol and to push for architectural planning for the actual construction of the rest of the building. As the author of the specifications for the Capitol competition of July 1792, which William Thornton won in April 1793, Jefferson envisioned a noble structure that through its dignity and architectural beauty would represent the ideals of the new republic.

It was not until Jefferson had been in office for two years, however—on March 3, 1803—that any sizable appropriation was made. Within three days, Jefferson wrote to Benjamin Henry Latrobe: "Congress has appropriated a sum of $50,000, to be applied to the public buildings under my direction. . . . The former

Presentation drawing of the U.S. Capitol, inscribed: "To Thomas Jefferson, Pres. U.S. B.H. Latrobe 1806."

post of surveyor of the public buildings, which Mr. Hoban held . . . will be revived. If you choose to accept it, you will be appointed to it. . . ." [2]

Jefferson had probably met Latrobe as early as March 1798 and knew the quality of his work, most recently from the plans for a naval arsenal and drydocks in the Federal City, prepared in November and December 1802 by "a person of skill and experience," to use Jefferson's own words. (These drawings are in the Prints and Photographs Division.) Latrobe was in fact the only well-trained professional architect in the country. The two men had much in common. Both were trained in the classics and had a knowledge of architecture, an interest in education, and a strong ambition to build a capitol that would be a national monument and a great artistic achievement.

During their six years of official collaboration, the amateur architect and the professional worked together, but they also had their differences of opinion. There were vigorous arguments and disagreements, mainly over questions of style, which are well recorded in their voluminous correspondence. For the first four years Latrobe could not afford to move his family from Philadelphia to live in Washington on his small salary of $1,700, and Jefferson went to Monticello each year for the spring planting. Hence there were many letters back and forth from their various places of residence.

Latrobe faced difficult practical problems with the Capitol building—the lack of adequate working drawings, discrepancies between existing drawings and what had actually been built, faulty construction that had to be torn down and rebuilt, the uncertainty and delay of the yearly congressional appropriations, the tremendous difficulties of getting, and keeping, trained and dependable workmen, and the problem of securing adequate supplies of building materials at the time they were needed. Jefferson's determination to follow as closely as possible the prizewinning Thornton design that George Washington had so admired, and his stubborn resistance to many of the changes suggested by his surveyor of public buildings, were problems of another dimension. Jefferson wrote later, "Another principle of conduct with me was to admit no innovations on the established plans, but on the strongest grounds." [3]

The major source of disagreement concerned the manner of covering and lighting the House of Representatives chamber in the south wing. Details such as this had not been resolved in the Thornton designs. Jefferson wanted a ceiling similar to the one he had seen in Paris in the Halle aux Blés, which he considered "the most superb thing on earth." It was constructed of great circular ribs—made up of small fir beams pegged together—which curved out and down from the

"Plan of the principal Dry Dock or Naval Arsenal, to contain Frigates in three tier of four ships each."
Watercolor drawing by B.H. Latrobe, December 4, 1802.

Benjamin Henry Latrobe. From Glenn Brown,
History of the United States Capitol, *vol. 1*
(Washington: U.S. Government Printing
Office, 1900).

center of the dome, the spaces in between being glazed, giving the effect of a radiating sunburst. Latrobe, on the other hand, argued for a "Lanthorn," or cupola, with vertical frames of glass, for he was considering practicality and comfort as well as beauty. The degree and quality of light and its appropriateness for the legislative chamber, heat and moisture condensation inside, accumulation of dirt and snow on the skylights, and breakage and consequent leaks constituted major problems in Jefferson's proposed ceiling.

The president appeared to yield, writing on September 8, 1805, "I cannot express to you the regret I feel on the subject of renouncing the Halle au bled lights of the Capitol dome. That single circumstance was to constitute the distinguishing merit of the room, and would solely have made it the handsomest room in the world without a single exception. . . . The only objection having any weight with me is the danger of leaking. . . . I leave therefore the decision on the abandonment of the idea entirely to yourself, and will acquiesce in that." [4]

Five days later Latrobe answered, "I cannot possibly venture to decide the point of the Halle aux Blés lights of myself. . . ." But, on the very same day he wrote to John Lenthall, his clerk of the works:

> The President very reluctantly gives up the skylights to my decision, which is placing me in a most unpleasant situation. I shall therefore let them lie over till it is absolutely necessary to decide, and then my conscience and my common sense I fear will reject them in spite of my desire to do as he wishes. . . .[5]

On October 23 he wrote: "I am very unfortunate to be obliged to oppose the man I most respect, and ought to obey, in so many points. I have, however, a queer scheme of lighting the House of Representatives which will please him." [6]

The new scheme proposed the substitution of five rectangular panel lights—to be spaced in each of the interstices between the great structural ribs of white pine—for each long glass skylight area. By this method the number of joints would be greatly reduced, and each panel of glass could be framed in wood on three sides with the fourth left free for drainage. Apparently this satisfied Jefferson, who wrote that "it would be beautiful . . . and a more mild mode of lighting, because it would be an original and unique." [7]

A drawing of this new arrangement, prepared for Lenthall's use, is dated November 28, 1805. Careful scrutiny shows, in addition to the panel lights, an octagonal frame on the center of the roof, with instructions that say it "must be made of Scantling sufficient to carry a Lanthorn if necessary."

By the summer of 1806 the south wing construction was ready for the dome ribbing, but the plate glass that had been ordered from Hamburg, Germany, the previous December had not arrived. Writing to Jefferson on August 27, Latrobe again gave notice that he was directing Lenthall to construct a "temporary" lantern that would be quickly placed over the center of the hall if the glass did not arrive before the onset of winter. On September 15 Lenthall reported that the framing for the cupola was ready. But it was not until October that Jefferson learned that the carpentry work for the skylights had not been touched and that "temporary" lantern was a misnomer. His displeasure is evident in a letter to Lenthall dated October 21: "The skylights in the dome of the House of Representatives' Chamber were a part of the plan as settled and communicated to Mr. Latrobe . . . they must be immediately prepared. . . ." [8]

Latrobe apologized, explaining that he had not wished to proceed with expensive construction until the glass had arrived. But he still persisted in his arguments and objections: "I am convinced by the evidence of my senses in inummerable cases, by all my professional experience for nearly 20 years, and by all my reasonings, that the panel lights must inevitably be destroyed after being made . . ." (October 29, 1806). [9]

The president's orders were obeyed, nevertheless, and at least half the roof had received its frames by mid-November. It was probably about this time that Latrobe completed for Jefferson the impressive presentation drawing of the Capitol, showing the building finished as he envisioned it, with the central domed rotunda, a splendid front portico, and cupolas over both the Senate and House wings. One can speculate about Latrobe's purpose in preparing the drawing. Was it a peace offering or subtle propaganda? He had been planning the drawing for several months, for he had written to Lenthall from Philadelphia on September 1, 1806, "I must beg Mr. [Robert] Mills to make a plan of the whole front of the Capitol & one side preparatory to my perspective view." [10]

The letter transmitting the drawing to President Jefferson, quoted at the beginning of this article, is dated 1806, on the 17th, but the month—presumably November—is omitted. Latrobe continues, "If I had had a good view of Monticello I would rather have employed my pencil upon that. . . . But as I had no other choice and am not satisfied with Mr. Mill's view of your house I have been obliged to chose a subject in which the President of the United States may perhaps have more interest than the individual—I beg therefore that you will please to accept the drawing as a contribution to the drawings of your own house. I

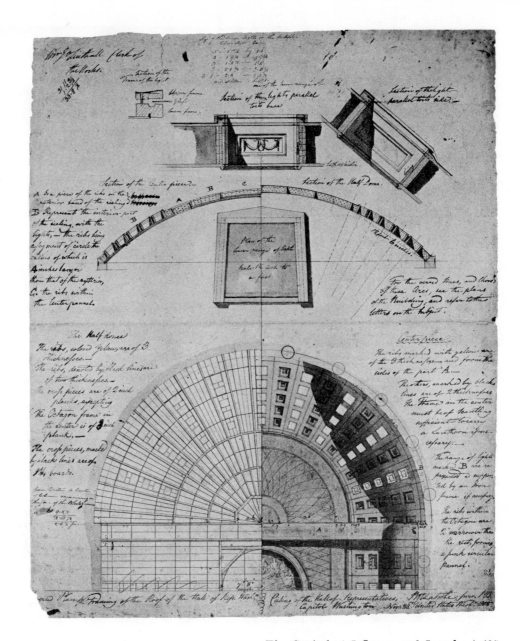

*Latrobe's plan for the framing of the roof of
the "Hall of Representatives." Watercolor
drawing, November 28, 1805.*

shall try to make a companion to it, from Mr. Mills drawing of Monticello during the winter. The frame will follow in a few days. . . ." [11]

Could this be the drawing referred to in Jefferson's letter to Latrobe of April 22, 1807? "It is with real pain I oppose myself to your passion for the lanthern, and that in a matter of taste, I differ from a professor in his own art. . . . You know my reverence for the Graecian & Roman style of architecture. I do not recollect ever to have seen in their buildings a single instance of a lanthern, cupola, or belfry. . . . one of the degeneracies of modern architecture. I confess they are most offensive to my eye, and a particular observation has strengthened my disgust at them. In the project for the central part of the Capitol which you were so kind as to give me, there is something of this kind on the crown of the dome. The drawing was exhibited for the view of the members, in the president's house, and the disapprobation of that feature in the drawing was very general." [12]

Latrobe replied on May 21: "In respect to the panel lights, I am acting diametrically contrary to my judgment. . . . In respect to the general subject of cupolas, I do not think that they are *always,* nor even *often,* ornamental. . . . I cannot admit that because the Greeks and Romans did not place elevated cupolas upon their temples, they may not when necessary be rendered also beautiful. . . . It is not the *ornament,* it is the use I want." [13]

Work progressed during the summer, and Latrobe reported to the president on August 13: "My whole time, excepting a few hours now and then devoted to the President's House, is occupied with drawing and directions for the north wing, in the arrangements for which I am pursuing the eventual plan approved and presented by you to Congress at the last session, and in pushing on the work of the south wing." [14]

Latrobe also prepared some designs for a cupola for the north wing, proposed to be carried up in 1807, which he felt was necessary to take care of the chimneys. Jefferson's reply was prompt: "I like well all your ideas except that of introducing a cupola to cover the chimnies. . . . It is evident that a cupola on the one wing necessarily calls for a corresponding one on the other. I need not here repeat the objections to that." [15]

Glass was at last obtained—from England—and the final glazing and puttying was completed in October 1807 in time for the opening session of Congress, sans cupola.

Latrobe's ideas prevailed in the end, however, for after the War of 1812 he was hired to rebuild the Capitol and, as Jefferson was no longer president, was able to construct his cupolas on both wings. They may be clearly seen in the

Left: The North Senate wing of the Capitol in 1880. Watercolor drawing by William Russell Birch.

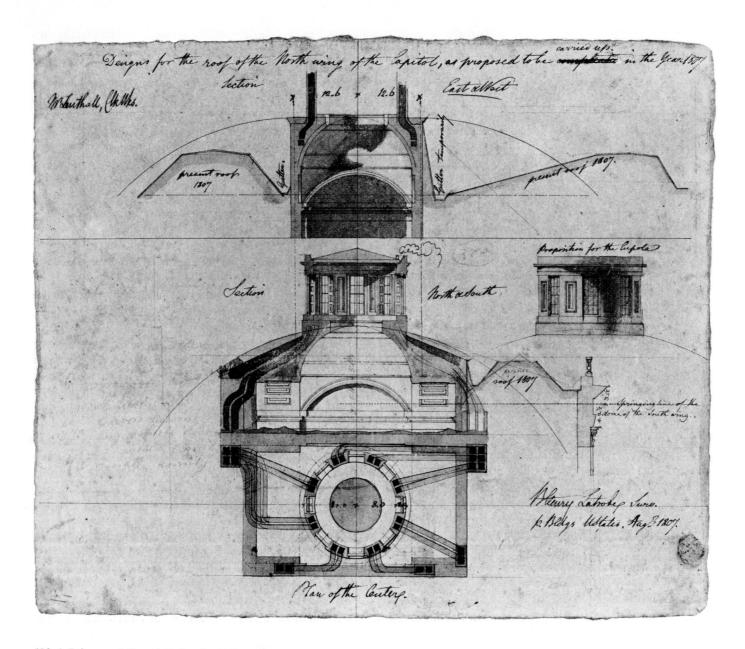

Plumbe daguerreotype of ca. 1846.

Despite all difficulties and disagreements, Latrobe and Jefferson remained friends, with a high regard for each other. On May 11, 1805, Latrobe wrote to Lenthall that Jefferson "is one of the best hearted men that ever came out of the hand of Nature and has one of the best heads also. . . . As a man, I never knew his superior in candor, kindness, and universal information; as a political character he has not his equal anywhere in patriotism, right intentions, and uniform perseverance in the system he has conceived to be the most beneficial for his country." [16]

In his report to the president on August 13, 1807, Latrobe stated: "Your administration, sir, in respect of public works, has hitherto claims of gratitude and respect from the public and from posterity. It is not flattery to say that you have planted the arts in your country. The works already erected in this city are the monuments of your judgment and of your zeal and of your taste." [17]

Jefferson likewise complimented Latrobe, writing to him on April 14, 1811, "Besides constant commendations of your taste in architecture, and science in execution, I declared on many and all occasions that I considered you the only person in the United States who could have executed the Representative chamber . . . ," [18] and again on July 12, 1812, ". . . the Representatives' Chamber will remain a durable monument of your talents as an architect. . . . I shall live in the hope that the day will come when an opportunity will be given you of finishing the middle building in a style worthy of the two wings, and worthy of the first temple dedicated to the sovereignty of the people, embellishing with Athenian taste the course of a nation looking far beyond the range of Athenian destinies." [19]

NOTES

1. Latrobe to Jefferson, [November] 17, 1806. Latrobe Papers, Manuscript Division.

2. Jefferson to Latrobe, March 6, 1803, in Glenn Brown, *History of the United States Capitol*, 2 vols. (Washington: U.S. Government Printing Office, 1900–1903), 1:32.

3. Jefferson to Latrobe, April 14, 1811, in *Thomas Jefferson and the National Capital, Containing Notes and Correspondence . . ., 1783–1813*, ed. Saul K. Padover (Washington: U.S. Government Printing Office, 1946), p. 469.

4. Jefferson to Latrobe, September 8, 1805, District of Columbia Letters and Papers on the Site and Buildings for the Federal City, Manuscript Division.

5. Latrobe to Jefferson, and to Lenthall. September 13, 1805, Latrobe Papers, Manuscript Division.

6. Latrobe to Lenthall, October 23, 1805, Latrobe Papers.

7. Jefferson to Latrobe, October 31, 1806, District of Columbia Papers.

8. Jefferson to Lenthall, October 21, 1806, Latrobe Papers.

9. Latrobe to Jefferson, October 29, 1806, Latrobe Papers.

10. Latrobe to Lenthall, September 1, 1806, Latrobe Papers.

11. Latrobe to Jefferson, [November] 17, 1806, Latrobe Papers.

12. Jefferson to Latrobe, April 22, 1807, in Padover, *Jefferson and the National Capital*, pp. 386–87.

13. Latrobe to Jefferson, May 21, 1807, Latrobe Papers.

14. Latrobe to Jefferson, August 13, 1807, Latrobe Papers.

15. Jefferson to Latrobe, September 20, 1807, District of Columbia Papers.

16. Latrobe to Lenthall, May 11, 1805, Latrobe Papers.

17. Latrobe to Jefferson, August 13, 1807, Latrobe Papers.

18. Jefferson to Latrobe, April 14, 1811, in Padover, *Jefferson and the National Capital*, p. 469.

19. Jefferson to Latrobe, July 12, 1812, in Padover, *Jefferson and the National Capital*, p. 471.

The Making of a Legend: Nicolas-Toussaint Charlet and the Napoleonic Era

BY KAREN F. BEALL

Nicolas-Toussaint Charlet, reproduced from Charlet et Son Oeuvre *by Armand Dayot, published by Libraries-Imprimeries Réunies, Paris, [1892].*

The figure of Napoleon Bonaparte seems to dominate the early years of the nineteenth century. Contributing to this impression is the depiction of his career in the graphic arts of the time. After his downfall in 1815 and death six years later, artists and writers began to glorify him, despite official censorship. The Library of Congress has recently acquired some six hundred lithographs associated with Napoleon and his era by Nicolas-Toussaint Charlet, one of the most popular propagators of the Napoleonic legend.

Charlet's father had served with the Republican Army and died for the Empire, and he himself had first-hand knowledge of military life. His serious artistic training was preceded by a period of service as sergeant-major in the Garde Nationale, during which he fought at the Barrière de Clichy. He then studied art briefly with Charles-Jacques Lebel, for whom he had little regard. In 1817 he enrolled in the atelier of Baron A. J. Gros, where he studied both painting and lithography until 1820.

Although lithography had been invented by Aloys Senefelder in Germany around 1798, it first came into prominence as an art form in France. Here men "seeking to emancipate themselves from the existing order [found] lithography with its spontaneous and versatile range of expression . . . more congenial to the new outlook than the strict techniques of copperplate engraving." [1]

It was while Charlet was studying with Baron Gros that he encountered the romantic painter Théodore Géricault, who had seen and admired his drawings. The two artists were to influence each other until Géricault's death in 1824.

Preceeding page: Cap-
tioned simply "1805" by
Charlet, this drawing
shows Napoleon brooding
over the battlefield that
was to become the scene
of one of his greatest
triumphs.

Left: Je suis prèt.
[I am ready.]

The French captions for the Charlet lithographs are copied literally from the prints in the Library of Congress.

Pleased with his pupil's work, Baron Gros showed some of Charlet's drawings to the lithographer Delpech. Soon after, the "Grenadier de Waterloo" appeared and was so successful that a second stone had to be prepared after the first one had worn out. It was the content of the print that attracted people, not the renown of the artist; Charlet had not then achieved a reputation.

As he was an admirer of Napoleon, dissatisfied with the reestablishment of the Bourbons, it is not surprising that Charlet participated in the July Revolution of 1830. Nevertheless he continued his artistic pursuits, and in 1836 he submitted a painting to the Salon entitled "Episode de la retraite de Russie." Official recognition came in 1838, when he was named professor at the Ecole Polytechnique and received the Legion of Honor.

Charlet remained at the Ecole Polytechnique until he died in 1845, leaving behind a small number of paintings, for which he is not particularly remembered, over one thousand prints,[2] and some fifteen hundred drawings.

During Charlet's lifetime, France had become indisputably a great military power. There had been numerous military painters, but until the nineteenth century they produced "official" pictures, portraits of kings and generals depicted at a secure distance from the actualities of war. Truth became increasingly important to the nineteenth-century artists, who were concerned with representing the essence of the times and portraying significant events.

Unlike his contemporaries Gros and Raffet, who tended to portray the epic of war or the panorama of the battlefield, Charlet presented the individual soldier in his daily life with all the trials and tribulations that were a part of it. Lighthearted realism and nostalgia for bygone times pervade his work. "Charlet . . . gives us the cheery, the amusing, often the grotesque view of the French Soldier."[3] There is an interplay of comedy and pathos, but rarely is tragedy portrayed. The pieces have an intimate quality, and one must be familiar with the social history of the times to appreciate fully each image with its accompanying caption, also supplied by Charlet. The artist recorded the many moods of the French soldier: his problems, his humor, his attitudes, his rivalries, his difficulties with women, his desire for drink, and his lack of funds. The drunkard in the lithograph reproduced here represents a recurring theme in Charlet's interpretation of military life.

Two of the lithographs, "O Amour" and "Je suis prèt," give some indication of Charlet's range when they are considered together. The first, more typical of his work, shows the lighter side of war and one of the advantages that may accrue to the man in uniform. The second is a powerful portrayal of war's darkest side.

Quoique fautive J'aime encore mieux être saoul que d'être bête, ça
dure moins longtems.
[Although a sinner, I'd rather be drunk than stupid: you get over it
sooner.]

"O amour!!!" with three eloquent exclamation points is Charlet's terse
caption for this print.

Écoute, Jean! If faut toujours préférer le pain noir de la Nation au gâteau de l'Etranger.
[*Listen, John, it is always better to eat black bread at home than cake abroad.*]

Artillerie légère allant prendre position.
[*Light artillery moving to position*]

It is clear that the man confronted by Death has not emotionally survived Waterloo and has never been able to make a new life.

Charlet made children the subject of many of his prints. In the two of them reproduced here the all-pervasive effect of the Napoleonic wars is evident. The children reflect their elders' preoccupation with war and with the intense nationalism it engenders.

The historical and satirical content of Charlet's works overshadows their artistic qualities, although their aesthetic merit is by no means inconsiderable. It seems curious that an artist working years after the events he portrayed became in effect a documentarian of the times. The very fact that his work does have this dimension is an interesting aspect of the cultural history of France between 1820 and 1840.

As an artist of the people, Charlet has some affinity with the poet Pierre Jean de Béranger (1780–1857). Béranger, often regarded as the national poet of France, enjoyed great popularity during his lifetime, but his reputation declined

Quand il n'y en aura plus, il y en aura
encore.
[*There are more where these came from.*]

after his death. Some of his songs and poems offer a gentle exposé of the Napoleonic era. He so irritated the Bourbon monarchy with poems published in 1821
that he was sentenced to a jail term, during which he continued to write. Another
series of poems brought a second sentence and another, a fine. His popularity was
such that the fine was paid by public subscription.

Like Béranger, Charlet enjoyed success despite censorship problems, working diligently with the collaboration of several lithographers and publishers:
Delpech, Gihaut, Motte, and Villain. His subject included military costume,
genre scenes, and some portraits, approximately half of which are of Napoleon.
The portrait reproduced here shows the solitary leader standing on a rock, over-

"Apothéose de Charlet," a lithograph by H. Bellangé, *shows a crowd of people typical of Charlet's own creations flocking to pay homage to him. Reproduced from* Charlet et Son Oeuvre *by* Armand Dayot, *published by Libraries-Imprimeries Reunies, Paris, [1892].*

looking a battlefield. The date 1805 refers to Austerlitz; the feeling conveyed is the heroism of the man standing alone in his decision, which was to lead to a brilliant victory.

Charlet also produced vignettes for poems and songs and numerous albums published from 1822 to 1845. The frontispiece for one of the albums, this one published in 1823, shows a man being inundated by hundreds of issues of albums deposited at his feet. He promises that if these are insufficient he will provide more.

Charlet worked until the last. On October 30, 1845, while he was drawing with his wife and sons looking on, his pencil stopped and he said, "Adieu, mes amis, je meurs, car je ne puis plus travailler." (Goodbye, my loved ones, I am dying because I can no longer work.) [4] With these words Nicolas-Toussaint Charlet died. He left us a great wealth of material. The Library of Congress staff hopes scholars of the Napoleonic era will find the large collection of his lithographs of use and interest.

In addition to the materials described here there are approximately 325 items on Napoleon and the French Revolution in the Gardiner Greene Hubbard Collection; several pertinent scrapbooks in the John Davis Batchelder Collection; and an uncounted group of pictures in the Joseph Verner Reed Collection, all in the Prints and Photographs Division.

NOTES

1. Felix Brunner, *A Handbook of Graphic Reproduction Processes* (New York: © 1962), pp. 177–78.

2. M. Joseph Félix Leblanc La Combe, *Charlet, sa vie, ses lettres suivi d'une description raisonnée de son oeuvre lithographique* (Paris: 1856), pp. 207–400.

3. Rose G. Kingsley, *A History of French Art, 1100–1899* (New York: 1899), p. 344.

4. La Combe, *Charlet*, p. 199.

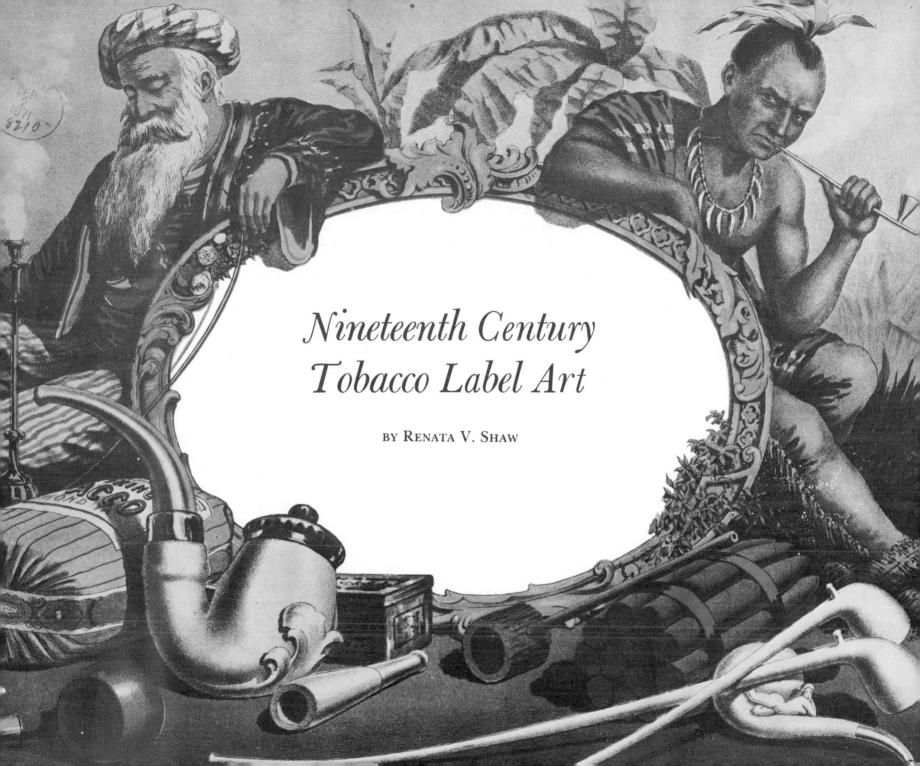

Nineteenth Century Tobacco Label Art

BY RENATA V. SHAW

American social history has been recorded in many ways, shapes, and forms—literature, music, art, drama. It can also be read on tobacco labels. Here portraits of political and military figures abound, sports personalities and stage scenes appear, paintings are reproduced and technological developments mirrored, the draft and evolution are satirized, and fashion and the feminine form are exalted.

The Prints and Photographs Division has among its nineteenth-century ephemera a collection of about a thousand tobacco labels acquired through copyright deposit from the 1840s to the 1880s, a period when all such deposits were retained. At the time, scant attention was paid to these seemingly worthless pieces of paper, because nobody then could see their value as a contribution to social history and industrial archeology. Today, they are precious examples of early American advertising and label "art."

Several important technical developments gave rise to the start of modern, colorful packaging of consumer goods; inexpensive machine-produced paper, cheap color lithography, and a vast network of shops with display shelves to accommodate a variety of individually packed wares.

From the beginning luxury goods, such as wine and tobacco, were the products on which the greatest ingenuity in advertising and presentation of goods was lavished. This was, of course, sound practice from the manufacturer's point of view. To tempt the consumer with goods not strictly life's necessities, he had to present packages that appealed to the buyer's snob sense, his yearning for elegance, and his desire for self-indulgence.

In the latter part of the nineteenth century, tobacco was sold mainly in the form of snuff, chewing tobacco, pipe tobacco, and cigars. Snuff was packaged in small cylindrical boxes; chewing tobacco was packed in wooden drums or in rectangular one-pound slabs, which were divided by the tobacconist into smaller chews, or plugs; pipe tobacco came in drawstring bags, and cigars in wooden boxes with lids ideal for fanciful illustrations, both inside and out. The different sizes and shapes of tobacco packages explain the variety of labels in use during the forty-year period that saw them transformed from relatively simple black-and-white designs into the garishly brilliant inventions of the late 1880s.

The earliest of the surviving commercial labels resembled title pages of books and consisted of the name of the product in italics and some discreet border design to finish off the composition. Their purpose was identification of the product, with no thought of commercial boasting. When pictures were added to the design, they usually showed the mill or factory where the products originated or the dignified, bearded countenance of the manufacturer, whose facsimile signature was

By picturing the American Indian and the turbaned Turk together, the manufacturer advertised his Turkish-American blend of tobacco, an innovation of the 1860s.

supposed to guarantee the purity and excellence of the product.

Eventually, competition between companies became too keen for the genteel approach. Something had to be done to attract the buyer's eye to the superior product. The most obvious device was to use more color to force the buyer to notice the package. Another was to choose an illustration that appealed to the special interests of the buyer—the male tobacco smoker.

There was no limitation to the subject matter considered suitable for decorating a tobacco label. It ranged from patriotic and lofty themes, current events of American life, and foreign historical events to personages, sports, and new inventions. On the lighter side, there appeared such favorites as sentimental portraits of maidens, children, and animals, Oriental nudes, goddesses and mermaids, foreign royalty, and spendidly attired Indians. The labels were not intended for a highly sophisticated public, although some were based on literary and artistic themes, and stars of the musical stage and the theater were frequently shown. The humor, often crude but always good natured, now seems touchingly naive and sentimental.

"Grecian Bend."

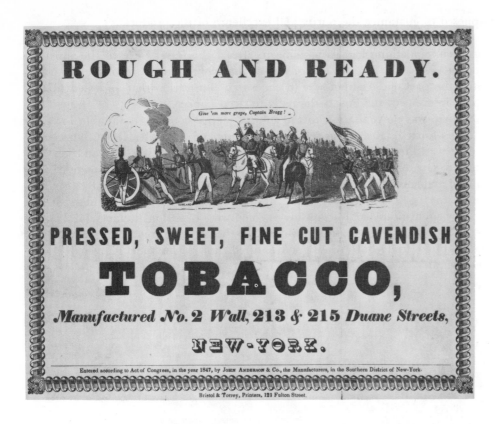

Although the 1840's had not evolved a true commercial style, advertisers already grasped the idea of timeliness in their sales message. What else would account for two different tobacco labels from 1847 both celebrating Gen. Zachary Taylor's victory at Buena Vista on February 23, 1847? Advertisers vied to be the first to publish a label celebrating some timely event: a military victory, a state visit, a new play or sports event, a new craze or fashion.

The oldest label in the collection is an 1844 black-and-white engraving for Maccoboy Snuff. Label art had not yet developed a pictorial language of its own but used traditional book-page composition for a new purpose.

Special interests of immigrants coming from Germany, Ireland, and England during the 1850s were also considered. Here, the Fenian movement is commemorated in an Irish label printed in green, with a verse designed to touch the sentiments of the Irish newcomer. The kilted Scot was another common symbol, for Scottish snuff manufacturers since the eighteenth century had sold their products widely in several countries. Thus the Scottish smoker could buy his American tobacco under a label well known to him from his homeland. Idealized portraits of Garibaldi —popular, perhaps, because he appealed to the democratic aspirations of the mid-nineteenth-century immigrant—appeared on many different labels, from tobacco to sewing silk.

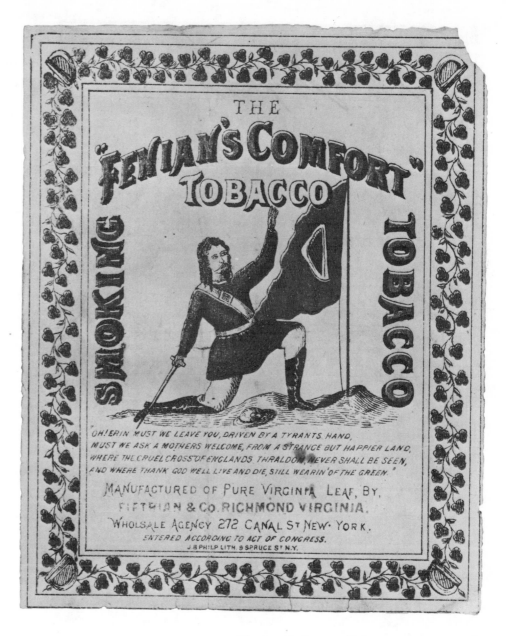

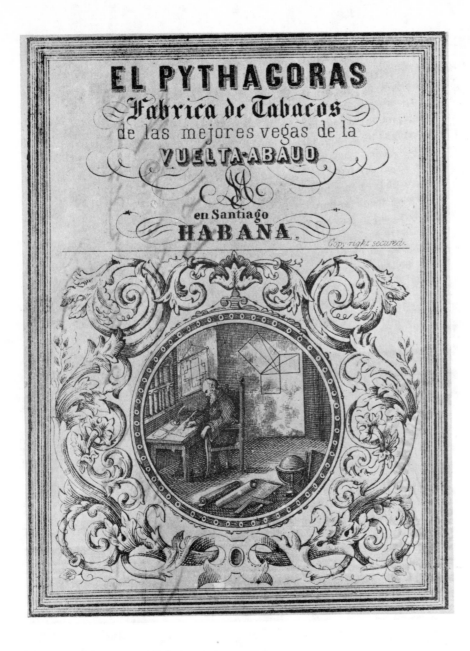

Political and military heroes were not the only famous figures to be found on tobacco labels. Dante, Goethe, and Tom Moore may not have had any connection with smoking, but they were an easily recognizable symbol of the "old country"; and familiar figures from classical history provided such unlikely label subjects as Seneca, Socrates, and Pythagoras.

It is understandable that inventions served as inspiration for labels in an age when everybody had faith in the improvement of life through better communications, rapid transportation, and other technological advances. The Library of Congress collection has three different labels—all poorly designed and hastily executed—commemorating submarine cable telegraphy, inaugurated in 1857. The trade name of the tobacco on the label shown suggests the importance popularly attached to this technological breakthrough.

Although tobacco labels were often copyrighted, the manufacturers had no qualms about adapting to their purposes any picture that caught their fancy. In the collection are several clear examples of this type of borrowing. The first is the famous portrait of the Indian scholar Sequoyah, who became known through a McKenny and Hall lithograph that shows him displaying the Cherokee syllabary he invented which paved the way to literacy for thousands of his people. The tobacco manufacturer simply obliterated the Cherokee characters and substituted his own name.

MANUFACTURED ONLY

YORKTOWN

YORKTOWN

BY PAULIN BYRD, RICHMOND VA

Lith. by A. Hoen & Co. Balto.

Entered according to act of Congress by Paulin Byrd in the year 1855.

In the Clerks office for the District Court of Maryland.

An equally significant development in the
1850s was the establishment of ocean steamship
lines, which made commerce and travel
speedier, safer, and more dependable. The
early vessels used steam only as auxiliary
power to sails; they were, nevertheless, a vast
improvement over sailing ships. A handsome
color lithograph of the side-wheeler *Yorktown*
shows large crates of tobacco on the pier waiting to be put aboard for shipment overseas.

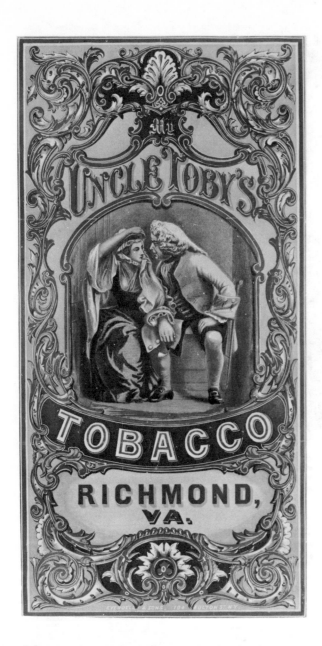

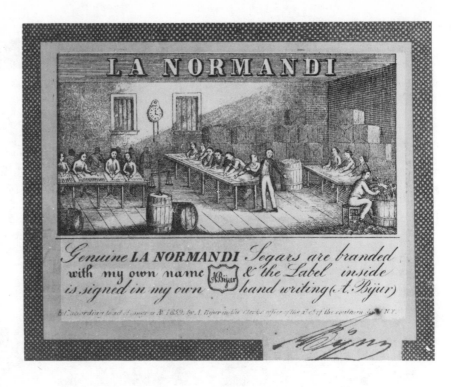

This handsome color lithograph was copied from Charles Robert Leslie's painting *Uncle Toby and Widow Wadman in the Sentry Box* (1851), today in the Tate Gallery in London. The painter based his genre scene on two important characters in Laurence Sterne's novel *Tristram Shandy*. Uncle Toby's long-stemmed pipe made the painting suitable for a tobacco advertisement.

The labels also tell the story of tobacco culture. A Cuban with a palm-thatched roof farmhouse and surrounded by palms and tobacco plants is pictured on several black-and-white labels. In another, bales of tobacco are being carried to a sailboat moored at the wharf directly below the fields. A small 1850 label showing a warehouse operator and a sailor exchanging papers for the hogsheads ready for shipping bears the optimistic mottoes: "Honest industry with enterprising perseverance shall succeed" and "Diligence is the mother of good luck!" In addition, the manufacturer promises to please "the taste of the most fastidious consumer of the weed." The scene here depicts a workroom, with cigarmakers rolling cigars by hand.

Toward the end of the 1850s color lithography achieved a high degree of technical proficiency, as seen in the large lithograph advertising the Empire State Brand, reminiscent of the seal of New York. The coloring is soft and rich, the design balanced and harmonious. The art of advertising was reaching a point of development where it was no longer dependent on the imitation of pictures created for other purposes.

JOHN C. HEENAN

ENTERED ACCORDING TO ACT OF CONGRESS A.D. 1860 BY F. ROSENBUSH IN THE CLERKS OFFICE OF THE DISTRICT COURT OF THE SOUTHERN DISTRICT OF N.Y.

In 1860 considerable curiosity was aroused when the first Japanese mission arrived in the United States carrying a treaty box containing a letter from the Tokugawa Shogun to the president and a treaty in Japanese and English. This momentous visit to exchange ratifications of the 1858 commercial treaty was a direct result of Commodore Perry's successful effort to open Japan to American trade. American ignorance of the customs and interests of the Japanese is reflected in the tobacco labels inspired by the visit. A curious error was made in naming one brand of tobacco Harikari. The label for it shows a pagodalike carriage used in the New York parade of the Japanese commissioners. Tame (Tommy) Tateishi, the popular Japanese interpreter, and some attendants sit with the treaty box on the platform.

An error of another type occurred in the brand name on a label honoring the visit of the Prince of Wales to New York in October 1860. The black-and-white engraved label is headed "El Principe de Wales" instead of "Gales," the Spanish form. The likeness is based on a well-known photograph from the famous Brady studios in New York.

Sports figures were also honored with tobacco labels displaying their names and portraits. Five different labels glorify John C. Heenan, American prizefighter, who returned to his homeland proudly sporting a championship belt after fighting the world champion, Tom Sayers, to a draw at Farnborough near London. Tom Sayers is shown sprawled on his back in the ring floored by a blow from the American. The fans eventually saved his life by pulling him out of Heenan's reach.

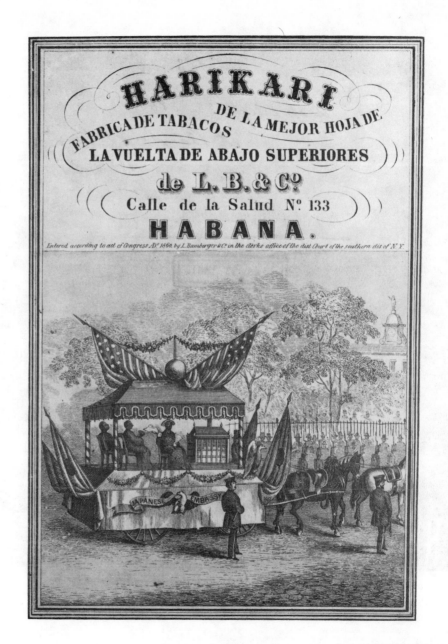

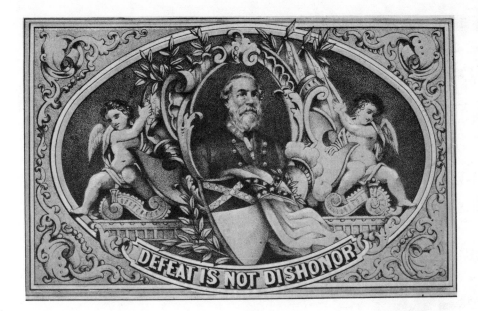

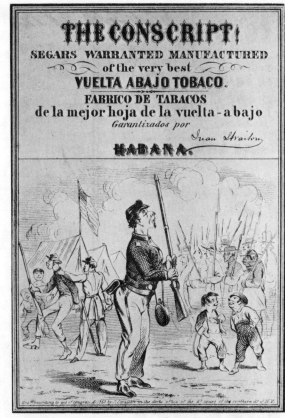

"Loyal," "Union," and "The Patriots Pride—the Old Flag" were Civil War period tobacco labels decorated with flags, American eagles, and liberty caps—all patriotic symbols designed to appeal to supporters of the Union. Only one label reflects dissenting opinion: a caricature of a draftee awkwardly holding his rifle while two street urchins poke fun at him in the background. An officer grabs another conscript by the collar to line him up with the rest of the new soldiers. The label was copyrighted in 1863, the year opposition developed to the newly passed conscription act. In the same year a label sympathetic to

the South and featuring Lee appeared. Another, "The Constitution," which shows a handshake below the flag of the United States surrounded by symbols of the Republic, expresses the spirit of conciliation appropriate to 1866.

With the start of the Civil War, the popular heroes were the military leaders. An early label devoted to one of the decisive events of the strife shows Fort Sumter in Charleston Harbor with Major Anderson in a medallion portrait surrounded by flags, cannon balls, and cannon. The label for "Our

Country's Pride" is a color lithograph of seven famous Union generals on horseback—Henry W. Halleck and George B. McClellan, left and right in the foreground, and George C. Meade, Philip H. Sheridan, Franz Sigel, Joseph Hooker, and Ambrose E. Burnside, left to right in the background. Individual labels were also devoted to McClellan and to Ulysses S. Grant, David S. Stanley, William Tecumseh Sherman, and Michael Corcoran, the commander of the "Irish Legion," and to the Confederate Generals Robert E. Lee, "Stonewall" Jackson, and Joseph E. Johnson.

Even during the Civil War years European political events and personalities were featured on tobacco labels. "Italia Unida" celebrated the unification of Italy in 1861, and "Schleswig Holstein" alluded to the events of 1864 when Austria joined with Prussia to separate Schleswig-Holstein from Denmark. "Alexander Imperials" shows the "Czar Liberator" Alexander II of Russia, whose reign was characterized by a cautious move toward liberalism. Other members of European royal houses, particularly beautiful princesses, were favorites of tobacco advertisers. Princess Alexandra of England and Empress Eugénie of France graced labels for chewing tobacco, the latter transformed into the "Belle of Kentucky."

The postbellum era introduced labels featuring sports and pastimes popular in all sections of the country, from baseball to billiards. Even before 1869, when the first professional team—the Cincinnati Red Stockings—was founded, labels advertised both tobacco and baseball, which had emerged as a national sport during the Civil War.

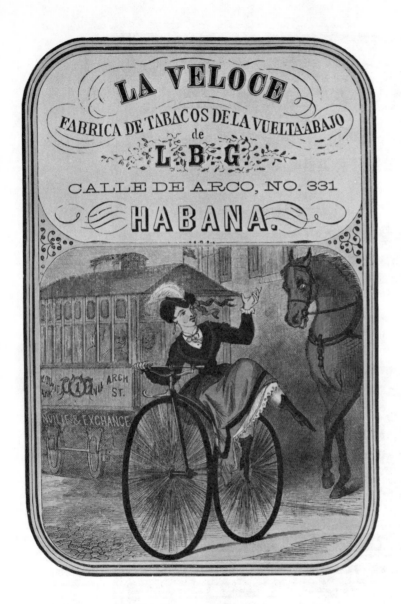

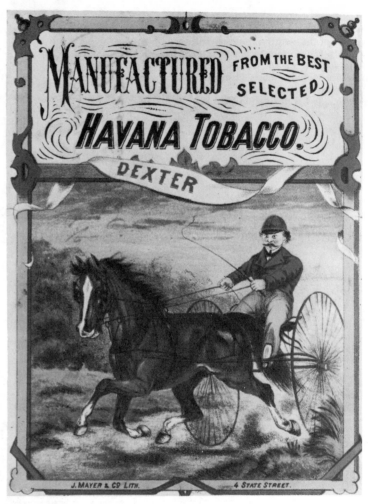

Another craze was introduced in 1869 when the rubber-tired velocipede arrived on the market. Earlier the wheels were of wood with iron rims, which offered such a bumpy ride that they were known as boneshakers. The new velocipede was a great improvement, as men and women, young and old, took to the wheels for a spin in the open air. The most humorous of these labels shows a bewildered lady in city traffic in the path of both a streetcar and a horse.

The first transatlantic yacht race from New York to the Isle of Wight was won by the American schooner *Henrietta* in thirteen days, twenty-one hours, and forty-five minutes in December 1866, an event recorded on several labels showing the proud winner. Light harness racing was a more folksy sport known to a large segment of the rural population. Several labels picture famous horses like Dexter and Hambletonian, the sire of many of America's famous racehorses. Both were immortalized by Currier and Ives.

The entertainment world of New York in the late 1860s had more variety to offer than the programs of today. Entertainers, singers, and stars of the opera and theater were imported every season from Europe. The discriminating public could enjoy plays and operas in the original German, French, or Italian in addition to English. The foreign language companies presented as many as a hundred different plays in one year. Copyrighted tobacco labels of these years display scenes from some of the most popular productions. In "The Grand Duchess" Lucille Tostée, star of Offenbach's *La Grande Duchesse de Gérolstein,* sings "Voici le tabac," an adaptation of the operetta's popular "Voici le sabre de mon père."

A ballet of eight tableaux called *White Fawn* was the source for five different labels of fairyland ballerinas. In contrast is the label inspired by *Fanchon*, another kind of spectacle which remained in the repertory for several decades.

Other labels show the British opera singer Euphrosyne Parepa-Rosa as Norma and scenes from *The Pickwick Papers, La Camille*, and *Falstaff*. These sophisticated themes from the entertainment world were intended to reach the tobacco smoker who preferred "Jerome Park," "Social," and "Grecian Bend," brands whose labels depicted high society. The "Grecian bend," a once-fashionable posture, often exaggerated by the bustle, is demonstrated by the lady who lights her cigar from a gentleman's pipe. This lighthearted reflection on the fashions of the day shows the return to more prosperous times, when people could devote their attention to amusements and outings.

By the 1870s there were two schools of tobacco label art: the traditional, reflecting events of the day such as the expansion of the frontier, the last skirmishes with the Indians, the changes brought about by railroads and balloons, the rapid extinction of the buffalo, and the gradual emancipation of women; and the sensual, emphasizing the female figure in a variety of settings, from classical mythology and romantic literature to the exotic Near East and modern West. Technically, the labels were larger and better executed than the earlier ones. More attention was paid to composition; the colors became softer and brighter. And an attempt was made to incorporate the lettering and advertising message into a harmonious whole. In most cases, however, the labels were too cluttered with different pictorial themes to achieve the impact of their modern counterparts.

Indian maidens were depicted as dark-haired beauties in feathered headdresses strolling along mountain streams or reclining in hammocks amidst ferns and palmettos, idealizations of the noble savage living in blissful innocence beyond the range of the civilized world.

Black Hawk and Red Cloud, chiefs who resisted the advance of the white man on their territories, were popularized in romantic poses in "Wild West" settings. Another timely brand, "Rivals," shows a fierce Indian and a white hunter chasing a buffalo over the open prairie. The "Echo" chewing tobacco label is decorated with the head of a magnificent buffalo, even then in danger of extinction.

The American Indian was also frequently used in juxtaposition with a turbaned Turk enjoying his waterpipe in a coffee shop. Turkish motifs appeared in tobacco labels when Turkish light tobacco became fashionable in the late 1860s. This coincided with the fad for cigarettes, manufactured from a Turkish-Virginia blend.

The Turkish themes of harem ladies reclining on soft cushions smoking the hookah or resting by lotus ponds in the moonlight gave the American advertising artist complete liberty to indulge in the most daring flights of imagination. He could safely portray lightly draped, dark-eyed temptresses in rich jewels and gold bangles without being criticized for exceeding the limits of good taste. In contrast are labels like "Crusader,' whose portrait was inspired by the Women's Christian Temperance Union, founded in 1874. She is fashionably dressed, but her mission in life is indicated by the women in the background who are preparing to storm a tavern.

No novelties of the 1870s escaped the commentary of the tobacco label artist. He showed a balloon rising above the globe and, in another label, the new Brooklyn Bridge, formally opened to traffic ten years after the label was copyrighted. An unknown artist made a drawing dedicated to the spirit of water in Fountain Square in Cincinnati for the label "Fountain Dew."

The ancient device of using animals dressed as humans to satirize contemporary life was also employed by label designers. "What Is It" may have been a veiled criticism of Darwin's controversial treatise *The Descent of Man,* which was then being earnestly debated by educated men. Another label, "Mule Ear," shows a mule standing on a porch of a southern mansion, in morning robe and cap, examining fresh tobacco leaves brought in from the fields on his estate. This label does not seem to carry any hidden message; it is only a humorous scene of an animal acting like a human.

There are also many labels which are merely pretty, sentimental pictures, without any story attached: a farmer pauses in his plowing to enjoy a plug of tobacco, a beautiful maiden dreamily admires a bouquet of forget-me-nots, exquisitely dressed young girls roll hoops in a quiet city street, and impeccably dressed hunters rest in a forest clearing.

But more and more it was the glamor girl who was front and center. Indeed, idealized beautiful women were becoming so important in advertising that artists had to turn to history, myth, romantic literature, and the stage for backgrounds. Two different companies depicted Leda, to whom Zeus appeared in the guise of a swan. Other used lightly draped ideal female nudes rising from the sea in a mist of pink clouds. "Jennie Hughes," a New York actress, is a less ethereal dream girl. These lithographs of the 1870s with their soft, chalky crayon outlines and delicately applied color testify to the designer's personal touch.

With the 1880s an obvious change took place in the technical as well as the artistic aspects of label art. The surface of the prints became slicker and smoother, acquiring an oily sheen. The illustrations deteriorated to the level of stereotyped cover girls, lacking subject interest and individuality, surrounded by animals and flowers; colors were now bright but garish. The decline of tobacco label art in the late 1880s must be attributed to a vastly greater demand for labels, with handprinting supplanted by mechanical processes and the introduction of new inks and new papers. Manufacturers also demanded greater speed, which meant that artistic quality had to be

sacrificed for faster production. An example of this type of label is "Prosperity," a symbolic figure surrounded by gold medals from trade fairs and an open box of cigars.

After 1890 chromolithographs on labels were gradually replaced by photomechanical reproductions, based on actual photographs of people and places. With the introduction of this new technique the era of tobacco label "art," which saw the modest black-and-white early designs develop into the flamboyant chromolithographs of the 1880s, came to an end.

Five Sketchbooks of Emanuel Leutze

BY RAYMOND L. STEHLE

In the summer of 1962 the Library of Congress received through Dr. Egon Hanfstaengl, a gift from his uncle Dr. Eberhard Hanfstaengl, the former Director of the Munich Pinakothek. The gift consisted of two sketchbooks of the artist Emanuel Leutze and fifteen letters addressed to him—ten of them written by Gen. Winfield S. Hancock and two by Frederick W. Seward. The letters are now in the custody of the Manuscript Division and the sketchbooks have been added to the collections of the Prints and Photographs Division, where they have joined a group of three other Leutze sketchbooks and a small portfolio of drawings that were presented to the Library by Dr. Eberhard Hanfstaengl in 1954. The Hanfstaengl family had been intimate friends of the family of Leutze's daughter Alice, who had married Carl Jooss of Munich; and it was from their children that Dr. Hanfstaengl obtained the Leutze items. He is still in possession of one or more Leutze sketchbooks and owns several of the artist's paintings.

Emanuel Leutze, who is best known for his picture *Washington Crossing the Delaware,* was born in Germany on May 24, 1816, and was nine years old when his parents emigrated to the United States and settled in Philadelphia, where he grew up. Even in his youth his talent for drawing was not to be doubted, and when he was only twenty he was elected to membership in the Artists' Fund Society of Philadelphia.

In 1837 young Leutze was engaged by Longacre and Herring to go to Washington and paint portraits of some of the men prominent in the Government for inclusion in their *National Portrait Gallery of Distinguished Americans.* The

Emanuel Leutze who painted Westward the Course of Empire Takes Its Way, *a mural in the Capitol. (Photograph from* Harper's Weekly, *August 8, 1868, p. 509.)*

167

depression of that year put a temporary end to the enterprise, and for a time Leutze became an itinerant portrait painter in Virginia. He then returned to Philadelphia and, after a short period of intense activity, he acquired the means to set out for Düsseldorf in 1840 for further study. During the next few years, he painted a number of pictures which found ready purchasers among American collectors, Toward the end of the year 1845, Leutze married the daughter of a German officer in Düsseldorf.

Sometime in 1849 he began work on *Washington Crossing the Delaware*, which occupied him for about two years. Before the painting was finished, it was purchased by Messrs. Goupil and Company of Paris, who planned to exhibit it in the United States and take orders for an engraving that was being made. When the picture was exhibited in Washington, Leutze was present. He had hoped to obtain a commission from the U.S. Congress to paint a replica and then bring his young family to America; however, other American artists and their friends thought that if Congress planned to award any commissions for paintings they would like to share in the distribution. So it is not surprising that the matter got mired in the Capitol and that when the 32d Congress came to an end on March 3, 1853, no one had been awarded a commission. Undoubtedly disappointed, Leutze returned to Düsseldorf. His next picture was another large one—*Washington Rallying the Troops at Monmouth*. That was followed by smaller works, many of which also found American purchasers.

In 1859 conditions again seemed propitious for a return to America. Since several of the sketchbooks reviewed in the following pages fall within this later period, some of the events of those years are related in a discussion of the books. For a few years subsequent to 1863, his life was uneventful, but there is reason to believe that those years were followed by a period characterized by ill health and debt. He died in Washington on July 18, 1868, and is buried in Glenwood Cemetery.

Leutze's paintings may be classified as follows: about sixty are historical pictures, nearly one hundred are portraits, around thirty are works inspired by literature, approximately fifty are products of his own fancy, and about ten are landscapes.

Considerable light is thrown upon Leutze's activities by the contents of Dr. Hanfstaengl's gifts, but the lack of place names and dates and even the arrangement of the sketches, which follow no particular chronological sequence, make their interpretation difficult and often uncertain. Leutze was not plagued by system—an unused page in any book was all that was important.

The contents of these books are confined to the years 1841 and 1859–61. They will be reviewed in what seems to be chronological order. As yet they have been assigned no definite designations, so they will be referred to as (1) the "green sketchbook," (2) the "dark brown sketchbook," (3) the "buff-colored sketchbook," (4) the "album," and (5) the "light brown sketchbook," or numerically in the same order.

The green sketchbook contains drawings made by Leutze soon after he had left Philadelphia at the age of twenty-four to study at Düsseldorf. (He registered with the authorities there on February 11, 1841.) Some of the sketches were probably made when he was a student at the Academy of Art in Düsseldorf. One is a caricature of himself painting. Examination of the sketch shows the varying character of his thoughts. That his homeland had not been forgotten is clear from the presence—among the subjects represented in his nebulous "thoughts"—of the Capitol at Washington and of an ear of corn. Also distinguishable are some pretty girls, a pair of fencing foils, a ship, a charioteer and, at the top of the page, food and drink. One of the sketches in this book is not by Leutze but by his friend Trevor McClurg of Pittsburgh. Someone has written beside this drawing "Self-portrait of Leutze." Whoever did this failed to recognize the significance of the "T. McC" written beneath it. The sketch is undated, but it was doubtless made in 1841. After a year or so at the academy, Leutze became dissatisfied with its routine and withdrew. It was then that he and his friends McClurg and J. G. Schwarze set up a studio of their own in Düsseldorf; the three had probably known each other in Philadelphia. Trevor McClurg must have been one of Leutze's most intimate friends, for the artist named one of his sons after him—Trevor McClurg Leutze, who became Engineer in Charge of the Eastern Division of the New York State Engineer's Office.

The earliest of the remaining four sketchbooks is probably the dark brown one (no. 2). From the earliest Düsseldorf period (1841), covered by the green book, one is transported to the period following his final return to America in 1859. Leutze had been home for the better part of a year during the period 1851–52 and would have remained in America had there been any prospect of obtaining commissions for the kind of painting that interested him—historical painting.

At the top of the first page of this sketchbook is written "Star of Empire, History." Beneath are listed subjects which he seems to have thought suitable for pictures illustrating the general title: "Moses slaying the taskmaster, feudalism, Knight feudal, right of inquiry, Luther, Brutus, Cromwell, Saul anointed king"

Sketch of Capt. James Stone of the steamship
Arabia.

Far left: A self-caricature by Leutze.

Left: A drawing by Leutze's friend, Trevor
McClurg. Note the initials "T. McC."

and two which the writer found illegible. Perhaps he was already thinking of a mural for the Capitol, encompassed by a border in which small pictures on these subjects would be incorporated. The oil sketch he later submitted to Capt. Montgomery C. Meigs, bearing the title "Westward the Course of Empire Takes Its Way" was such a composition; the border contains many sketches. The mural itself is another such composition; it has an elaborate border, but the subjects incorporated in it are different from those of the oil sketch.

Following several sketches which are of such a nature that only Leutze could explain their presence (procurators of St. Mark, a Franciscan cardinal, and other specimens of aristocratic faces) there are many portrait sketches, some dated, of passengers and crew aboard the steamship *Arabia* on which he returned to America in 1859.[1] That of Capt. James Stone, dated January 26, 1859, is reproduced here as representative of this group.

Other entries of significance concern a picture that Leutze painted in 1860, the *Founding of Maryland,* which now hangs in the headquarters of the Maryland Historical Society in Baltimore. He made a trip to the region of the first settlement on the lower Potomac to obtain firsthand information for the setting he was to represent. Actually, the landscape had changed considerably since the settlement. There are several sketches devoted to the plants of the region, a grouse and heads of other birds, a turtle, and several broad sweeps showing the lay of the land and the Potomac estuary. Among this group is an undated sketch of a warship; on it is written "Old Ironsides, Constitution, Point Lookout." The log of this ship shows that it was at Point Lookout, St. Mary's County, Maryland, on April 14–15, 1860. Dates are so rare in these books that it is a pleasure to find something which can be dated and which fixes the artist momentarily in time and place. Finally, among the oddities that occur is a little sketch which is identifiable as the Doge's Palace; it probably represents a pleasant memory of his visit to Venice as a young man. Later, in 1864, he painted a picture entitled *Venice Victorious,* in which the palace is conspicuous.

The three remaining sketchbooks (nos. 3–5) fall within the period 1859–61. The dominant theme of the subjects represented is emigration to the West, which eventually culminated in the Capitol mural *Westward the Course of Empire Takes Its Way.*

In a letter of January 12, 1854,[2] which Meigs addressed to Leutze in Düsseldorf, he had said:

My dear sir.

The reputation you bear as an artist induces me to address you this letter.

In designing the Extension of the U.S. Capitol there are spaces provided on the walls of some of the Rooms & Halls but more particularly on the marble stairways which seem almost to require decoration by the hand of the Painter.

Now are there any American artists capable of executing a fresco painting of large size. Would it not be well for some of them yourself for instance to turn their attention to this art with a view to this building.

I believe that I shall be supported by Congress in calling to our aid all the best talent & skill in art which our country can boast. And should you be disposed to risk the loss of time incurred in the study if unsuccessful I will be glad to communicate with you on the subject to send you tracings of our designs & receive from you hints in relation to decoration.

I believe that suitable designs would be accepted by Congress & the President in whose hands the building is by law placed

> *Very respectfully*
> *Your obt svt*
> *M. C. Meigs*
> **Captain U.S. Engineers**
> **in charge of Wash. Aq. & Cap[1] extension**

It was not until three years later—in a letter received by the architect on February 8, 1857—that Leutze submitted a long list of subjects he considered to be suitable for paintings; among them was "Emigration to the West." When he returned to the United States in 1859, he probably expected, or at any rate hoped, that he would soon be at work in the Capitol; the walls were about ready for the artist. Meigs wrote to Leutze on February 12,[3] shortly after his arrival in New York, urging him to come to Washington at once.

Capitol Extension & Washington
Aqueduct Office
Washington 12 Feby 1859.

E. Leutze
Artist
New York

My dear sir.

The newspapers inform me of your arrival in this country & I write to express to you my gratification at the news & to suggest the importance, in view of the great work on which I doubt not you are bound, of your losing as little time as possible, in coming to Washington.

It has been my earnest desire so to arrange the works of the Great Public building under my charge that it would be necessary to employ artists in filling up the outlines I have sketched. Fields for pictures, niches & pediments for statues have been liberally provided.

What is needed here is an artist capable of occupying the field.

I have been annoyed by pretenders by quacks by scoundrels (?)

I have not received from any American artist a sketch or design for a picture fit to go into a county court house much less into the Capitol of the U States. From one American sculptor however I have received valuable aid & his recommendation (?) rests upon a firm foundation of able historical works executed for his country.

I know Congress to be liberal & I doubt not that a good artist, located here, painting here & able to paint a picture when commissioned—instead of being obliged to go abroad to study his art before he fills his commission, would find himself fully occupied with works for the decoration of the Capitol. To such a one I should gladly lend all the aid in my power believing that my own reputation is benefited by whatever exalts the character for art of the building on which I have spent so much thought & labor.

The session passes away—Members of committees are occupied and liable to be sick & thus business is delayed. If anything is to be done time is precious.

Assuring you of a hearty welcome and all the aid in my power, for in your works I recognize a true artist's power and genius, I am very truly and sincerely yours,

M. C. Meigs.

For a time, however, the deliberations of an Art Commission prevented any contracts being awarded, and after the demise of the Art Commission Congress itself forbade the expenditure of any money for paintings or sculpture before July 1, 1861. This state of affairs did not prevent Meigs and Leutze from making comprehensive plans for paintings in the Capitol. Meigs had evidently liked the subject "Emigration to the West," and they may have agreed that it would be the theme of the first mural if and when the embellishment of the building were allowed to proceed.

In the spring of 1861 Leutze submitted to Meigs an oil sketch which pleased the latter immensely, and on July 9, 1861, the two entered into a contract calling for Leutze to paint "upon the western wall of the eastern stairs of the Capitol a picture on Emigration." This sketch, if we are not mistaken, was based upon information gathered during the course of an undocumented trip which Leutze made to the West, probably in the summer of 1860. This trip was doubtless made on his own initiative and in spite of the fact that he no longer had "a friend at court," for Meigs had been relieved of his duties in connection with the extensions to the Capitol on November 1, 1859. In his book *The National Capitol* (1897), George C. Hazelton, Jr., states on page 196 that ". . . in disregard of the letter of the law, money had been advanced to the artist to enable him to visit the frontier for the purpose of studying its scenes and making his sketches from life." Obviously, in 1860 Meigs was in no position to do this; and the record shows that no payment was made to Leutze until after he had submitted his sketch. This he seems to have done after February 27, 1861, when Meigs resumed the supervision of the extensions to the Capitol; it is, however, within the realm of possibility that the sketch was submitted before that date, since Meigs must have known for some time what was in the offing. The prospect for proceeding with the mural was good, and the money to pay for it would be available in the unspent balance of an appropriation as soon as the congressional ban had expired. A payment to Leutze, whose trip to the West had probably been made at considerable cost, would not appear to have been outside Meigs's authority. The beginning of the Civil War delayed the signing of the contract for about a month.

The contract itself supports the idea of a trip to the West, made before Leutze submitted his oil sketch. It states that $3,500 already received "for completing the design" is to be deducted from the contract price.

The scant information which the writer has gleaned concerning Leutze's movements in 1860 also supports the idea that he went West in that year. He is known to have planned to spend the summer at West Point, where he had spent the previous summer, but no evidence that he carried out this intention has been found. His family was in Europe, so he was free to travel, and he was undoubtedly anxious to submit a sketch which would bring him a commission.

After he received the commission, Leutze made a trip to the West which is well authenticated. It resulted, however, in no important changes in the design; in essentials the mural is like the preliminary sketch.

The three remaining books are also especially interesting for the evidence they provide regarding the early, undocumented trip to the West.

The first sketch in the buff-colored book is useful in providing the approximate date on which this book was put into use. About the end of 1859, Leutze was commissioned by Secretary of State Lewis Cass to design a medal which would be awarded to foreigners who had assisted in saving the lives of American sailors ship-wrecked in foreign parts. A sketch of the reverse side of this medal appears as the first item. Nearly all of the following page has been torn out, but enough remains to indicate that whatever was on it concerned the medal too—possibly the obverse, which would have been more interesting than the reverse.

Having used the first pages of the third book at the end of the year 1859, Leutze seems to have set it aside in favor of the one just reviewed (no. 2), and later to have reverted to it.

Following the medal, the objects portrayed pertain to the West. The first is a sketch of two figures, possibly emigrants, with their belongings beside them; they are followed by studies of cattle. The next few are more significant. One depicts a rocky mass that is easily recognizable as the central feature in the Capitol mural. Another is a drawing of a mountainous landscape which resembles one of the distant mountains of the mural. Close after this is a sketch of a man who has scaled the rocks and is now waving his kerchief with one hand, while holding a flag in the other. Several pages are devoted to small western animals—a skunk, a coyote, a burrowing owl, and others. The animal studies, in particular, lead one to suppose that all these sketches were made in the West and, since some of them recur in the preliminary sketch given to Meigs, they must have been made on a trip which occurred before that of 1861.

The fourth book (the album) contains many miscellaneous trifles which seem to have occupied Leutze's mind, and therefore his pencil, while he was in the West. The most interesting of its contents depict western objects—a camp including two tents and horses, horses feeding at a covered wagon, stacked harnesses, and legs and paws of animals of the region. Of much greater significance

Above: The rocky mass which forms the central features of the mural in the Capitol. Above right: One of the distant mountainous scenes in the mural.

for the support they give to a trip made in 1860 are five sketches of the West. These carry more weight in favor of such a trip than do the sketches in the third book, because two of them bear place names and therefore identify the region visited. They indicate that Leutze journeyed to the northwest boundary between the United States and Canada, the survey of which was just being completed. One of the two sketches on which the locations are noted bears the legend "Sierra Nevada, Cascade, near the Pacific coast, North." It was made, therefore, near the western end of the boundary. The notation on the other is simply "Mt. Kish-e-nehn." This mountain was found to be in the Rockies, hence near the eastern end of the boundary.[4]

In the course of his search for Mt. Kish-e-nehn, the writer learned that the boundary survey material in the National Archives includes sixty-six sketches made by James M. Alden, the artist of the expedition. It is a matter of interest to compare these with the sketches in Leutze's book. Two of the Alden sketches have the same subjects as the two of Leutze's just mentioned, but the drawings of the two artists differ in detail. Alden's sketch (no. 46) of the valley of Kish-e-nehn Creek was made from quite a different position than was the Leutze sketch bearing the caption "Mt. Kish-e-nehn"; and Leutze's sketch of the Cascade covers a much wider sweep of territory than does Alden's sketch (no. 6), of the Langley

Buttes. (These are without doubt different names for the same feature.) Alden's sketch no. 51 is limited to Mt. Kish-e-nehn and differs greatly in detail from the mountain represented in the left-hand portion of Leutze's drawing. Three of Leutze's sketches have no counterparts among Alden's.

One may ask why Leutze went to the Northwest to gather his information instead of the region he visited in 1861. There is reason to believe that Leutze was acquainted with A. D. Bache, Superintendent of the Coast Survey, whose office was involved in the survey of the western end of the boundary, where it became a tortuous line among islands. The boundary would have been a natural subject of conversation and the possibilities offered by the survey to anyone interested in the western terrain could scarcely have escaped Leutze.

In the oil sketch which Leutze submitted to Meigs, mentioned above, the mountain mass in the right background has no counterpart in the sketchbooks. In the mural itself, however, the writer is inclined to think that the quite different mass represented there is a modified composite of two of the sketches—the left-hand part being based upon the sketch shown in one of the mural's mountain scenes and the right-hand part on that shown in the Sierra Nevada drawing or the Rockies sketch, all illustrated in this article. The idea of a relationship between sketch and mural is perhaps more acceptable in the case of the left-hand portion. If Leutze had his sketch of Mt. Kish-e-nehn in mind for the right-hand portion, he employed it with considerable artistic license. The reader may find that this portion resembles the Cascade more than Mt. Kish-e-nehn. The whole matter is extremely speculative, and what has been said here is to be regarded as nothing more than an attempt to see in the mural something more than the pure imagination of the artist.

The last of the sketchbooks seems to have been used at two periods separated in time by more than a year. The first pages contain several sketches of heads of Indians which Leutze copied from the portraits by Carl Bodmer published in the Prince of Wied-Neuwied's *Travels in the Interior of North America, 1832–1834.*[5] The motive which impelled him to make these copies is not evident. They are followed by a sketch of an ox bearing a yoke and then by a sketch of a man wielding an ax. In the oil sketch given to Meigs, Leutze used the latter figure, but he did not use it in the mural. The character of the sketches in this book then changes. The next one, a drawing of a tree, bears the legend "Fredericksburg, Apr. 4, 1861," just a week before the beginning of the Civil War at Fort Sumter. Another is a sketch of a picturesque rail fence. Then follow a field of soldiers and a man in a Zouave uniform. There are also several sketches of horses, one bear-

Sketch of a central figure in the mural, the man who has scaled the rocks.

A drawing with Leutze's notation: "Sierra Nevada, Cascade, near the Pacific coast, North."

ing the caption "old Bob," and another sketch of a Conestoga wagon.

The small portfolio contains sketches relating to the war. It was probably the artist S. R. Gifford, a member of the Seventh New York Regiment, who mentions in an unsigned letter of May 17, 1861 (published in *The Crayon* for June 1861, vol. 8, pp. 134–35), visits that Leutze made to Camp Cameron on Meridian Hill in Washington, D.C., where he was stationed, and a visit he himself made to Leutze's studio in Washington. One of the sketches in the portfolio, dated May 7, 1861, was made at Camp Cameron. Another pictures five soldiers occupied in various ways at desks. This was probably made between May 2 and 10, 1861, when several companies of Col. Elmer E. Ellsworth's Fire Zouaves were quartered in the Capitol—some in the House of Representatives. At this time Leutze must have been a frequent visitor at the Capitol. Meigs probably had his preliminary "Westward the Course of Empire Takes Its Way" under consideration, though no commission could be given without the approval of the secretary of war, who had

Westward the Course of Empire Takes Its Way, *the mural by Emanuel Leutze which stands above the landing of the grand marble staircase leading from the west corridor of the Nation's Capitol. (From a negative in the Office of the Architect of the Capitol.)*

Above: Leutze's sketch of Mt. Kish-e-nehn in the Rockies.

Left: Probably Leutze's sketch of some of Col. Elmer E. Ellsworth's Fire Zouaves who were quartered at the Capitol in 1861. The drawing is in the portfolio.

more pressing matters than paintings to think about. On the occasion of one of these visits, Leutze may have made this sketch; the wall of the stairway on which he hoped to paint his mural was just across the corridor from the quarters of the Zouaves.

The camp of these same Zouaves at Alexandria, named Camp Ellsworth after the colonel's death on May 24, 1861, upon the invasion of Virginia by Union troops, is also the subject of a sketch. It was probably made about the end of that month. Another sketch bears the legend "de Trobriand's Camp." This was Fort Gaines, which was built on land belonging at the time to William D. C. Murdock and now to the American University. A tablet marks the approximate position of the fort, and therefore of the Leutze sketch. The leafless trees indicate that it was made in winter—the winter of 1861–62.

Among the letters from General Hancock to Leutze are several which are of interest because they show the general's desire to see Leutze selected to paint a picture representing the Battle of Gettysburg, in which he had played a role. General Hancock seems to have known that certain influential Pennsylvanians were thinking of having such a picture painted. He invited Leutze and the historian Bancroft to visit the battlefield with him in October 1865. Actually, the Pennsylvania legislature did not decide to take definite action until early in 1866, when it appointed a committee to select the artist. Notification of this step was received by Leutze from Gen. Samuel W. Crawford in a letter dated March 14, [1866] at Harrisburg, Pa., which reads:

My dear Sir:

> *The Legislature of Pennsylvania have authorized the painting of a battle scene of some part of the battle of Gettysburg. Your name has been mentioned but the resolve of the Committee is to ask for battle scene studies from different artists & I now write to you asking that you may take advantage of this request. It is proposed to offer a prize of $500 for the successful picture.*
> *I write you now but I hope to be in your studio next week.*

> *Sincerely your friend*
> *S. W. CRAWFORD*

An effort to insure that the artist be a Pennsylvanian failed, but when the time came to award the commission the committee did select a native son—Peter F.

Rothermel. Leutze seems to have made no effort to procure the commission.

Another letter, dated June 21, 1866, was written by S. P. Hanscom, publisher of the *National Republican,* a Washington, D.C., newspaper. Leutze had traveled from New York to Washington to paint a portrait of Pres. Andrew Johnson and had been rebuffed by one of the president's secretaries, Col. W. J. Moore, who told him that the president was busy. Upon his return to New York, Leutze directed an account of the episode to Mr. Hanscom, who evidently made a visit to the president to bring the matter to his attention. Hanscom's reply to Leutze, written on "Executive Mansion" stationery, is most apologetic. It reads:

My Dear LEUTZE

Upon my return found your letter. Its contents very much impressed me and surprised the President still more, who desires me to say to you that he was not aware that you had been there, but on the contrary inquired once of Col. Moore why you did not call and was told that your things were there and that you had called once but that the President being busy was not notified. The President felt very much annoyed about the matter, scolded Moore severely and assures me if you are in the city to be sure and let him know. You will have no difficulty hereafter I can assure you.

The President sat today at the request of Mr. Seward for the artist sent here by Switzerland. I have seen his rough [sketch] and it promises well.

Let me know if you propose coming again and I will not go away. I would not have gone as it was had I supposed the matter was not completely arranged.

I hope to see you soon here or in New York.

Sincerely regretting your disappointment, which the President regrets on his own account, I remain.

Very Truly
S. P. HANSCOM

The letters written by Frederick W. Seward, the son of the secretary of state, pertain primarily to the design for a monument which his father wished Leutze to make for the grave of his daughter. Leutze had already designed the monument for his wife. In the second of these letters, dated March 14, 1867, in which the son thanks Leutze for his design, there is reference to the artist's health.

My Dear LEUTZE

I have received your letter of the 12th enclosing your beautiful design for the monument of my sister, for which we all thank you gratefully and sincerely.

And we are very glad to thus learn from you that [you] are recovering from your late serious illness and threatened affection of the eyesight which had occasioned grave apprehensions—now happily relieved.

Yours very truly,
F. W. SEWARD

Notice of an illness he was suffering early in 1867 had been published in the February 7 issue of the *New York Evening Post*. This letter makes it clear that the erysipelas which had afflicted him had been a serious affair and that his eyesight had been endangered.

In concluding this review, mention of the last drawing in the third book would seem fitting. It is a sketch of a portion of the steamship *Teutonia* and must have been made in May 1863. It was on this ship that, after finishing the mural in the Capitol, Leutze returned to Germany to bring his family to America. There can be no doubt that he thought the mural he had just finished was only the first of several he would do in the same building. He did not have the opportunity to decorate even the side walls of the stairway where he painted "Westward Ho!" This picture was the beginning and end of the plans of Meigs and Leutze for murals in the Capitol.

NOTES

1. Leutze arrived in Boston on January 30, 1859, and reached Washington approximately two weeks later, on February 16.

2. This letter (scarcely decipherable in parts) and Leutze's reply are in the files of the Office of the Architect of the Capitol.

3. This is among the private letters of Montgomery C. Meigs in the Library's Manuscript Division.

4. Shown on sheet no. 1 of the boundary survey maps in the Cartographic Branch of the Office of Civil Archives at the National Archives.

5. The original German work by Maximilian, Prince of Wied-Neuwied was published in two volumes at Coblenz in 1839–41.

Caricatures and Cartoons: The 1848 Revolution in Europe

BY RENATA V. SHAW

The three prints discussed here are political cartoons from the German pre-revolutionary and revolutionary period of the 1840s. This was an age of reawakening from the peaceful Biedermeier slumber of cozy domesticity following the wars of liberation of the Napoleonic era. Prussia was now openly challenging the supremacy of Austria in central Europe. At the same time political forces within the country were stirring and demanding the right to participate in political affairs.

In 1840 when Friedrich Wilhelm IV inherited the throne of Prussia from his aged father, the hopes and expectations of his restless subjects were concentrated on the new monarch. The population yearned for a reign of liberalism, freedom, and German unity under the idealistic young sovereign. Friedrich Wilhelm, indeed, retracted the strict censorship laws of his predecessors. The new freedom of expression gave rise to a German satirical press based on the examples of *Punch* in London and *La Caricature* and *Charivari* in Paris. Political cartoons were also published separately as broadsides. These were either steel engravings or hand-colored lithographs, which had recently been introduced as an inexpensive and popular technique for quick print distribution. Three of these prints were recently received on exchange from a New York print dealer.

The first two prints satirize the position of Friedrich Wilhelm IV on the political stage of Europe in a strikingly similar fashion. This resemblance may derive from a common source, or one of our prints may have influenced the other. A connection between the first lithograph printed in Magdeburg and the second in Königsberg seems probable, although the two cities were for the period geographically far apart.

Cities such as Cologne and Königsberg expressed their yearnings for freedom more directly than Berlin. This may explain the anticipation which greeted the reign of Friedrich Wilhelm IV in the provincial towns.

The first cartoon, a hand-colored crayon lithograph, was designed and lithographed by H. Schäfer and published by Emil Baensch in Magdeburg. It shows a ruddy and energetic young man jumping up from a jerrybuilt wooden throne wielding a club, while various figures surrounding him retreat in poses of surprised indignation. Prince Metternich leaves the scene in disgust, while a Russian peasant is crouching in the background in an attitude of respectful supplication. Italy is shown as a soldier grinding away on his street organ. France in uniform (with the gallic cock on his helmet) has been knocked over, and England, the bulldog, sneaks away from the scene. The Pope sits on his golden throne observing surreptitiously the rise of the new Protestant king.

This cartoon includes a great many additional allusions to the shift of political power in Europe. Friedrich Wilhelm IV appears in the guise of a clumsy peasant boy, *"der deutsche Michel"* (a folklore figure of the time), who tramples on a family tree with his stocking cap at his feet. The tree apparently signifies the decline of the ancient Hapsburg dynasty and the ascent of the Hohenzollern family. The pouch of 50,000 talers in the king's pocket had been pledged by him for the finishing of Cologne Cathedral, a project undertaken at his initiative not for religious reasons but as a gesture of common effort of the German states symbolizing a new patriotic unity. The map of these German states is printed on Friedrich Wilhelm's shirtfront and the Prussian eagle is embossed on his boots. This seems to indicate that Prussia is now ready to take over leadership in the German states.

The second cartoon, a black-and-white pen lithograph published by W. Winckler of Königsberg, expands the idea expressed in the Magdeburg drawing. Friedrich Wilhelm IV, again depicted as "der deutsche Michel," is standing in front of his homemade wooden throne swinging a heavy club at representatives of neighboring states. He steps on Metternich, who is lying on his back with his feet in the air, a torn Hapsburg family tree underneath him. The Russian serf recoils from the threat of a blow, the Pope abandons his throne and flees to the Castel Sant' Angelo, the Italian soldier drops his sword, the Frenchman, hit by a blow, loses his kepi, while the English bulldog is sneering at the Prussian monarch. Again Friedrich Wilhelm has tossed off his cap, but here his dreams for the future tumble forth: the building of Cologne Cathedral is advancing,

The hand-colored crayon lithograph by H. Schäfer, published by Emil Baensch in Magdeburg.

Father Rhine has been captured and is being held by Prussian troops while the King and Queen of Prussia receive a joyous welcome from their enthusiastic subjects. The Prussian clergy, Prussian bureaucracy, and the Hohenzollern family are taking a new place in the sun.

Friedrich Wilhelm IV has one arm inside the sleeve of his coat as if on the

The black-and-white pen lithograph published by W. Winckler of Königsberg, expands the idea presented in the cartoon.

verge of taking over control of German leadership. His shirtfront bears a map with the member states of the German confederation numbered on it. The pouch containing 50,000 talers is at the king's feet as a reminder of the spirit of German unity and power which he expected to complete the building of Cologne Cathedral.

Published a hundred years before the date at the bottom, this hand-colored cartoon by an anonymous artist shows France and Germany clasping hands across the border, and the middle class has over-thrown both ecclesiastic and political rulers.

Both of these undated cartoons must have been created at the beginning of the reign of Friedrich Wilhelm IV because they show him as a forceful leader of Germany, a role he never succeeded in playing. His rule was characterized by an unrealistic reactionary spirit harking back to the supposedly idyllic Middle Ages. In 1847 he refused to grant his people the constitution promised them in 1815 by his father, because he could not "allow a scribbled sheet of paper to intervene like a second Providence between our God in Heaven and this land of ours, to rule us by paragraphs and oust our time-honoured and sacred fidelity to each other." [1] He kept a deaf ear to the people and continued to follow his own autocratic ideals. The obtuse nature of the king led to political unrest in his country and explains the spontaneous riots of 1848 sparked by the overthrow of Louis Philippe in France.

Our third cartoon is a political phophecy, hence the caption *1942*. The attack on the established power of 1842, monarchy and church, is so strong that neither the artist nor the publisher reveals his name.

In this hand-colored cartoon Friedrich Wilhelm IV is no longer the central figure. "Der deutsche Michel," the robust peasant, now transformed into a personification of the German nation, is proudly brandishing a club sprouting buds of fresh oak leaves. He grabs the outstretched hand of France extended to him across the border. Father Rhine sits peacefully on the river bank where old conflicts are forgotten in the revolutionary fervor. In the background young men, celebrating the victory of the bourgeoisie over the local princes, are dancing joyfully around a May tree decorated with green wreaths. Three men are hacking away at Cologne Cathedral—to them a symbol of the reactionary spirit of all churches. The church is on fire, stone slabs with carved portraits of bishops lie abandoned on the ground. Not only the sovereign princes but also the ecclesiatic hierarchy dominated by the nobility are being forcefully overthrown by the newly triumphant middle class.

The Library of Congress has a vast collection of political caricatures and cartoons mainly covering the history of the United States, England, and France. These three German cartoons illustrate turning points in European history not previously covered by the collection of documentary prints.

NOTE

1. J. G. Legge, *Rhyme and Revolution in Germany* (London: 1918), p. 150.

Historical Prints: Lithographed Letterheads

BY MILTON KAPLAN

"Dear Mother: The above picture is a very good view of the city [San Francisco] at the present time."

So begins a letter dated April 28, 1854, which is reproduced in Harry T. Peters's *California on Stone* (New York: Doubleday, Doran, 1935). The letter represents an important group of nineteenth-century American prints—the illustrated letter paper or letterhead, lithographed or engraved with views which often are the only ones of a locality or of an event. Peters referred to them as the "godparents of the illustrated postal card of today."

Although they seem to have been printed in fairly large numbers during the middle decades of the nineteenth century—Peters listed 109 different sheets in *California on Stone* and in his *America on Stone*, 1931, he observed that "the East was literally flooded with myriads of these lithographic letterheads"—their very nature seems to have precluded the survival of any substantial quantity. Once read, the letters were thrown away. Relatively few exist today and most of them are to be found in the various manuscript collections throughout the United States. Unused letterheads are even rarer. This past year the division was fortunate in acquiring nine to add to our small but growing collection which now contains the following examples:

Bankettsaal und Gabentempel des dritten Amerikanischen Bundes-Schiessens, New York, 27. Juni bis 6. Juli. Lithograph by Charles Magnus.
Bowling Green. Lithograph by Charles Magnus.

Letterheads

1. Washington, D.C. Engraving by Charles Magnus & Co.

2. Norfolk, Portsmouth, Va. Lithograph by Charles Magnus.

3. Bankettsaal und Gabentempel des dritten Amerikanischen Bundes—Schiessens, New York, 27 Juni bis 6 Juli. Lithograph by Charles Magnus.

4. United States Firemen. Engraving by Charles Magnus & Co.

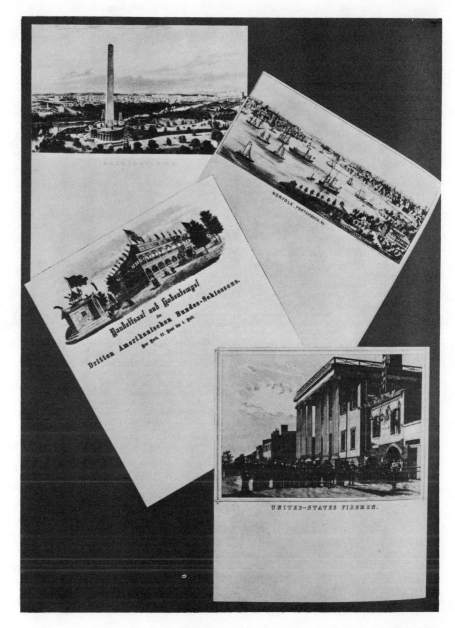

A Representation of the GREAT STORM *at Providence Sept 23 1815.*

A representation of the great storm at Providence, September 23, 1815. Engraving by James Kidder, 1816.

Kingston, Lake Ontario. Engraving by Charles Magnus & Co.
Louisville, Ky. Engraving by Charles Magnus & Co.
Lowell, Mass. Woodcut by Franklin Hedge, 1848.
Norfolk, Portsmouth, Va. Lithograph by Charles Magnus.
Rochester, Engraving by Charles Magnus.
Syracuse, N.Y. Engraving by Capewell & Kimmel.
Toledo, Ohio. Engraving by Charles Magnus & Co.
Troy, N.Y. Engraving by Charles Magnus & Co.
The 25th of April in New York. Lithograph by Charles Magnus, 1865.

The funeral of Abraham Lincoln.

Washington, D.C. Engraving by Charles Magnus & Co. This view is an almost exact copy of a large folio lithograph "Washington, D. C., with projected improvements," copyrighted by Smith & Jenkins in 1852. Did Magnus & Co. arrange with Smith & Jenkins to use the print, or was it outright piracy?

The cities of these letterheads are always shown in their most tranquil aspect. In contrast, a very rare engraving just acquired is possibly the first American print depicting a natural calamity. On September 23, 1815, a violent storm struck Providence, R.I. In a burst of prose which probably matched the intensity of the storm, the *Rhode Island American and General Advertiser,* September 26, 1815, commented:

> Whether we consider the violence of the late storm, or the desolation which ensued, we do not incur the hazard of contradiction in pronouncing it the most sublime and tremendous elemental strife that has been witnessed for centuries by the inhabitants of this town. It seemed as if He, who "rides the whirlwind and directs the storm" had permitted sea and air to combine their strength and terror to give us an impressive assurance of His power, to humble our pride and to discipline our affections. . . . Had there lived a being whose bosom was tenanted by misanthropic feelings, he could have ascended some lofty hill, and apostrophized with the exultation of a demon the sublime desolation which surrounded him—but he who inherits the sensibilities or the weaknesses of our nature, must have viewed, with revolting feelings, "the wild and wasteful scene."

On June 13, 1916, the following announcement appeared in the Boston *Independent Chronicle:*

> Bowen's Phoenix Museum, will commence at Franklin Hall . . . June 13. . . . The collection consists of a great variety of the ingenuous [sic] works of art . . . among which are . . . large and elegant paintings, executed by J. Kidder, from correct drawings, taken from nature. First view—a very natural representation of the great storm at Providence, September 23, 1815. . . . This painting was taken on the spot, a short time after the storm, from the appearance of the many remaining objects of ruin, and, from information of

facts, given by some of the most intelligent and respectable gentlemen in Providence, who were witnesses to this distressing event.

James Kidder is described in *The New York Historical Society's Dictionary of Artists in America* (New Haven: Yale University Press, 1957, p. 369) as a "landscape artist, engraver, and aquatintist of Boston." Little is known of his career except that he was active in the 1830s and produced an aquatint of Boston Common which was published in the *Polyanthus* for June 1813.

Kidder's painting of the great storm was well received by the public not only in Boston but later that same year in Providence. The November 9, 1816, issue of the *Providence Gazette and Country Journal* noted:

> The following remarks, from the Newport Republican, coincide so exactly with our own sentiments, that we cannot but give them an insertion: "A correspondent, who last week visited the Museum of Messrs. Bowen and Kidder, at Providence, recommends it in the warmest terms, to public patronage. He speaks of the grand panoramic view of the great storm in Providence, as a proud specimen of American genius, in which the awful effects of that terrible hurricane, are speaking delineated with a bold hand."

The success of the painting probably prompted Daniel Bowen and James Kidder to publish an engraving of it so that copies would be available to the public. The engraving was copyrighted October 8, 1816, and priced to sell at one dollar. In the October 8, 1816, issue of the *New England Palladium Commercial Advertiser,* there appeared the following:

> Messrs. Bowen & Kidder have completed a very elegant print of the great storm at Providence, on Sept. last. It does honor to the genius of Mr. Kidder, who designed and executed the same; and binds another wreath of laurel on the brows of our native artists. A few copies only of this admirable print are as yet struck off, which are left for examination.

This engraving seems to be an unlisted one. Neither the Old Print Shop nor the Kennedy Galleries, both major dealers in New York City, has had the print in stock according to their records. We have located only one other proof, that in the collection of the Rhode Island Historical Society, Providence.

Japanese Picture Scrolls of the First Americans in Japan

BY RENATA V. SHAW

Within the last year several scrolls and other materials relating mainly to Commodore Matthew C. Perry's expedition to Japan in 1853–54 were transferred to the Prints and Photographs Division from the Manuscript Division, where they had been since their purchase in 1926 from a Minneapolis dealer. It has thus been possible for the first time to study them as pictorial materials. The Prints and Photographs Division was also fortunate in being able to have translations made of the Japanese text appearing with the illustrations. While many questions remain as to the origin of the drawings, the results of this first attempt to describe them are presented in this article.

In the middle of the nineteenth century Japan had been shut off from the Western world for over two hundred years. The only exception to this policy of exclusion was a small enclave of Dutch merchants allowed to remain in Nagasaki. The Dutch traders functioned as intermediaries between Japan and the Western world and taught the Japanese the rudiments of Western science and technology. Several nations had tried to approach Japan in order to start trade negotiations, but all foreign ships had been driven off by the Japanese, who were determined not to open their country to foreign powers or revolutionary ideas.

When Commodore Perry in 1853 succeeded in bringing his boats to the forbidden coast and actually stepped on the soil of Japan, the audacity of his venture created a tremendous upheaval in the country. He had been sent with a letter from President Fillmore, which suggested that ports should be opened for trade between the two countries. The Japanese suspected, however, that the arrival of

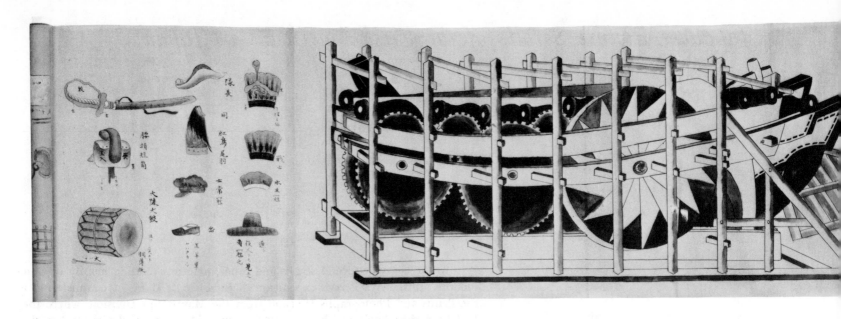

Commodore Perry's first landing at Kurihama in 1853 was recorded by Japanese observers on scrolls like this, which, typical of oriental writings, reads from right to left.

the U.S. Navy, albeit with only four ships, meant an attempt to attack and conquer the islands. But the commodore, who had studied the customs and traditions of the Far East as thoroughly as it was possible at this period, succeeded by firmness, inscrutability, and impressive pomp to break the resistance of the Japanese.

The emperor of Japan, whose court was still in Kyoto, had lost his sovereignty and become a figurehead. The executive power had been seized by the Tokugawa Shogunate, which had its seat in Edo, the city today known as Tokyo. This political situation was successfully concealed from foreign observers, who believed that they had to deal with the emperor as the supreme ruler of the country. The shogun and his closest advisers kept themselves carefully hidden in Edo. They chose the governor and vice-governor of Uraga, as their emissaries to deal with Perry and named them for the occasion Toda, "Lord of Idzu," and Ido, "Lord of Iwami."

The two noblemen were given careful instructions from Edo to try to stall the Americans and discourage them from any hope of meeting the emperor. But the more evasive the Japanese became, the more pressing became the demands of the Americans, who threatened to take their ships all the way to Edo harbor if their requests were not granted.

After many discussions between the representatives of Perry and those of the shogun, July 14, 1853, was finally agreed upon for Commodore Perry's landing and delivery of President Fillmore's letter to the Japanese emperor. This first meeting was carefully planned and ended in a way which saved the honor of both parties.

During the brief stay of the American ships in July 1853 and again during the four and a half months of 1854 that they were in Japanese waters, the American visitors were under constant close observation by the Japanese. Not only was every move they made reported to the governor of the province, but artists were sent to the harbor to make sketches of the invading barbarians and their boats.

The first approach to the Susquehanna from the Shore was that of a boat at early sunrise next morning (July 9th, 1853), apparently containing a corps of artists, who came close to the ship's side, but making no attempt to come on board, busied themselves in taking sketches of the strange vessels.[1]

Japanese Picture Scrolls of the First Americans in Japan | 197

The sketches served two purposes. The first was to create a lasting historical record for the archives, and the second was to give accurate information to the shogun in Edo of the invaders and their military equipment.

PERRY'S FIRST LANDING

Three of the scrolls and parts of a large sketchbook and of a small printed book relate to the first landing of Commodore Perry at Kurihama in 1853.

The identical choice of subject matter as well as a similar succession of events shown on the scrolls proves that although several artists were commissioned to portray the coming of the barbarians, many of the picture scrolls known today are partially or wholly copied from the first authorized sketches of eyewitnesses.

Only a few of the drawings are signed. It is known that Sadahide, a master of the popular woodcut, was employed by the shogunate in an official capacity at other times, and he may therefore also have made sketches of the Perry expedition by official appointment. None of the drawings on the Library's scrolls, however, can definitely be attributed to him.

Susquehanna Scroll

The scroll showing the steamships *Susquehanna* and *Mississippi* bears the following revealing note:

> This sketch was done by a new friend of mine, Taguchi Shumpei, who accompanied the Lord of Shimosone to Uraga and saw the ships on the spot; when he asked where the ships came from, he was told in our country's language that the ships carried an envoy sent by the President of America to Edo; Shumpei told this to me yesterday, the 9th, on his return from Uraga.[2]

The scroll of the two steamers shows that the draftsman was very much impressed with the black smoke coming out of the chimney, the paddle wheels, and the American ensign flying at the stern with "about 30 white crests on navy blue background, said to be the number of the states." The U.S. Navy jack at the

Above: The Susquehanna.

Right: Commodore Perry. This portrait is from a printed Japanese book that was acquired with the scrolls.

bow is also properly represented as well as Perry's command pennant on the masthead. The point of the drawing is not phtographic accuracy so much as it is an attempt to quickly record the first impression made by the "black ships."

Machinery Scroll

The second scroll begins also with illustrations of two steamers, probably the *Susquehanna* and the *Mississippi*. The picture of the first ship (at right) does not show its construction accurately, but the pennants are gay—white, green, and red—and the rope ladders form an attractive pattern against the masts. Reddish smoke is belching from the smokestack. The total impression of this paddle wheeler is gay and decorative and shows the hand of a competent painter. The

The paddle wheel from the machinery scroll.

second steamer has obviously been copied from the first and painted by a much less accomplished artist, perhaps an apprentice. The color is flatter and the design altogether less convincing.

The most interesting part of this scroll, however, is the third panel, which purports to show the paddle wheel and its connected machinery. Intended to be a "technical drawing," it does not really explain the workings of a steam vessel, but it shows us the passionate interest with which the Japanese studied every detail of the black ships.

The fourth panel is devoted to American hats, caps, weapons, and musical instruments. This is one of five versions of these designs in our scrolls, differing only in detail and pointing to their common origin.

Large Scroll of the First Landing

This scroll contains a picture series that might be called "Commodore Perry's First Landing at Kurihama, 1853." It is made up of the following nine scenes:

Two American marines and one of the two officers shown on the large scroll.

1) two American marines and two officers; 2) headgear of marines and naval officers; 3) musical instruments used by the Americans; 4) two small surveying boats, one with a canvas roof; 5) steamboat *Susquehanna* with commodore's quarters marked; 6) American troops parading at Kurihama with Perry; 7) Japanese defense forces arriving carrying banners; 8) reception hall erected at Kurihama; 9) Kurihama harbor with American boats anchored on the bay.

Another version of these same scenes appears in the large sketchbook, described below, and still another in a scroll in the New York Public Library.[3] Thus we can speak of a real iconography of the first landing. All of these scrolls may have been copied almost simultaneously from the government-sponsored original versions, which today are in the Tokyo University Historiographical Institute. There was, of course, a great popular demand for the scrolls. In speculating on the order in which they were produced, we have to consider the skill of the individual draftsman and the speed with which he was forced to finish his copy.

It is obviously more than coincidence that the sequence of the nine scenes in the Library of Congress scroll is the same as that of the New York Public Library scroll. The New York scroll is superior in execution, and watercolor has been applied to the brush drawing of each scene. The Kurihama harbor picture in that scroll shows correct use of Western perspective and true understanding of the placement of buildings to achieve a three-dimensional effect.

The draftsman of the scroll at the Library of Congress has done his best to follow a more sophisticated model. He has succeeded in the simpler scenes, but in copying the "harbor of Kurihama from a bird's-eye view," he does not quite succeed in mastering the technique of Western perspective and lets his houses and boats follow the contours of the coastline.

The captions on both scrolls are placed in similar positions and the wording is nearly identical. It is amusing to see how the American troops have been drawn with caps, swords, and bayonets clearly shown, where the Japanese contingent is shown as a succession of circles instead of heads and bodies. Pennants and banners identify Toda, "Lord of Idzu," and Ido, "Lord of Iwami." The Japanese public, for whom these scrolls were intended, was well enough acquainted with their own lords and their attendants and were not interested in knowing how these men were dressed. It was sufficient to have pennants to mark their places in the procession and to show the respective rank and responsibility of the participants. Unfortunately, the American viewer is unable to fill in the missing details from his imagination.

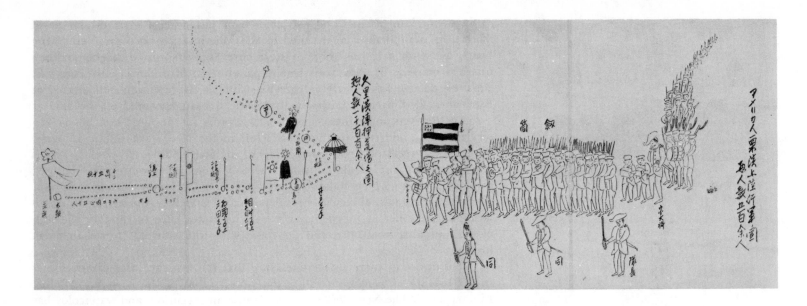

火星漢渾押荒備之図
熟人数一千百余人

叙首

アメリカ人粟渓上陸行軍之図
悉人数五百余人

同 同 隊長

Japanese troops, at the left, and American troops at Kurihama.

A prominent feature of the drawing of the reception hall is the large screen in the background that shows the emblems of Japanese negotiators and other officials. The placement of the troops is again indicated without much detail. The drawing on the Library's scroll may be based on an original sketch made from a boat in the harbor.

The first scenes on this scroll, at the right, are in full color, but the last four have only a few touches of red color added to the basic brush drawing. For some reason the artist did not finish coloring them. The scroll in the Library of Congress measures 11 feet 7 inches as compared to the 13 feet 5¼ inches of the other, but both are about 11 inches high.

Large Sketchbook

While not in scroll form today, the drawings pasted in this sketchbook were once part of several scrolls. They are not all by the same hand, nor are they limited to the first landing or even to the Perry expedition, but they depict the first official contacts between Americans and Japanese. The drawings that relate to the landing at Kurihama in July 1853 are described here; the other contents of the sketchbook are mentioned later in connection with the events to which they relate.

After a page of text that unaccountably relates to Perry's second landing, page 2 of the sketchbook shows the floor plan of the "Resting place of the Defense Forces," located in the boat house of the Ii clan at Kurihama. It is sketched with quick brush strokes, leading to the inference that it was made at or about the time of the 1853 landing. The same page includes thoroughly captioned but quickly executed black and white drawings of American caps and hats. The Japanese artist has emphasized the distinction between officers' hats and soldiers' hats, and the caption describes the eagle on the officer's hat as "like a single-petaled peony or a bird."

A rough sketch of Edo Bay follows on page 3. Its Japanese caption may be translated "Forts of local lords; the number of guns according to an old map; not to be deemed accurate." On the map is traced the route of Perry's second ship, the *Mississippi*, which he had dispatched on a surveying trip in the Bay

The reception hall at Kurihama as depicted on the large scroll.

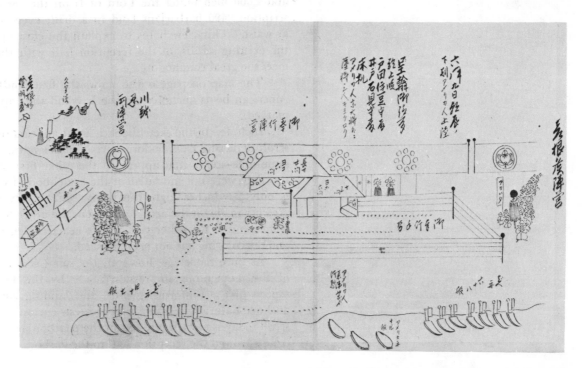

of Edo to make a show of force. Behind their fortifications on shore the Japanese were no doubt watching every move the Americans made. So many Japanese defense vessels surrounded the *Mississippi* and the smaller surveying boats that they returned to their original anchorage.

On page 4 is a map of the Japanese defenses closer to the city of Edo. The shore was protected by strategically placed forts in the sea, and the map gives distances between the individual forts and the forts and shore. Perry would no doubt have been delighted to have had a copy even of this crude map, for he had arrived on the Japanese coast without accurate maps of the area. The Japanese were reluctant to inform him of the names of the towns he passed, let alone help him navigate the waters.

The drawing on page 5, partially map and partially bird's-eye view, shows the scene at Kurihama when Perry came ashore to deliver the president's letter. By the use of cloth screens on either side of the pavilion and the Japanese text, the artist shows that 800 men of the Kawagoe clan were stationed on the left and 2,000 men under the Lord of Ii on the right. At the shore line is the inscription "400 barbarians land in a drill; even the soldiers carry a pistol each at waist." This view helps to explain the close-up views, appearing in many of the existing scrolls, of the reception hall with the Japanese forces lined up to meet the great commodore.

The map on page 6 also shows the first landing site of Kurihama with the American boats anchored on the bay and the Japanese defense positions clearly marked.

Included in the sketchbook is what appears to be a complete, though small, scroll depicting Commodore Perry's first landing at Kurihama. It contains the same nine scenes that appear in the other first landing scrolls discussed above, but they were not mounted in the sketchbook in the same order. As this scroll is only 5½ inches high, the paper could easily have been rolled up and the sketches made on the actual scene. On the other hand, it might have been copied from some of the other versions. It bears evidence of having been done hastily, and the coloring has not been finished.

As pure reportage, however, the small scroll gives a good pictorial account of the momentous impression made by the landing invaders. The physical aspects of the uniforms, swords, and landing cutters with steering chains and anchors naturally evoked the greatest curiosity. The American studying the scroll today is more interested in the pavilion and the distribution of the defense troops around the reception hall in the harbor.

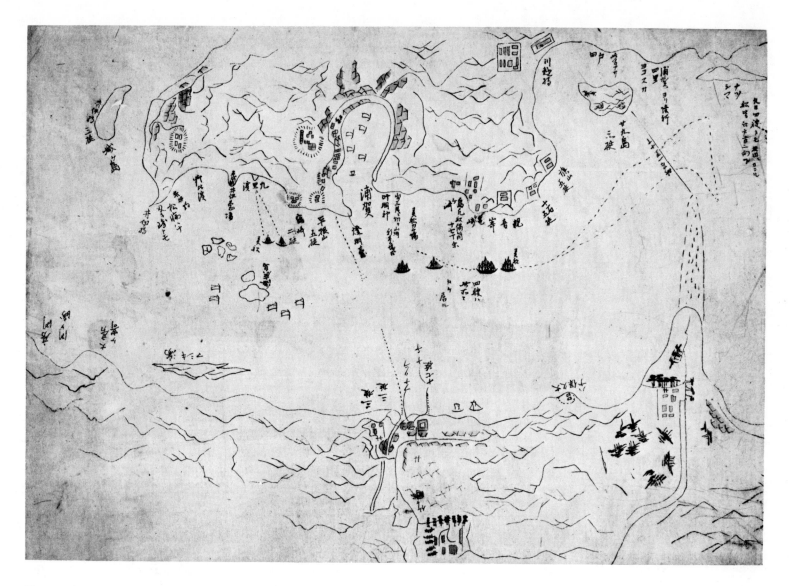

Map of Edo Bay, from page 6 of the large sketchbook.

The familiar weapons, musical instruments, and hats as they appeared in the printed volume.

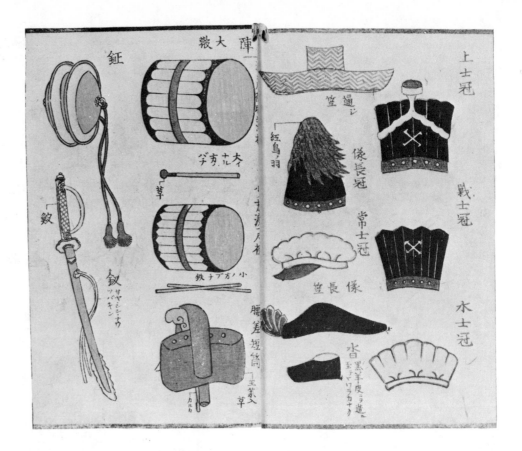

The Scrolls in Printed Form

The Library is fortunate to have acquired along with the scrolls a small printed book that utilizes the drawings, but in a more finished and detailed form. Entitled *Ikoku Ochiba Kago* (A Basket of Fallen Leaves from Abroad), it was written by Miki Kosai and published by Ingakudo, probably soon after Perry negotiated the treaty with the Japanese. After a discussion of world geography and the position of the Japanese Islands in relation to North America, the author presents a map of that continent and then a map of Edo Bay with the forts of defense and the distances from shore to shore clearly marked. He continues with a list of Japanese defense encampments and the names of local lords assigned to man the fortifications.

Among the illustrations are several that are familiar because of their appearance on the "first landing" scrolls: woodcuts of two American marines and two officers, the hats and caps, the musical instruments, and the woodcut of the *Susquehanna,* a lively and colorful double-page illustration. A small detail, the head of an eagle that serves as the figurehead of the ship, appears in the woodcut in a form similar to that on the small scroll in the sketchbook.

THE SECOND LANDING

The second widely illustrated incident of the Perry story is the "second landing," which took place at Yokohama on March 8, 1954. Commodore Perry had spent the winter in Chinese waters. He decided to return to Japan to force an answer to President Fillmore's letter somewhat earlier than he had planned, before any of the interested European nations could disturb his plans by profiting from his initial friendly contact with the Japanese. Again he encountered much resistance and evasion from representatives of the Shogun, but with the help of his old ruse of moving his fleet closer to Edo, he forced the Japanese into agreeing to a meeting place at Yokohama.

Here on March 8, 1854, Perry came ashore with great ceremony and received a reply to the president's letter. In the days that followed presents were exchanged between the Americans and the Japanese, and negotiations were carried on that led to the signing of a treaty on March 31.

The Lexington, Saratoga, and Macedonian Scroll

The Library's first scroll of the second landing starts with two illustrations of sailboats captioned "Photograph of American Ships." The artist obviously had access to pictures taken by the American official photographer. The proportions of these two boats are more in keeping with the true proportions of sailboats and, except for the American flag and pennants, the coloring is confined to black ink with white highlights. The front view of the *Saratoga,* next on the scroll, may also have been copied from a photograph, because the foreshortening is very convincing.

The fourth drawing shows the *Macedonian* firing a salute in honor of Com-

The sailboat Saratoga *on a scroll depicting Perry's return trip to Japan in 1854.*

The Macedonian, *firing a salute in honor of Commodore Perry.*

modore Perry. The corvette is half hidden in dramatic clouds of billowing smoke—part of the spectacle carefully planned to impress the waiting Japanese commissioners. The story continues with the landing of twenty-seven launches firing salutes from the guns mounted in their bows. Here again the illustration rises to the level of exciting reportage, with flags waving in the wind and marines loading the guns almost hidden in gray clouds of smoke.

The last four panels of this scroll are not by the same draftsman. They consist of pictures of a section of a vessel's hull, an iron anchor, and a water barrel drawn in a matter-of-fact way, as if for inclusion in an encyclopedia. The last panel, however, is a charming little vignette of a straw roof protecting one of the American presents to the emperor. The caption reads, "neither its content nor its use is known."

The American Doll Scroll

The second scroll of the Yokohama landing begins with a puzzling drawing of an American doll labeled, in English, "AN OWNER WANTED." The original sketch, made at the reception hall on March 8, 1854, by an anonymous Japanese artist, is in the Tokyo University Historiographical Institute. As the doll was not listed in the official narrative as a gift for the emperor, it may have been intended as a gift for a Japanese child.

In his published account Perry told about the Japanese habit of making sketches of everything observed in the American camp: [4]

> They [the Japanese] were not contented with merely observing with their eyes, but were constantly taking out their writing materials, their mulberry-bark paper, and their Indian ink and hair pencils, which they always carried in a pocket within the left breast of their loose robes, and making notes and sketches. The Japanese had all apparently a strong pictorial taste, and looked with great delight upon the engravings and pictures which were shown them, but their own performances appeared exceedingly rude and unartistic. Every man, however, seemed anxious to try his skill at drawing, and they were constantly taking the portraits of the Americans, and sketches of the various articles that appeared curious to them, with a result, which, however satisfactory it might have been to the artist (and it must be conceded they exhibited no little exultation), was far from showing

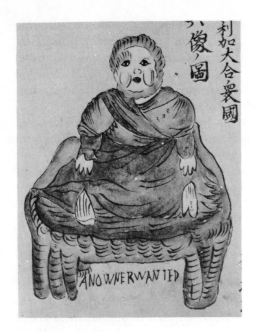

利加大合衆國
ノ像ノ圖

ANOWNERWANTED

The American doll.

any encouraging advance in art. It should, however, be remarked that the artists were not professional.

Today we do not judge the artistic abilities of these anonymous Japanese artists as severely as the Americans of a hundred years ago did. The scrolls are regarded as a form of lively folk art and appreciated as such. How much poorer would our knowledge of the American impact on Japan be without these spontaneous pictorial documents! The choice of subject matter alone gives us an idea of the features which excited the Japanese the most.

The doll scroll continues its story with a picture of the landing boats filled with marines armed with pistols and bayonets. The Commodore's white boat is decorated with a gold star. The artist took obvious delight in retelling the landing story. He spent a great deal of effort in painting the flagship *Powhatan* and decorating its paddle wheel with gold and green ornaments. The steamboat panel is followed by an illustration of marines marching in single file with their rifles and led by four musicians and two officers with huge epaulets. The scroll continues with bust portraits of Commodore Perry and Commander Adams. These portraits were a popular theme among the second landing scrolls, and there are several examples in the Library's collection. Double portraits of Commodore Perry and his son, as well as Commander Adams and his son, were also popular. These illustrations sometimes achieved almost photographic likeness, but sometimes they deteriorated into simple views of fearsome-looking hirsute barbarians. This particular scroll includes poorly drawn portraits where no attempt at characterization is evident.

The scroll ends with a jolly illustration of a bearded marine smoking a yellow pipe. A caption in American handwriting and large block letters attempts to show the Japanese a sample of the Americans' language, but it conveys no meaning to us.

This scroll is the work of one artist. It is consistent in style and full of naive wonder at the strange things taking place in Yokohama. It must have once been a favorite souvenir of a visitor to that town.

Locomotive, Tender, and Passenger Car

On March 13, 1854, the American presents were carried from the ships and the small ones were laid out in the main hall of the reception center. The gift that excited the greatest curiosity and wonder was a miniature train with its own circular track, which was set up on a piece of level ground.

The delicately painted sketch of the train includes enough details to convince us that the artist had seen the actual gift. As the cars are shown in perspective from above and the side, the artist has added the trade name "NORRIS WORKS 1853" to the edge of the scroll so that the front view will not be missed. The drawing is so competent that it was probably executed by a professional artist. Of all the scrolls under discussion here, it is the closest to being a truly finished illustration. The colors are not necessarily those of the original train, but they create a pleasant composition and add life to the otherwise technical subject.

Two more panels from the doll scroll: a marine at ease, smoking his pipe, and a column of marines on parade during the negotiations at Yokohama.

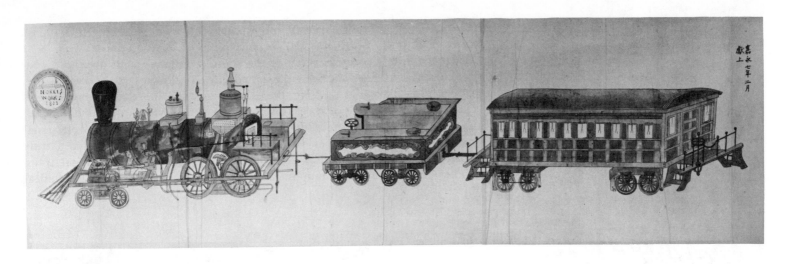

Small Hand-Painted Book

The Library also has a small handmade booklet, damaged by bookworms, which includes full-color miniature paintings with touches of gold, done in a delicate style with hairline outlines in black ink. Each page is enclosed in a gray painted frame. The illustrations are gay and informal as if intended for a children's book. The first page shows a Navy band complete with drummer boy and young flutist marching to the tune of *The Star-Spangled Banner*. The artist has taken great delight in accurately copying the true colors of the uniforms, the red cock feathers of the officer's hat, the golden epaulets, and the buttons. Space was left for a caption, but the text was not inserted, so that we have to interpret the picture from our knowledge of the second landing.

We know from the published account that the marines and the seamen were drawn up to form an honor guard when Commodore Perry stepped from his barge. A double-page illustration shows some of them in stiff, tight ranks led by two officers. The composition is a diagonal slash across two pages in a non-symmetric arrangement. Some shading has been used in the uniforms and a touch of flesh color added on the cheeks, but the background has been left empty.

The next double page is devoted to a painting of five American officers, one of them carrying a black umbrella. It show the same informal Japanese composition in which the figures seem to be arbitrarily arranged in space although the composition maintains a perfect balance. Each hair has been individually

Left: The train would actually run, and although it was too small for the passengers to get inside, they sat on top of the car and rode merrily around the circular track.

Five American officers as shown in the hand-pointed book.

painted. Fierce whiskers give the men a determined look. The epaulets, which must have fascinated the artist, are much exaggerated compared to the rest of the uniforms.

The flagship *Powhatan* is shown in such a way that a profile view and an end view can be seen simultaneously. This is a pictorial device that is common in Japanese art and is accepted as a traditional way of seeing objects. The masts of the *Powhatan* cut the frame of the illustration, which is not disturbing to the Japanese artist, who simply extended his drawing as far as his subject demanded. This freedom in design was adopted by Western artists only after a prolonged acquaintance with Japanese prints and their composition.

The booklet ends with an illustration of a minstrel show presented as an entertainment on the *Powhatan* to a group of distinguished Japanese visitors. The actors were American sailors, who had improvised the musical program as a climax to a convivial dinner party. The Japanese were no more prepared to understand this entertainment than the Americans were to judge the fine points of the Japanese Sumo wrestlers, but they entered into the spirit of the performance and were carried away by the lively rhythms.

Large Sketchbook

In the first contacts between the Americans and the Japanese, the intense interest shown by each party toward the other was quite naturally heightened by the fact that each nation knew so little about life in the other. The explanations on the Japanese illustrations that seem naive to us were obviously sincere and were intended to enlighten the buyer.

The large sketchbook, already discussed in connection with the first landing, contains several drawings relating to the second landing that illustrate this point.

A painting of a red-haired man in a blue frock coat drinking wine bears the following eyewitness description of the Americans: "Their faces were paler than our women, their hair was as red as a palm; their eyes and eyebrows were close and the hollows about the eyes were deep; their noses were tall; they looked so much alike that they might be taken for brothers."

The artist has observed his model well. He has emphasized the foreign details of the suit such as the way the wrinkles are formed around the buttonholes of the coat. As the Japanese fastened their clothing with ties rather than buttons, all buttons were in great demand by them as souvenirs.

The red-haired American.

Also in the sketchbook is a finely drawn sketch of an American Negro dressed in a parade uniform with gold buttons and epaulets and wearing a sword. That the artist has sketched a paddle boat on the same sheet of paper may indicate that he was preparing a whole picture story on the men of the black ships. This theory is strengthened by a drawing of four marines with muskets and bayonets, which seems to be by the same artist. The color has been carefully applied and every detail is thoroughly observed. The faces are not caricatures and the Western features have been individualized.

In the double portrait of Commander Henry A. Adams and his son in this same sketchbook an attempt has been made to make the portraits true likenesses. At the same time certain traditionally accepted codes have been followed. This explains the pink cheeks of the young man and the ruddy complexion of the father. The noses are large and the eyes slanted; this is the accepted way a Japanese artist drew an American. The portraits are distinguished by having captions written above them in legible English script: "The Son of Adams 18 ys" and "Adams 50 years."

AMERICANS IN JAPAN AFTER COMMODORE PERRY

The treaty of Kanagawa, which was the result of Commodore Perry's voyages to Japan, opened two ports on the Japanese coast to American vessels. The port of Shimoda, south of Edo, was the first. The second, Hakodate, on the northern island of Hokkaido, was suggested for its geographical location, because it was convenient to the whalers, who needed a port in which to replenish their supplies.

"Caroline E. Foote" Scroll

In the winter of 1855 the first American commercial schooner, the *Caroline E. Foote,* arrived in Shimoda on its way to Hakodate to establish a trading post. The Library has a scroll of six scenes inspired by this visit, which aroused the greatest curiosity among the Japanese because of the presence of three American ladies and some children. The scroll begins with a family picture of Mr. and Mrs. Reed with their five-year-old daughter and the wife of the captain, Mrs. Worth.

The drawing is obviously copied from a more competently made scroll. It is of interest to us because it shows the first American women in Japan through the eyes of a Japanese observer. The ladies are wrapped in fringed shawls, and they wear demure bonnets and voluminous skirts to protect them against the cold of the harbor. The child is dressed in a miniature version of the clothes worn by the grownups.

The scroll then presents a reproduction of one of the well-known portraits of Commodore Perry, for sale at Shimoda according to a contemporary letter: "I send you a Japanese drawing of Commodore Perry and two of his officers done in a high style of art, which I procured at Simoda, and I think will make you laugh." [5]

A portrait of Commander Adams and his son with captions in English is

Below: This picture of Adams and his son from the large sketchbook is more finished than one in the Caroline E. Foote *scroll.*

Below right: Mrs. Doty in her finery.

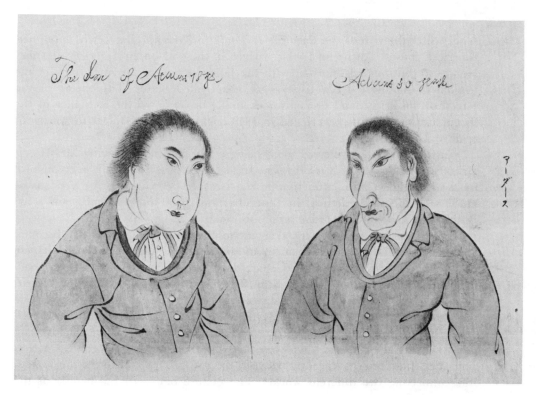

added to this scroll. The full-figure portrait of Mrs. Doty in casual dress is followed by a portrait of her dressed up in special finery for the "Girl's Festival." Her three-tiered skirt and her fancy parasol indicate that she is prepared for a special outing. The facial features are not individualized and thus tell us little about the lady's true physiognomy.

The last panel of the scroll shows a group of foreigners as they might have been observed on a Shimoda street corner. There are three officers, two marines, and a Chinese gentleman, who may be modeled on Mr. Lo, the assistant to the American interpreter, Samuel Wells Williams. Mr. Lo had made himself very popular among the Japanese by his ability to write suitable verses as mementos on their fans. For this reason his portrait also appears in other drawings of the Americans made in Hakodate.

Large Sketchbook

A year after the visit of the *Caroline E. Foote* to Shimoda, the newly appointed American consul, Townsend Harris, arrived in the port on an American steamer. He was to continue negotiations with the Japanese and to convince them of the wisdom of signing a trade treaty with the United States. The threat of the arrival of the British and French forces finally broke down the resistance of the shogunate, and a treaty was signed in 1858 opening Japanese ports to American trade.

In the sketchbook referred to earlier are two paintings showing Mr. Harris and officers of the U.S.S. *Mississippi* at an audience in the Goshoin, a conference room in the Edo Castle, after signing the treaty. The paintings are versions of much more detailed pictures in the collections of Tsuneo Tamba and Carl Boehringer, some of which have been published.

In comparing the Library's sketches to the finished paintings, it becomes apparent that the basic arrangement of the figures is identical. The Japanese court officials wear the prescribed court dress, including a black lacquer headdress and wide pantaloons with a train. In comparison to their colorful appearance, the American naval officers appear somber in their black uniforms. The only break in the monotony is the red diplomatic sash of the minister-in-residence, Townsend Harris. The picture is dominated by a mood of courtly ceremonial. Every actor knows his place in the drama and plays his role to perfection. The interpreter is kneeling between the two groups and forms the human link connecting two different worlds. The picture omits all the details of the

Minister-in-Residence Townsend Harris,
identified by a ceremonial sash, in the first of
two pictures at an audience in the Goshoin.

walls and floor mats, but the essential character of the scene is preserved.

The second illustration, which depicts the acceptance of the Japanese gifts, continues in the same tone of solemn ceremony. The Japanese nobles are attended by kneeling sword bearers. Minister Harris and two American naval officers are stepping forward to receive a gift of rolls of silk presented on trays. The Library's painting does not show all the details of the more complete version of the painting, although the colors of the court costumes in the two paintings match. They seem to be based on a common source.

The study of these Japanese documentary pictures leads to a fascination with the story behind them. The arrival of the Americans created a turmoil which eventually led to the dissolution of the feudal power of the shogunate. It also gave rise to a new school of popular art. Pictures describing Americans and foreigners in Japan after the opening of the country are called Yokohama-e. Our scrolls and illustrations fall into this category of popular art. For many years they were not appreciated by the Japanese public, because they were considered only crude and common popularizations. Today more and more attention is being paid to the Yokohama-e. The Library of Congress is fortunate in having a representative collection of these early pictures which record the first contacts between the United States and Japan.

The Susquehanna *as depicted in the large scroll of the first landing.*

NOTES

1. Matthew C. Perry, *Narrative of the Expedition of an American Squadron to the China Seas and Japan, Performed in the Years 1852, 1853 and 1854*, vol. 1, (Washington: 1856), p. 237.

2. Like the other translations of the text appearing on the scrolls, this one was made by Miss Akiko Murakata, a participant in the doctoral program in American thought and culture conducted jointly by the Smithsonian Institute and the George Washington University.

3. See the reproduction of the New York Public Library scroll on the double-page insert between pages 10 and 11 of Harold A. Mattice's *Perry and Japan* (New York: 1942).

4. Vol. 1, pp. 358–59.

5. George Henry Preble, *The Opening of Japan; a Diary of Discovery in the Far East, 1853–1856* (Norman: 1962), p. 274.

PICTORIAL ESSAYS ON WOMEN

BY MILTON KAPLAN

Stages of Woman's life from infancy to the brink of the grave.

1

2

3

1. Shake Hands? Lithograph by Lafosse. Painted by Mrs. Lily Martin Spencer. William Schaus, 1854. LC–USZ62–16771.

2. W. F. Shaw's Patent Gas Cooking & Ironing Apparatus. Gas Smoothing-Iron, and Miniature Gas Furnace, 1858. LC–USZ62–40704.

3. [Woman with Hoe.] Drawing by Alice Barber Stephens. LC–USZ62–54590.

4. The Kitchen. Prang's Aids for Object Teaching; Trades & Occupations, plate 6. Lithograph by L. Prang & Co., 1874. LC–USZ62–478.

4

5

6

7

8

5. The Young Housekeepers. The Day after Marriage.
Lithographed by Nathaniel Currier, 1848. LC–USZ6–361.

6. Hovey's Cocoa Glycerine For Preserving & Dressing the Hair.
Lithograph by John H. Bufford, 1860. LC–USZ62–4624.

7. The last Request. Lithograph by Fenderich & Wild, n.d.
LC–USZ62–54598.

8. Reading the Scriptures. Lithographed by Nathaniel Currier,
n.d. LC–USZ62–02874.

WOMAN AS MOTHER

9

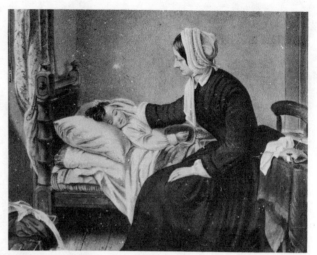

10

11

12

13

14

9. And The Star-Spangled Banner. Engraved by George E. Perine. Published by William Pate, 1861. LC–USZ62–5264.

10. The Mother's Blessing. Lithograph by Currier & Ives, n.d. LC–USZ6–354.

11. "Her face was dark with heat and streaked with perspiration," a drawing by F. C. Yohn for *Mother* by Kathleen Norris. reproduced in *The Ladies' Home Journal,* August 1912. LC–USZ62–54595.

12. Chippeway Squaw & Child. Lithographed by John T. Bowen. Published in Thomas L. McKenny and James Hall's *History of the Indian Tribes of North America, 1838–44.* LC–USZ62–54593.

13. Mother and Child. Lithographed by Nathaniel Currier, 1846. LC–USZ6–353.

14. An Increase of Family. Lithograph by Currier & Ives, 1863. LC–USZ62–8931.

WOMAN AS MENTOR

15. "I received an appointment as teacher in a district school," drawing by John Wolcott Adams, for "The Log Cabin Lady," in *The Delineator*, December 1921. LC–USZ62–34839.

16. One of the Wards of the Hospital at Scutari. Lithograph by E. Walker of a drawing by W. Simpson. Printed by Day & Son, 1856. LC–USZ62–11313.

17. Mrs. Juliann Jane Tilman. Preacher of the A.M.E. Church. Lithograph by A. Hoffy. Printed by P.S. Duval, 1844. LC–USZ62–54596.

18. The Slum Work of the Salvation Army—Scene at a Prayer-Service in the Slum District of New York. Reproduction in *Frank Leslie's Illustrated Newspaper*, December 20, 1894, of a drawing by Miss G. A. Davis. LC–USZ62–2173.

19. "Dorothy Busy in the Library," drawing by Alice Barber Stephens for George Eliot's *Middlemarch*. LC–USZ62–54592.

15

16

17

18

19

WOMAN AS BREADWINNER

20

22

21

20. Baker, Prang's Aids for Object Teaching; Trades & Occupations, plate 10. Lithograph by L. Prang & Co., 1875. LC–USZ62–4218.

21. Milliner, Woodcut in Edward Hazen's *Panorama of Professsions & Trades,* 1836. LC–USZ62–32031.

22. Jas. B. Smith & Co. Booksellers and Blank Book Manufacturers. Lithograph by August Köllner. Printed by H. Camp, 1850. LC–USZ62–02169.

23. Glimpses at the Freedmen—The Freedmen's Union Industrial School, Richmond Virginia. "From a Sketch by Our Special Artist, Jas. E. Taylor." Wood engraving, *Frank Leslie's Illustrated Newspaper,* September 22, 1866. LC–USZ62–33264.

24. W. S. & C. H. Thomson's Skirt Manufactory. Wood engraving in *Harper's Weekly,* February 19, 1859, LC–USZ62–2035.

25. Match-Makers. Wood engraving in *Harper's Weekly,* June 17, 1871. LC–USZ62–5375.

23

24

25

26

27

28

29

30

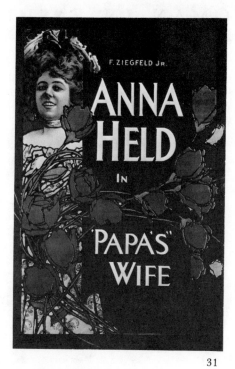

F. ZIEGFELD JR.

ANNA HELD

IN

'PAPA'S' WIFE

31

26. John W. Isham's Grand Opera Celebrities. Great Singers of the Century. Lithograph by the Strobridge Lith. Co., 1896. LC–USZ61–1016.

27. Greeting to America. Jenny Lind. Lithograph by A. Shwartz & F. Moné. Printed by Nagel & Weingaertner, 1850. LC–USZ62–01295.

28. [Animal Tamer] Lithograph by Gibson & Co., 1872. LC–USZ62–1146.

29. Ellen Tree in the Character of Mariane in "The Wreckers Daughter." Lithograph by Henri Heidemans. Printed by Nathaniel Currier, 1837. LC–USZ62–54601.

30. Madame Celeste as Miami, in Buckstone's Celebrated Drama "Green Bushes." Lithograph by Nathaniel Currier, 1848. LC–USZ62–15674.

31. Anna Held in "Papa's Wife." Lithograph by Strobridge Lith. Co., 1900. LC–USZ62–11878.

WOMAN IN FASHION

32

32. A Daughter of the South. Drawing by Charles Dana Gibson, for *Collier's; the National Weekly*, July 31, 1909. LC–USZ62–5536.

33. Mary. Lithographed by James Baillie, 1846. LC–USZ62–54600.

34. American Fashions. Spring and Summer 1886. Lithograph by Major, Knapp & Co., 1886. LC–USZ62–54279.

35. The Colored Beauty. Lithograph by Currier & Ives, 1877. LC–USZ62–35745.

36. The Grecian Bend, "She Stoops to Conquer." Lithograph by Studley & Co., 1868. LC–USZ62–02308.

37. "Bloomerism," or the New Female Costume of 1851, As it has appeared in the various Cities and Towns. Woodcut in *Bloomerism,* published by S. W. Wheeler, 1851. LC–USZ62–050171.

33

34

35

"BLOOMERISM,"
OR THE
NEW FEMALE COSTUME OF 1851,

As it has appeared in the various Cities and Towns.

BOSTON: S. W. WHEELER, 66 Cornhill—1851.

36

37

WOMAN IN SPORTS

38

39

38. The Stormer Bicycle. Lithograph by Strobridge Lith. Co., 1896. LC–USZ62–29633.

39. Bending Her Beau! Lithograph by Currier & Ives, 1880. LC–USZ62–17673.

40. Rower. Lithography by Knapp & Co., 1889. LC–USZ62–54599.

41. [Skating] Cover for *Vanity Fair,* January 1916. LC–USZ62–45907.

42. [Her First Tee] Watercolor by William T. Smedley for "Colonel Bogie, a Golf Story," by Gustav Kobbé, in *Harper's Weekly,* July 31, 1897. LC–USZ62–15735.

43. Lawn Tennis. Lithograph by L. Prang & Co. of painting by Henry Sandham, 1887. LC–USZ62–1244.

40

41

42

43

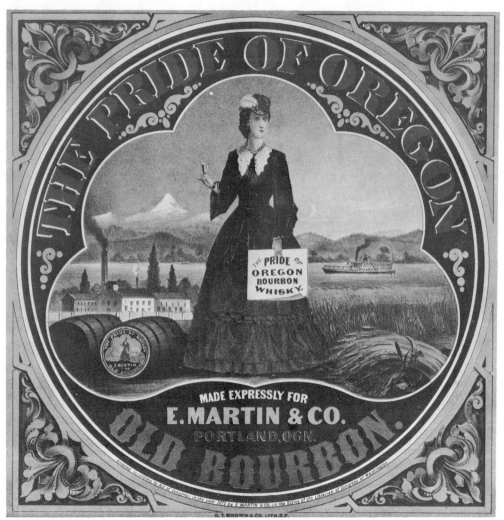

44

45

44. The Pride of Oregon Old Bourbon. Lithograph by G. T. Brown & Co., 1871. LC–USZ62–12429.

45. Granulated 7 O'clock Breakfast Coffee. Lithograph by Britton, Rey & Co., 1876. LC–USZ62–16777.

46. The Best in the Market. Lithograph by Currier & Ives, 1880. LC–USZ62–19533.

47. The Quality of Rob Roy, Lithograph by Julius Bien & Company, 1895. LC–USZ62–20485.

THE BEST IN THE MARKET.

46

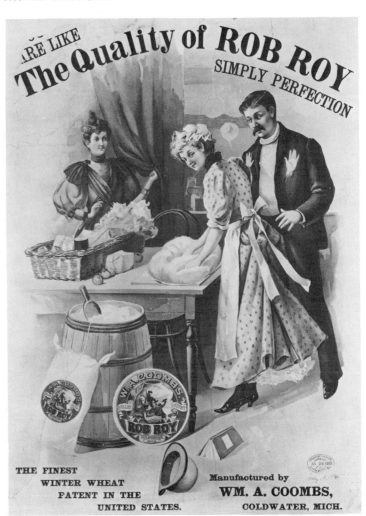

47

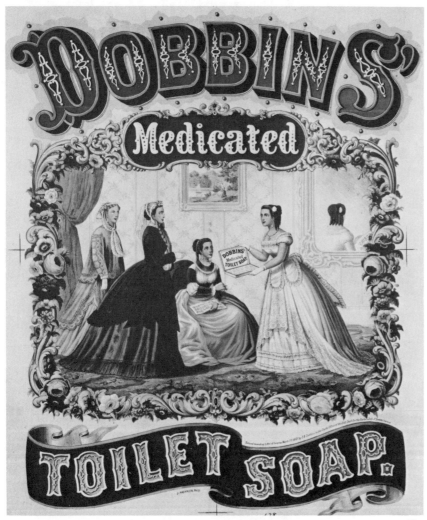

48

49

48. Dobbins' Medicated Toilet Soap. Lithograph by J. Haehnlen, 1869. LC–USZ62–12432.

49. Domestic Sewing Machine. Lithograph by W. J. Morgan & Co., 1882. LC–USZ62–38598.

50. Dobbins' Vegetable Hair Renewer. Woodcut by Ringwalt & Brown, 1870. LC–USZ62–12861.

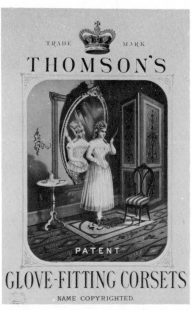

51

52

51. Thomson's Glove-Fitting Corsets. Lithograph by The Graphic Co., 1874. LC–USZ62–54597.

52. Lenox Soap Lathers Freely in Hard Water. Lithograph by the Strobridge Litho. Co., 1898. LC–USZ62–28613.

53. Home Washing Machine & Wringer. Lithograph, 1869. LC–USZ62–2589.

53

III PRINTS, DRAWINGS, AND PAINTINGS
FROM THE TURN OF THE CENTURY
TO THE SIXTIES

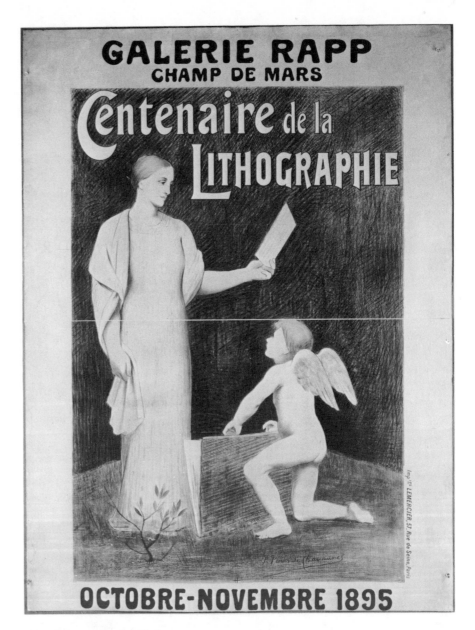

Pierre Cécile Puvis de Chavannes, the French mural
painter, designed this poster for the exhibition
marking the centenary of the invention of lithography. His first critical acclaim was won by
his paintings entitled War and Peace. His murals
decorated many buildings in France, and in 1895
he began a series of panels for the Boston public
Library.

244 / Prints, Drawings, and Paintings from the Turn of the Century to the Sixties

American Artist Prints

BY KAREN F. BEALL

The Library of Congress recently acquired for the Pennell Collection one of the six rare lithographs made by John Singer Sargent (1856–1925), the well-known painter of portraits.

Sargent was a truly cosmopolitan figure. Born in Florence of parents with Boston and Philadelphia backgrounds, Sargent, thus an American, remained an expatriate throughout his life. His childhood was spent moving about Europe before settling in Paris in 1874. Here the eighteen-year-old artist enrolled in the atelier of Carolus-Duran where he received the academic training suitable for portraiture—the most readily acceptable outlet in the field in the eyes of his parents.

Sargent worked diligently and in 1877 submitted the first of his many salon entries. Early in 1885 he gave up his Paris studio and made London his permanent headquarters although he continued to make numerous trips abroad. During his lifetime many honors were bestowed on him, yet acclaim does not seem to have dampened his vigor and enthusiasm. In his later years he devoted himself to landscapes and figure studies in watercolor, abandoning portraiture, which had been both his forte and his livelihood.

During the 1890s a great interest in lithography was stirring as the centennial year of the discovery of the process by Aloys Senefelder (1771–1834) approached. In 1895 an exhibition in celebration of this anniversary was arranged in Paris at the Galerie Rapp. A poster by Puvis de Chavannes (1824 98) in the Library's collections advertises this exhibition. The master printer

Frederick Goulding (1842–1909) was particularly interested in this venture and offered to provide the necessary lithographic materials for the participating artists as well as do the actual printing.

There are two methods for producing lithographs. Using a greasy crayon or ink, the artist can draw either directly on the stone or on specially prepared paper, which is then transferred to the stone by the printer. In an interview which appeared in *The Studio* in 1898 (vol. 6, p. 86), Goulding was asked if he preferred the method of drawing on paper and replied, "Yes, you can draw on paper with much greater freedom and with less mechanical grain being apparent than upon stone." Aside from any personal preference for drawing on paper, it was also a practical matter as many of the participating artists would not have had easy access to the cumbersome lithographic stones. An impressive array of artist's names appears in the catalog of the centennial exhibition. (The only copy of this catalog known to us is in Boston at the Museum of Fine Arts.) Among the artists included are Edouard Manet (1832–1883), Honoré Daumier (1808–1879), Henri de Toulouse-Lautrec (1864–1901), Phil May (1864–1903), Odilon Redon (1840–1916), and, of particular interest for these notes, Sargent.

Although he had done much drawing, Sargent was not quite at home with the stickiness of the lithographic crayon, which differed so radically from his familiar media, pencil and charcoal. Despite this, he found he was able to maintain his usual high standard of draftsmanship and his prints have a directness and spontaneity that have an immediate appeal to the observer. In his *Study of a Young Man (Seated)*, 1895, as in all of his lithographs, he used the specially prepared transfer paper. Goulding remarked, "To all intents and purposes this bold drawing of Sargent's is his actual work, every dot and gradation he set down is there."[1] The print is signed and dated on the stone and the Library's impression is also signed in pencil with the insription, "To Miss Stephens, John S. Sargent." The date on the stone is nearly illegible, yet there is no doubt of its execution in 1895 at Goulding's instigation. The figure, rather artificially draped, sits on a bed or couch, his right arm extended behind him, his hand resting on a pillow. The compositional device of receding diagonal lines creates a feeling of space. The figure leans forward and seems to project almost before the picture plane, a pose very rare in works by Sargent. An illusion of depth is further created by the contrast between the light striking the bed in the left foreground and the darkness of the upper right background. The sparkling effect of light is achieved through the use of the white of the paper and the print has a fresh, vital quality. The black lines and areas of the background are quite rich but some of the fainter ones of the drapery are nearly lost, which may be due to the fact that the drawing was not done directly on the stone. Stylistically this is freer and looser than the portraits Sargent was doing at this time and is closer in this respect to some of his later watercolors.

The inscription to Miss Stephens refers to Emily Henrietta Stephens of Eastington. Letter's written by Sargent and seen, courtesy of David McKibbin, at the Boston Athenaeum, indicate that a friendship between the artist and the Stephens family existed for many years (see Burke's *Landed Gentry*, 1952, for the Stephens family). After Miss Stephens's death in 1952 at the age of ninety-six, her pictures passed to her niece, and her papers were sold by a bookseller to a relative of Sargent. The lithograph, however, was placed by the bookseller at auction at Sotheby's in London, where it was acquired by the Library of Congress.

The identity of the model is also uncertain. It is known that in the early 1890s a young London Italian, Nicola d'Inverno, came into Sargent's service as his valet, an association that was maintained for over twenty years—during which he often posed for the artist. He is known to have posed for the painting *Man Reading,* dated after 1895. Both this picture (in the Reading Public Museum and Art Gallery) and an impression of our lithograph (in the Philadelphia Museum of Art) were lent to an exhibition in 1964 at the Corcoran Gallery of Art.[2]

In the painting, Nicola leans on his elbow and reads from a book held in his left hand. He wears a mustache and appears somewhat older than the model for our lithograph or for a second one, *Study of a Young Man (Drawing)*, believed to have been done at the same time and from the same model. In this the model leans across a table, the head is in profile, and he is sketching. His profile view and the indication of a mustache even more convincingly relate to the *Man Reading* and suggest that Nicola may have been the model. In each instance, the line of the nose, the position of the eyes, the hairline, and the structure of the forearm are much the same. Nicola has been described as lithe and muscular—a description certainly fitting the model for our study. Sargent had received a commission for murals in the Boston Public Library in 1890 and was developing his ideas for them at the time his lithographs were made, so a connection between the murals and the prints is possible. Nicola is known to have posed for the murals, in which Sargent painted numerous nude and partially draped figures. Being very contained, these figures are stylistically quite different from the lithograph; yet the similarity of the pose of the

Above: Study of a Young Man (Drawing).

Left, Sargent's Study of a Young Man (Seated), *acquired by the Library of Congress.*

Left: Man Reading (*The Reading Public Museum and Art Gallery, Reading, Pa.*) ; *center:* Philosophy, *section of the murals on the stair vault of the Museum of Fine Arts at Boston (courtesy of Museum of Fine Arts, Boston. Francis Bartlett donation); right: the variant* Study of a Young Man (Seated) *from the collection at Boston* (*Museum of Fine Arts*) .

Philosophy panel and our seated study is striking.

Two lithographs have already been mentioned; in addition, Sargent did two portaits of Albert Belleroche (one in 1905, the other, head only, undated), one of William Rothenstein, and one of Beatrice Stewart. According to Campbell Dodgson the British Museum has all six. The Boston Museum of Fine Arts has the *Study of a Young Man* (*Seated*), *Head of a Young Woman* (Beatrice Stewart in two impressions, one on white the other on pink paper), and *William Rothenstein,* 1897 (in two states—one done after the print was canceled; approximately eight impressions were made before cancellation) . In addition to the *Study of a Young Man* (*Seated*) a remarkable print similar in proportion but certainly different in technique is in the collection at Boston. The relationship between the print and ours is ambiguous; perhaps it is a copy, perhaps an adaptation in which the original was drawn over or in which the proof lost its separation of tones and was allowed to become too dark. In any case the technique of scraping into the dark areas gives an effect that is utterly different.

In this version a distinct paper texture appears unlike lithographic paper. This variant was exhibited together with the other one in a lithography show held at the Boston Museum, October 7–December 21, 1937. Through the generosity of Frederick Goulding, the Victoria and Albert Museum received in 1906 a set of seventy-six signed proofs from the centennial exhibition, among which is included the Sargent print. The Metropolitan Museum of Art has two impressions of our study; the Cleveland Museum of Art, the Philadelphia Museum of Art and, of course, the Library of Congress each have an impression as well.

Nothing further has been written about these prints since Albert Belleroche did an article and Campbell Dodgson compiled a catalog of Sargent's lithographs.[3]

NOTES

1. Martin Hardie, *Frederick Goulding* (Stirling, Eng.: 1910), p. 110.
2. Donelson F. Hoopes, *The Private World of John Singer Sargent* (New York: 1964).
3. *Print Collector's Quarterly* 13 (1926): 30–45.

Drawings by William Glackens

BY ALAN M. FERN

In this day of picture magazines and illustrated newspapers, it is difficult to remember that only fifty years ago the speedy, direct reproduction of photographs was relatively uncommon. A commercially practical method of making printing plates from photographs without using hand engraving was developed only after 1880, and it was not until the founding of the New York *Daily Mirror* in 1904 that a newspaper was illustrated exclusively with photographs. Until then, most pictorial journals employed skilled artists as reporters and retained large crews of wood engravers to transform into printing blocks the drawings made on the scene of a news story.

Since 1932 the Library of Congress has actively collected the original drawings of these reporters and illustrators. The Cabinet of American Illustration, the Civil War drawings of Edwin Forbes, Alfred Waud, and William Waud, and the collection of original political cartoons comprise about ten thousand drawings originally prepared for reproduction. The recent gift of eleven drawings—augmented by fourteen others deposited with them—made during the Spanish-American War by William Glackens is a notable addition to these collections, and the Library is grateful to the artist's son, Mr. Ira Glackens, for his generosity.

Although he is best known for his paintings, which are in many American museums and private collections, William Glackens started his career as an artist reporter.[1] Born in Philadelphia in 1870, he enrolled at the Pennsylvania Academy of the Fine Arts at the age of twenty-one to begin the serious study of painting. At the same time, he supported himself by doing drawings for the Philadelphia *Record,* a job which gave him an unparalleled opportunity to develop a sharp eye, a keen memory, and a deft touch. These qualities never deserted him even when, in his later career, he turned away from reporting. The painter Everett Shinn, writing in 1943, recalls of his friend, "All things within the range of William J. Glackens' vision were . . . unconsciously absorbed and catalogued in orderly fashion for any immediate usage. His eyes were veritable harvesters of the total limits of his sight." [2] Shinn was deeply impressed with the artist's ability to record accurately the rigging of ships or the details of machinery, as well as the sense of a crowd in a street which he might have observed in passing. To a considerable extent, delight in observation was the basis of Glackens's painting as well as of his reportorial drawing, and unquestionably it is this which raises the Spanish-American War series above the ordinary level of journalistic sketching.

After a few years of newspaper work, Glackens wished to expand his artistic horizons and to develop for himself a style of painting more mature and responsive than he was able to evolve in his spare time in Philadelphia. In 1895 he went to Paris and was deeply impressed by what he saw of the painting of Edouard Manet, Auguste Renoir, and the other independent artists who had broken with the anecdotal painting of the Académie des Beaux-Arts and the official Salon. These men had taken their subjects from everyday life, not from ancient Greece or medieval Europe, and for their landscapes and genre scenes they created a radically new technique of painting—free and vivid, giving the effect of an immediate transcription of their observations from nature.

Glackens responded immediately to this kind of painting and felt at least that he had found his proper medium of expression. He returned to the United States late in 1895, settled in New York, and—as in Philadelphia—found that he had to earn his living as an illustrator. He worked for the *New York Herald* and, briefly, for the *Sunday World;* but now his painting was going well and he wished to devote more time to it. He exhibited his paintings for the first time at the Pennsylvania Academy's exhibition in 1896, and in the following year resigned from the *Herald.* From this time onward, with the single exception of the Spanish-American War, Glackens accepted only freelance assignments to augment his income from the sale of paintings.

His skilled draftsmanship and painterly handling of composition (along with an engaging sense of humor) made Glackens' illustrations outstanding among those published in American periodicals during the 1890s, with the result that his work became well known to art editors in New York. With the outbreak of the Spanish-American War there was a scramble for increased circulation by all papers and magazines covering the event. Writers, artists, and photographers were hired for their ability to attract readers either by the quality of their work or by their personal reputation. *McClure's Magazine* evidently hoped to find correspondents who would provide both attractions. Stephen Crane, whose *Red Badge of Courage* and intricate personal life had made him famous and notorious, was engaged to write from the battlefront. William Glackens was the only artist-reporter employed to work exclusively for *McClure's*. Since his life was reasonably conventional, it may be assumed that he was hired for his extraordinary talents as a draftsman.

A letter from the manager of *McClure's* art department (quoted in Ira Glackens's biography, page 23) assigned Glackens to "go to Cuba with the American troops" and send "illustrations telling the story of the departure, voyage and arrival and subsequent work and fights of the U.S. troops in Cuba."

Evidently Glackens took his assignment seriously, for in the twenty-five drawings which survive (now in the Library of Congress, as noted in the appended checklist) and in six others which were reproduced but later disappeared, every aspect of the campaign mentioned in the letter is represented. The artist arrived in Florida early in May 1898, and his scenes in Tampa include the marshalling and feeding of troops, the delivery of a captured Spanish spy, and general views of the transports anchored in the bay. Crossing with the troops in June, he recorded life aboard the transport *Vigilancia;* arriving at Daiquiri, he showed the debarkation of troops and horses, the shelling of the woods above the harbor, and the battle headquarters. Glackens followed the troops to El Pozo and San Juan Hill, and sent back drawings of life in the trenches, of the surrneder, and of the ceremonies before the Governor's Palace in Santiago de Cuba at the close of hostilities.

Taken as a group, the drawings exhibit remarkable contrasts of character. At an early point in the campaign (possibly just after the troops had landed in Cuba). Glackens depicted a spruce, orderly squad of soldiers proceeding across a field, led by an officer on horseback (Fig. 1). The neatness of the men's bedrolls and packs is reinforced by the composition of the picture, in which the artist-reporter repeated the shapes of the packs and the men in numerious parallel series. Strikingly different is the drawing of a scene late in the battle at El Pozo, in which the condition of the men in battle is eloquently expressed through the artist's use of scattered, jagged lines and shapes (Fig. 2). It is doubt-

Troops and man on horse, Cuba.

ful that these details of composition would have asserted themselves consciously to the artist during the excitement and danger of battle, but Glackens's early experience as an artist-reporter had so thoroughly trained him to respond directly to the scenes and actions before him that he instinctively could communicate with all possible force what he had seen and felt.

A less sensitive artist might have been satisfied to portray the ordinary activities of an army in battle without attempting to convey a sense of atmosphere or mood. Glackens's drawings, on the contrary, communicate a striking sense of time and weather. The superb drawing of a night view of the field hospital after San Juan (Fig. 3) and the scene of the transports in Tampa Bay under an overcast sky (Fig. 4) are but two examples of this mood setting so surely handled that even the process of reproductive engraving could not destroy it.

Of necessity, the drawings had to be made into printing blocks before they were useful to *McClure's*, and to do this involved a complex process. Many of the drawings were done on toned paper, using bold strokes of black-and-white watercolor to model the basic shapes and tonal areas. On all the drawings, Glackens used a crisp line of either pen and ink or crayon. When the drawings were received in New York, they were photographed and made into metal halftone blocks; that is, a photographic and chemical procedure was used which divided all areas of gray into tiny raised dots, equally spaced but varying in size with the depth of value in each part of the drawing. The dots in dark portions were large, in light portions small, so that an approximation of the original tonalities could be obtained in printing.

Up to this point, no handwork was done on the plate, but since only limited contrasts of black and white are easily attainable in the primitive halftone process, the plate then went to an engraver who added highlights by hand and reinforced the vigorous lines of the artist's drawing. When the plates were finally printed on the high-speed presses used for *McClure's* a reasonable facsimile of the original drawing resulted, although—as can be noticed in Figures 5a and b— the intervention of another hand somewhat altered the character of Glackens's drafsmanship.

Of the drawings in the present gift, those published appeared in *McClure's Magazine*. Ira Glackens records that an agreement had been reached with the *World* for his father to use the newspaper's special boat in return for publication rights to some of the drawings—the sole exception to the exclusive contract with *McClure's*. So far, no drawings have been identified in the *World*, and it may be assumed that Glackens never took advantage of the arrangement.

"El Pozo (fighting up hill)."

"Night after San Juan—Field Hospital."

"Transports anchored in the bay (Tampa]."

"Raising the flag . . . Santiago"—*detail of original drawing.*

"Raising the flag . . . Santiago"—*detail of reproduction in* MCCLURE'S.

Several drawings remained unpublished owing to the time it took to send them by ship from Cuba to New York, or so Glackens was told when he arrived home, ill with malaria, to learn that he was to be paid only for the drawings actually used. Since most of his drawings did not appear in *McClure's* until October and December 1898 and February 1899 issues (the fighting had ended in July, the treaty of peace was signed in December 1898), it may be that readers lost interest before all of them had been used. Nonetheless, it is difficult to believe that the artist greeted this news with as much equanimity as Ira Glackens suggests, and the fact remains that he did no more work for the magazine.

The drawings—used or unused—were never returned to the artist. In a note accompanying his gift of the drawings, Ira Glackens wrote: "The history of these drawings is curious. *McClure's* retained them and my father never saw them again. After his death in 1938, a stranger wrote my mother that he had the collection, and felt she should have it, and presented it to her. He had saved the drawings from destruction forty years before. Unfortunately I do not know his name."

Although Glackens continued to make illustrations—nine of his drawings for *Scribner's Magazine* or for books are in the Library's Cabinet of American Illustration—from this time onward he concentrated more and more on painting. In 1901 he participated in his first group exhibition, in contrast to the large Academy exhibitions in which only one or two paintings by each artist could be shown. After his marriage in 1904 and a belated wedding trip to Europe, a series of events brought him into the national prominence he enjoyed until his death in 1938.

Excluded from the New York Academy Exhibition of 1907, Glackens and seven others showed their pictures independently at the Macbeth Gallery in 1908.[3] "The Eight," as they came to be called, undertook to paint pictures that vibrated with the life around them. Portrayals of children in the park, people in crowded streets, scenes of homelife in humble apartments earned them the epithet "Ashcan Painters." The extraordinary power of their brushwork and draftsmanship, however, gave nobility to their subjects and raised their work far above the level of the mere chronicle.

Today the paintings of "The Eight" still live. Much of the art-loving public is pleased, rather than shocked, by portrayals of familiar life, while it finds it increasingly difficult to accept the sentimental and artificial studies produced by the Academicians against whom Glackens and his associates revolted. The drawings of the Spanish-American War belong to this tradition. Indeed, because they came in a period of Glackens's career when he was turning away from reporting and finding his way as a painter, so they are important documents in American art as well as significant records of a war.

"Raising the flag over the Governor's Palace, Santiago."

NOTES

1. A full biography of the artist has been published by his son Ira in *William Glackens and the Ashcan Group* (New York: 1957). Most of the biographical material in this article is based on this work.

2. Everett Shinn, "Recollections of the Eight," in Brooklyn Institute of Arts and Sciences Museum, *The Eight* (Brooklyn, N.Y.: 1943), p. 18.

3. The other participants in this famous exhibition were Arthur B. Davies, Robert Henri, Ernest Lawson, George Luks, William Prendergast, Everett Shinn, and John Sloan.

Portrait of Arnold Schönberg.
LC–USZ62–52575

Arnold Schonberg and the Blaue Reiter

BY EDGAR BREITENBACH

Schönberg's Vision.
LC–USZ62–60632

The purpose of this essay is to restore a remarkable pedigree to a painting which for many years has been displayed in the Whittall Pavilion in the Library of Congress. I am referring to the painting by Arnold Schönberg which was presented to the Library in October 1954 by Leopold Stokowski, the famous conductor. Schönberg completed the painting in 1910, and in 1949 he dedicated it to Stokowski, who believed it to be a self-portrait.[1] This conclusion, however, is in error and, as we shall see, the correct title is *Vision*.

In the decades preceding the First World War, Germany enjoyed a high degree of prosperity, unprecedented in her history, that reached far down into the lower strata of society. Yet for all the material well-being, there was widespread uneasiness among German intellectuals, accompanied by tensions which increased year by year after the turn of the century. It was not so much social unrest as a deep disgust with crass materialism. There were demands for a new spirituality, for a simpler form of life, reminiscent of Rousseau's "back to nature." As one of the contemporaries put it:

> We are standing today at the turning point of two long epochs, similar to the state of the world fifteen hundred years ago, when there was also a transitional period without art and religion—a period in which great and traditional ideas died and new and unexpected ones took their place. . . . The hour is unique. Is it too daring to call attention to the small, unique signs of the time?[2]

These words were written in 1911; five years later, their author was dead on the battlefields of France. By that time the chiliastic enthusiasm was spent.

During the latter half of the nineteenth century Munich replaced Düsseldorf as the center of the German art world. Its Academy of Art was the most renowned in the country and the bastion of the art establishment. The first revolt against the traditional ways occurred in 1892, when a group of dissident artists formed the *Sezession*. It did not take very long before the secessionists became academicians in their turn, and thus a new anti-establishment movement was created. Even more short-lived and today all but forgotten, it carried the significant name *Die Scholle* ("the soil"), thereby indicating the belief of its members in the regenerating influence of communion with nature. Finally, in January 1909, a new group was formed under the intentionally neutral name of Neue Künstlervereinigung München ("New Artists' Association of Munich"). Its leader was Wassily Kandinsky.

Kandinsky, a lawyer by training and a professor of economics in Moscow, came to Munich in 1896 to become an artist. He enrolled in the private art school of Anton Azbé and later established a similar school himself, called Phalanx. In the spring of 1909 the Neue Künstlervereinigung sent a letter to prospective patrons, probably drafted by Kandinsky, which outlined the association's programs.

> We take the liberty of drawing your attention to an artists' organization formed in January 1909 which hopes, through the exhibition of serious works of art, to work for the promotion of art to the best of its ability. It is our belief that an artist, in addition to the impressions he receives from the external world, that is to say nature, is constantly collecting experiences from an inner world. The search for artistic forms, which express the interpenetration of all these experiences, forms freed from everything superfluous, expressing nothing but what is essential, in short a search for an artistic synthesis, seems in our opinion a solution which today spiritually links more and more artists to each other.[3]

The first major problem which the new association faced was to find a gallery willing to accept their exhibitions. After much prodding on the part of Hugo von Tschudi, the newly appointed director of the Bavarian State Museums, Heinrich Thannhauser, owner of the largest commercial art gallery, finally agreed to accept the group. The first exhibition took place in December

1909 and was followed by a second one nine months later. Both were complete failures in the eyes of the public and the critics. Practically the only words of understanding and sympathy came from Hugo von Tschudi and from an outsider, a young painter who valiantly defended the group in the press and who subsequently was offered a membership and given a voice in the association's affairs. His name was Franz Marc.

In contrast to the first exhibition, which included only sixteen Munich painters, the second exhibition was international. Many of the French painters who subsequently enjoyed global fame were represented: Braque and Picasso, Derain, Vlaminck, and Odilon Redon. When the time came to hold a third exhibition, tension among the members of the association became noticeable. It is easy to blame the more conservative members for being too stodgy. They evidently felt that the two previous failures proved that the group had become too experimental and thus had lost touch with the critics and public alike. When the jury met, they voted down Kandinsky's entry. This rejection was the signal for Kandinsky, Marc, Alfred Kubin, Gabriele Münter, and several others to leave the association in protest. The new dissidents frantically arranged an exhibition of their own, held in two rooms of the Thannhauser Gallery, adjacent to the third exhibition of the New Artists' Association. It opened on December 18, 1911, and closed early in January 1912. Its title was "First Exhibition of the Editors of the Blaue Reiter." The *Blaue Reiter Almanac*, which Kandinsky and Marc had been working on since the summer of 1911, was finally published in May 1912. Both the exhibition and almanac were of seminal importance. They were a landmark in the history of modern art, and their impact was comparable to that of the Armory Show in New York in 1913. It was at this exhibition that Arnold Schönberg's painting, which is now in the possession of the Library, was displayed, while a reproduction was included in the almanac.

Kandinsky became acquainted with Schönberg's music through the latter's famous book *Harmonielehre,* which before it appeared in book form was published in installments in the Berlin periodical *Die Musik* in 1910. Kandinsky quotes from it in his book *Über das Geistige in der Kunst* . . . [On the Spiritual in Art], written in 1910 and published the following year, and goes on to say: "Schönberg's music opens a new realm to us where musical experiences are not acoustical ones but experiences of the soul." [4] What Kandinsky evidently felt to be the common denominator between his own art and Schönberg's music was later poignantly expressed by Franz Marc, who, after listening to Schönberg's music, observed: "Can you imagine a kind of music in which tonality (i.e., the

Gabriele Munter's 1906 portrait of Wassily Kandinsky. The Solomon R.
Guggenheim Museum, New York.

Kandinsky sketched this design in 1911 for the cover of the Blaue Reiter
Almanac. Städtische Galerie im Lenbachhaus, Munich. A 1912 copy of
the almanac is in the collections of the Rare Book and Special Collections
Division in the Library of Congress.

use of one key) is completely absent? I was constantly reminded of Kandinsky's "Large Composition" in which there is also not a trace of a key. . . ." [5]

But this is not all. Kandinsky and other artists around him believed that there was a close relationship between music and the visual arts—so close, indeed, that each note corresponded to a definite color; thus, music could be translated into painting and painting into music. Therefore, it is not by chance that Kandinsky frequently chose musical terms as titles for his abstract compositions, as in "Klänge." Kandinsky and his friends believed in the totality of art. For this reason the *Blaue Reiter Almanac* is devoted not only to the visual arts but also to music and the performing arts, the latter being represented by Kandinsky's own dramatic piece. Significantly, he called it *Der Gelbe Ton* [The Yellow Sound], thus emphasizing the synthesis of the arts he had in mind. The music for this play was written by Theodor von Hartmann, a Russian composer.

In 1912, after the appearance of Schönberg's *Harmonielehre,* some of his devoted friends compiled a small volume of testimonials in his honor which was published by Kandinsky's Munich publisher, R. Piper. This book contains an essay by Kandinsky on Schönberg as a painter. He tells us that Schönberg produced two kinds of pictures: figures or landscapes painted from nature, which their creator considered mere "finger exercises" and on which he placed no particular value, and "visions," consisting of intuitively conceived heads, which he painted to give form to emotions he was unable to express through music. He then goes on to say:

> Schönberg does not paint in order to create a "beautiful" or a "pleasing" picture, but while he paints he does not actually think of the picture at all. His aim is not to represent an objective image but rather to fix his subjective "feeling," and in order to do this he uses only such means as appear to him unavoidable at the moment. Not every professional painter can pride himself on this creative manner. . . . We see that in all of Schönberg's pictures the inner desire of the artist is expressed through its corresponding form. Just as in his music (if I may say so as a layman) he disregards in his paintings everything that is superfluous (that is to say, harmful). He goes directly to the essential (i.e., the necessary), shunning all "beautifications" and fine details. [6]

Concerning our painting, Kandinsky says: "Painted on a small piece of canvas (or a piece of carton), this 'vision' is merely a head in which only the eyes outlined in red speak to us strongly."

Kandinsky designed this poster for the first exhibition of the Neue Künstlervereinigung München ("New Artists' Association of Munich") . Fondation Marguerite et Aimé Maeght, Paris.

People, of course, react differently when they look at a painting. August Macke (1887–1914), the youngest among the contributors to the almanac, had helped to edit the book in its final stages. He was a man firmly rooted in this world. Neither Marc's quasi-religious philosophy nor Kandinsky's often involved theories concerning aesthetics and art had much appeal for him. When he received his copy of the *Blaue Reiter Almanac* he wrote to his friend Franz Marc, commenting on the book: "And finally that Schönberg. He made me really mad. These green-eyed watery buns [*Wasserbrötchen*] with an astral glance. I won't say anything against the Self-Portrait from Behind. But do these tidbits [*Bröckchen*] really justify all the fuss about the 'painter' Schönberg?" [7]

Arnold Schönberg, who painted intermittently until about 1940, does not have a place in the history of art, nor does he need one. His greatness as a musician is uncontested. Painting was for him a sideline, pursued partly as a diversion, partly from inner necessity. We look at his paintings with the same interest with which we look at the watercolors of Goethe, whom nobody would classify as a painter either. The Library of Congress is proud to own one of Schönberg's paintings. Now that the pedigree of the picture has been reestablished, we hope that a future edition of the *Blaue Reiter Almanac* will correct the footnote "Now untraceable." [8]

NOTES

1. The inscription in Schönberg's hand in the lower left reads: To Leopold Stokowski; Arnold Schoenberg, September 1949; that in the lower right reads: Arnold Schönberg, 16. III. 1910.

2. Franz Marc, "Two Pictures," in *The Blaue Reiter Almanac,* ed. Wassily Kandinsky and Franz Marc. New documentary edition . . . by Klaus Lankheit (New York: Viking Press, 1974), p. 69.

3. Rosel Gollek, *Der Blaue Reiter im Lenbachhaus München; Katalog der Sammlung in der Städtischen Galerie* (Munich: Prestel-Verlag, 1974, p. 2. Author's translation.

4. Wassily Kandinsky, *Über das Geistige in der Kunst, insbesondere in der Malerei; mit acht Tafeln und zehn Originalholzschnitten* (Munich: R. Piper & Co., 1912), p. 29. Author's translation.

5. Lothar Günther Buchheim, *Der Blaue Reiter und die "Neue Künstlervereinigung München"* (Feldafing: Buchheim Verlag, 1959), p. 146. Author's translation.

6. Wassily Kandinsky, "Die Bilder," in Arnold Schönberg, *Arnold Schönberg* (Munich: R. Piper & Co., 1912), pp. 59–64. Author's translation.

7. Buchheim, *Der Blaue Reiter,* p. 52. This picture, showing Schönberg from behind, walking down a path, was included in both the almanac and the exhibition. Author's translation.

8. Kandinsky and Marc, eds., *The Blaue Reiter Almanac,* p. 276, no. 85.

The Drawings of C. K. Berryman

BY MARY R. MEARNS

Clifford Kennedy Berryman, for half a century Washington's best known and most beloved graphic commentator on politics, began on January 19, 1945, the transfer of the corpus of his cartoons to the Library of Congress, where they constitute an important addition to the Cabinet of American Illustration. Thus far almost twelve hundred drawings have been received. When the remainder of those in Mr. Berryman's home and office come to the Library, it is believed that the Berryman Archive will contain some five thousand sketches. Though there are notable small collections in other institutions,[1] a great many original drawings are owned by individuals. Many public figures, pleased or pricked by Mr. Berryman's caricatured portraits of them, have sought the originals and the artist has always acceded generously to their requests. It is hoped that many of these widely scattered drawings eventually will find their way to the master collection in the Library of Congress.

On June 1, 1945, an exhibition of cartoons illustrating the political scene in Washington from 1896 to 1945 was opened at the Library. It aroused and sustained so much public interest and pleasure that, although scheduled to remain on view only until August 1st, it was continued until August 17th.

Mr. Berryman's first thought of the Library of Congress as the appropriate repository for the collection was aroused by a casual query from Dr. Herbert Putnam as they journeyed together on a streetcar, bound for desks symbolic of widely diverse public service. Zest for matutinal attack on each day's duties was not all the two men had in common. Contrasting in appearance and personality, each had served some of the same constituency for nearly fifty years, each had

1912.

achieved unique distinction, each had found his keenest enjoyment in his work. Soon after his conversation, Mr. Berryman made up his mind ultimately to present the collection to the national library but gave no more attention to the matter until the spring of 1944 when Archibald MacLeish, then Librarian, asked Mr. Berryman to deposit the originals of his drawings in the Library. On January 19, 1945, Mr. Berryman brought the first installment of the gift to the Library himself, and remained for an hour's visit in the office of the Acting Librarian, Dr. Luther H. Evans, reminiscing about his career and sketching swiftly in pencil as he talked, impervious to flashlights and cameras, while a few privileged members of the staff looked on.

The story of his career is typically American. He was born in Woodford County, Kentucky, on April 2, 1869, and was graduated from Professor Henry's School for Boys in 1886. A talent for drawing, combined with an avid and amused interest in politics, was one of his youthful characteristics. At thirteen, he once absented himself from school in order to hear a campaign speech delivered by Rep. Joseph C. S. Blackburn, who has been described as "chivalrous, courteous and gallant, withal possessed of a personality the magnetism of which is rarely excelled . . . petted and idolized by his constituency." Young Berryman apparently succumbed to "Joe" Blackburn's charm from that moment. He made a sketch of the gentleman and fashioned it into a bust by mounting it on a cigar box and trimming it with a jigsaw which he had purchased from his earnings as a clerk in the country store. A few years later, Blackburn, who had become a senator, chanced upon it in the office of Clifford's uncle. Impressed by the lad's abilities as a draftsman, he arranged for him (then seventeen years of age) to come to Washington to a position in the Patent Office at thirty dollars a month.

Once on the spot, the youthful Berryman found time to study the folk habits of Capitol Hill and to record his impressions in humorous sketches drawn for his own enjoyment. Moreover, he contrived to inform himself of the work of the foremost caricaturists as represented in the pages of *Puck* and *Fudge,* making a weekly investment of ten cents for each new number as it was published. Unconsciously but effectively, he was preparing himself for a field of endeavor just beginning to develop.

William Murrell has written that "it was not until the middle and late nineties that cartoons became a regular feature in a few of the great American daily newspapers," although they had occasionally appeared as early as 1872

NEWS NOTE — PRESIDENT WILSON'S ANNUAL MESSAGE TO CONGRESS IS COMPLETED

Above right: Berryman's view of the Balkan hostilities, July 28, 1914.

and "first became a force through Walt McDougall's efforts in the *New York World* at the end of the presidential campaign in 1884." [2] In 1891 Mr. Berryman sold a cartoon to *The Washington Post* for twenty-five dollars; it proved so successful that shortly thereafter his cartoons began to appear regularly in the pages of this newspaper. In January 1907 he joined the staff of *The Evening and Sunday Star* where for nearly forty years he delighted daily in an arch examination of the political fabric in the making, isolating a thread or two for discussion with, and approval of, his colleagues before turning to his drawing board and composing the final product.

The Drawings of C. K. Berryman / 273

A few weeks after arriving in Washington, he met Miss Kate G. Durfee, who seven years later was to become Mrs. Clifford Berryman. They were honored on their fiftieth wedding anniversary, July 5, 1943, by the Corcoran Gallery of Art with a reception and an exhibition of some three hundred Berryman cartoons. His daughter, Miss Florence Berryman, is known for her art notes; and his son, James, who inherited his father's pencil penchant to so remarkable a degree, alternated with him in supplying Washington daily with a visual editorial. Mr. Berryman says pridefully of his son, "He *has* had lessons, he is a superior draftsman and can portray action." His own father had talent, too, Mr. Berryman recalls, but his sketches were not preserved, to his son's everlasting disappointment.

Mr. Berryman's sense of responsibility in the exercise of his great talents has given a special character to his work. In 1926 he declared in an address delivered at the School of Journalism of the University of Missouri:

> There is nothing in our modern life so alarming as the power which reckless and dissolute talent has to make virtuous life seem provincial and ridiculous, vicious life graceful and metropolitan. The cartoonist's pencil cannot, however, defeat a good measure. Caricature is powerless against an administration that is honest and competent; powerless against a public official who does his duty in his place.

Certainly, his smiling caricatures could be drawn only by a genial, smiling man; his technique of emphasizing rather than exaggerating the salient characteristics of his subjects is the mark of his lack of malice;[3] the fluent sweep of his major strokes indicates his generous spirit; his enthusiasm for each diurnal episode is reflected in work at once fresh and charming and (by reason of its contemporaneity) historically important. He has an ability unsurpassed to catch likenesses[4] and to endow a figure or countenance with emotional quality. One cartoon, typical of many others, appeared on December 17, 1944. Former Senator Clark (opposing the nomination of Archibald MacLeish as an assistant secretary of state) is reading uncomprehendingly the lines "and watched infinities of things careen with shouted laughter down the startled air" and pointing a derisive finger at the distinguished author who, seated dejectedly on the floor, gives actual meaning to his words in an appearance of reluctant and puzzled disillusion.

Stark and sudden national tragedy endowed the cartoon of April 12, 1945, with unequalled dramatic force. This commended Vice President Truman's devotion to duty as president of the Senate and hence his presence on the floor of the Senate chamber two days earlier when the administration needed help in breaking a tie vote on the Taft amendment to the bill for extending Lend Lease. It appeared in *The Star* an hour or two before word of Franklin Delano Roosevelt's tragic death flashed to an incredulous world. The man pictured as a schoolboy receiving Professor Barkley's approval for good behavior was destined to be sworn in as president of the United States a few hours later!

Both of the drawings described above are privately owned. A few others, selected from the Library's collection, are reproduced in this issue as examples from other periods of Mr. Berryman's long career. Several more, also selected from the Library's collection, are described here to illustrate Mr. Berryman's humor, his adept use of familiar literary simile, his light treatment of tense moments in party affairs, his sense of international import, his presentation of labor problems, and his whimsy:

Mama (*F. D. R.*) returns from a vacation to find her small boy and girl (*Senate and House*) greeting her with welcome signs, smirks, and flowers amidst the shambles of broken mirrors, careened furniture, smashed vases, and portraits desecrated with ink—testimony to their brattish behavior during her absence. (April 13, 1934) .

Bloated, disheveled, mammoth in size, Alice (labeled *Deficit*) slumps in an easy chair indulging herself with a bottle of disastrous *Recovery Expenditure* while tiny white rabbit Douglas (Director of the Budget) wails, "The trouble is I can't make her stop drinking." (December 30, 1933.)

Roosevelt watches the heels of the Democratic mule and the havoc they've wrought: broken fence, crashed flower pots, and overturned barrels, as he explains, "All I said was 'Gimme six more Justices'." (March 9, 1937.)

Chamberlain is shown flinging away his umbrella to reach for a sturdy cane-length club from a nearby rack, exclaiming, "I have carried that thing too long." (March 20, 1939) .

Ferdinand the Bull as *Anti Strike Legislation* is kept contented and smiling by *F. D. R.* who pats him while matadors Lewis, Murray and Kennedy tease for a fight in spite of the President's protest, "If you boys keep that up, I'm not going to be responsible for Ferdinand any longer." (November 13, 1941.)

A large squirrel with his nuts under his paws for provident burial tells

Conant, Baruch and Compton seated on a bench in Lafayette Park, non-plussed by a mandate from the President to get some rubber, "Looks like a hard winter, boys, you'd better get going." (August 9, 1942.)

House in hunter's garb with a large game pouch (*U. S. Budget*) on his hip says, "Watch me bring down a big bag" as he trains his blunderbuss on a puny bird (*Government Clerk*) on a distant limb though swollen beasts —*Pork, Veteran* and *Farm Relief,* and *State Aid*—cluster at his very knees. (April 27, 1932.)

Clifford Berryman has used many of the symbols originated by famous early political cartoonists whose work appeared in weekly and monthly serials, notably those of Sir John Tenniel: the Eagle, the Russian Bear, the British Lion, the New Year; and those of Thomas Nast: the G. O. P. Elephant, the Tammany Tiger, the "ragbaby" of inflation and the cap and dinner pail emblematic of labor. He has created many of his own: Miss Democracy, a giggling, befrilled, cork-screw-curled spinster; the District of Columbia, a stalwart male in eighteenth-century dress; the Squash Center farmers; and, most widely known, the Teddy Bear. Both the people of Squash Center and their setting were suggested by real characters who assembled around the stove in the country store in Kentucky where Mr. Berryman, aged twelve, once measured sugar and flour. Over and over again he has sketched these homely and homespun persons, loafing, smoking, and commenting shrewdly on the news of the day.

Mark Sullivan in *Our Times* has given an account of the origin of the Teddy Bear:

On November 10, 1902, Roosevelt went on a bear hunt in Mississippi. While he was in camp near Smedes, Miss., a newspaper dispatch described him as refusing to shoot a small bear that had been brought into camp for him to kill. The cartoonist of the Washington POST, Clifford K. Berryman, pictured the incident. For one reason or another, whimsical or symbolic, the public saw in the bear episode a quality that it pleased to associate with Roosevelt's personality. The "Teddy-bear", beginning with Berryman's original cartoon, was repeated thousands of times and printed literally thousands of millions of times; in countless variations, pictorial and verbal, prose and verse; on the stage and in political debate; in satire or in humorous friendliness. Toy-makers took advantage of its vogue: it became more common in the hands of children than the woolly lamb. For Republican

KEEP THE FLAG AFLOAT!

Above: March 17, 1917.

Above right: World War I.

conventions, and meetings associated with Roosevelt, the "Teddy-bear" became the standard decoration, more in evidence than the eagle and only less usual than the Stars and Stripes. (Vol. II, p. 445.)

Mr. Berryman has plied his pencil so industriously through the years that he has found time to illustrate many works,[5] including possibly two dozen Gridiron Club dinner souvenirs. Satirical tidbits for those thousands denied entree to Gridiron Club dinners have been provided nearly a hundred times by Mr. Berryman through his cartoon reports in *The Washington Post* and *The Star*. A monument both to his industry and to his ability to gauge and project personality is *Berryman's Cartoons of the 58th House; a Collection of Original Sketches of the Complete Membership* . . . Washington, D. C., 1903.[6]

Many honors have been conferred upon him. Perhaps he has delighted most in membership in the Gridiron Club, "the most famous dining club in the world," organized by Washington correspondents whose object has been stated

Above: In Honor of the Birthday of "Uncle" Joseph G. Cannon, May 7, 1922.

Above right: 1923.

"to prevent" pompous persons "from taking themselves too seriously." He has a valuable collection of letters and memorabilia from notables, including the eight presidents of the United States from Theodore Roosevelt to Harry S. Truman.

In May 1944, he won a Pulitzer Prize for his cartoon of August 28, 1943, *But Where is the Boat Going?* which presented the "manpower mobilization muddle." A dinghy is shown crowded with seven sturdy male figures in sailor togs. *Congress,* in the bow, wants to drop the *Ban-on-draft-of-fathers* anchor while McNutt restrains him. Hershey, Green and Murray pull oars on the port side, while Lewis, towering and glowering above them on the starboard side, is not lending a hand. *Captain F. D. R.* nonchalantly smokes a cigarette (in the inevitable long holder) standing in the stern and gazing serenely at his fractious crew.

The boyhood admiration aroused by Senator Blackburn has remained constant, for Mr. Berryman today wears flowing bow ties and modified sombreros identical in style with those worn by the Kentucky legislator. He, too, has become "idolized by his constituency." Perhaps some of the qualities for which Blackburn was beloved have been bequeathed as a spiritual legacy to his protégé. Magnetism, modesty and generosity are conspicuous in his nature. He is majestic yet benign, an individualist wholly without guile or affectation, a busy man, with time for "people." Spontaneity seems to motivate his life and work. He has given continuously: laughs, ideas, drawings, time, and talent, not only to the Gridiron Club but to lesser groups and causes. It never occurred to him to copyright the Teddy Bear though he might have profited richly. "I have made thousands of children happy; that is enough for me," is one of his responses to the "Why not?".

There are those, and they are legion, who recognize in this gentle, deflating critic a force which incisively, intelligently and with vast good humor, is forever restoring American feet to the ground where they belong.

NOTES

1. Among these are the British Museum, Corcoran Gallery of Art, Folger Shakespeare Library, Franklin D. Roosevelt Library, Henry E. Huntington Library and Art Gallery, U.S. Supreme Court, University of Idaho, University of Missouri, and the University of Texas, as well as numerous clubs and public offices.

2. *A History of American Graphic Humor* (1865–1938). vol. II, (Macmillan, 1938), pp. 129–30.

3. In Mr. Berryman's cherished collection of signed photographs is one from William Howard Taft inscribed, "To the cartoonist who resisted always the common temptation to exaggerate a corporosity already too large and who made me better looking than I was."

4. Will Rogers once joined an audience to which Mr. Berryman was giving one of his famous "chalk talks." When prodded to speak to the group he finally acquiesced with the comment that "These drawings are excellent, you can recognize the people." He told of having watched another cartoonist who "couldn't even tell you himself who he was sketching."

5. Among them are: his own "Development of the Cartoon," in University of Missouri *Bulletin, Journalism Series,* no. 41 (June 7, 1926) ; Arthur Wallace Dunn's *Gridiron Nights;* Louis Ludlow's *From Cornfield to Press Gallery,* and *In the Heart of Hoosierland;* J. Hampton Moore's *Roosevelt and the Old Guard; Pictorial History of the Schley Court of Inquiry,* reproduced from *The Washington Post;* O. O. Stealey's *Twenty Years in the Press Gallery;* Charlotte Stellwagen's *Mrs. Andrew Johnson Jones' Handmaid;* and Jean Wilson's *Dovey Sary.*

6. Mr. Macon of Arkansas is said to have defied the artist to portray him and to have refused to supply him with a picture. He is sketched behind his desk with only his hands and one elbow showing.

Portrait of the Artist in Love With the Book

BY FRITZ EICHENBERG

Looking back is fraught with danger—as Lot's wife learned to her chagrin. An artist, looking back over forty years of living with, in, and off books of all descriptions, sees a long column of them stretching well into his dim past, an awesome sight which could easily turn him into a pillar of salt. There are nearly a hundred books to which this artist has lent his hand and mind and heart, not all of them worth preserving or talking about.

My assignment, however, is to talk about the Artist and the Book, and I must stand or fall on my record, those solidly bound pieces of evidence on many bookshelves across the country.

No doubt, the book and I were made for each other. There has never been a dull or lonely moment in my life when a book could keep me company. From the moment I could read I became totally committed and addicted to books. They were to me friends and teachers, a constant source of inspiration, joy, and solace, and incidentally of work and bread and sometimes butter.

My reading was wild and untutored. What poured out of the pages of my odd collection of borrowed books and into my mind was a fantastic procession of characters, players in the great tragicomedy we call life. To me books are like a stage and I watch with endless fascination the actors coming out of the wings and slipping into the pages of my books. *My* books, I say with a bow to the authors whose words I try to interpret visually and reverently.

Infinitely varied are the ingredients that make up an artist.

In my case, I guess they are an odd mixture, composed of an all too graphic

"And she became a pillar of salt," wood engraving by Fritz Eichenberg for the Old Testament. (Pennell Collection, Prints and Photographs Division)

mind, a love for the drama and the comedy, an insatiable curiosity about people of all kinds, and the urge to study and recreate their images. Add to this a love for men and beasts, for all living organisms, for plants and trees, for sand and rocks, for clouds and waves, and for the music and the poetry of the drama of life—full of pathos and savagery, often redeemed by laughter and compassion.

I was born with a graphic mind and a graphic eye, with ink in my blood and on my fingers—a gregarious introvert. The print has always been my medium, perhaps because it is such an ideal companion to the printed letter. I always thought in black and white, and soon discovered the infinite variety of shades between the two. The excitement of lifting a piece of paper off the inked surface of a block, creating a multiple image, has never worn off. To see my engravings in the matchless company of letters, each a little symbol in itself, within the covers of a book that goes out into the world to seek friends—and influence people—continues to be a memorable experience.

Perhaps my love for trees and rocks made me quite naturally turn to the woodblock and the lithographic stone. I never cared for the cold glitter of the copper plate because I never cared for the metallic gadgets of our machine age.

To me a book is not just a succession of printed pages on which a story is unfolding. The ideal book is a work of art, a vessel perfectly made to fit its contents, a pleasure to hold, to cherish, and to possess. As a harmonious whole, it becomes a thing of beauty and permanence. A book poorly made is like an ill-fitting suit, embarrassing to the tailor and the wearer. A book poorly bound opens reluctantly; you have to fight it in order to read it. A book poorly printed hurts the eye; poorly designed, it offends your senses. I believe that books seek out their readers—and their illustrators.

Books helped me through the worst years of my childhood and adolescence, coinciding with years of war and depression. Ill at ease in a world at odds with all the fine and noble things I hungered for, I met up with Kafka and Dostoevsky who had dealt creatively with the same problems that tortured me. I submerged my fears and doubts in the savage humor of Voltaire and Swift, of de Coster and Grimmelshausen. To live by your wits in a world turned upside down, not to despair but to make the best of "this best of all possible worlds," was a lesson never to be forgotten.

Here were human beings who understood my own predicament—the Raskolnikoffs and Candides, the Gullivers and the Ulenspiegels—a motley crew among whom I managed to grow up. And so it happened that the first books I ever illustrated were *Tyll Ulenspiegel, Gulliver's Travels,* and *Crime and Punish-*

ment. They were published while I was still a student at the Academy of Graphic Arts in Leipzig.

Predestination? Coincidence? Who knows. Ten years later, starting a new life in the New World, it was again *Tyll Ulenspiegel, Gulliver's Travels,* and *Crime and Punishment* which came my way, this time with a new challenge to an artist somewhat more mature and better able to cope with his task.

Illustration is a bad word these days, debased by ill-usage. This is one of the reasons why I would rather be called a graphic artist, a book artist, an artist in search of characters.

Many books have crossed my path. Publishers may believe they have a hand in this, which is true up to a point. But I believe that books seek me out, stop me, fascinate me, often torture me. Their characters surround me, hold me, seduce me. If that sound like the beginning of a passionate affair, that's what it is.

This is how I met Cathy and Heathcliff in *Wuthering Heights,* that is how I got involved with Jane Eyre, Eugene Onegin, and Tatyana, with Bazarov in *Fathers and Sons,* with Tolstoi's princes and prostitutes, and with all those saints and sinners, the chaste and the passionate, the devils and the redeemers, that file past your eyes in an eloquent procession out of the pages of *The Brothers Karamazov.*

Only recently, on my first trip to the USSR for the State Department, I met my characters in the flesh, right out of Tolstoi and Dostoevsky, in the dark streets of Moscow, on the embankment of the Neva, on a park bench in Kiev, around the Cathedral of Alma Ata, a sleepy frontier town in Kazakhstan. But the acid test came when thousands of Russians looked at my illustrations and found in them what I had hoped to have captured: the spirit of their great writers, the soul of their people.

There are other books that cross your path: Shakespeare, Edgar Allan Poe, the Bible, each challenging one's capacity for understanding the human tragedy and translating it into what one hopes are meaningful images. And to provide needed relief from these heavy burdens, one can always try another children's book, for your child, for everybody's children.

Here we come to the questions most frequently asked of the illustrator: How do you grapple with a book? Where do you start? Why do you prefer certain passages to others, one medium to another?

In the beginning is the word! You read the book, once, twice, three times; you absorb it, it absorbs you. You slip into the time, the place, the characters.

MEMO *from:*

TO:

Russian ornaments

"*You . . . make thumbnail sketches. . . .
Every bit of the environment becomes important. . . .*" *Some of the ornaments sketched here are reflected in designs for half titles and headpieces in* The Brothers Karamazov (*The Limited Editions Club, The George Macy Companies, Inc.*) .

Your interest widens. You read books about the author and the background of his time. You explore the special problems he was concerned with—the Patriotic Wars of 1812, the political exile system of Czarist Russia, as Tolstoi studied them for his *War and Peace* and for *Resurrection*. This is the test whether or not the book is meant for you. Does it hold your interest as you work your way into it or does it begin to pall?

You begin to discover things you had overlooked at first reading. You take notes while you read, make thumbnail sketches. You note details of the passing of seasons, of time and places. Every bit of the environment becomes important, the native landscape, the trees and plants, the furniture and the architecture of the period.

You set the stage, the actors are waiting in the wings, the spotlights are turned on, the actors emerge, take their places, and begin to act. The artist is the director, the stage and costume designer. He must take an interest in the actors' makeup, their hairdo, their acting methods. He recreates the illusion of the stage on his woodblock or in any other graphic medium, a trompe l'oeil finally achieved on a little square of paper in the printed book. After accumulating hundreds of sketches, the conception of the total book slowly emerges—the format, a type face that fits the mood of the book and the character of the illustrations. The title page, the half title, the chapter headings, the end paper, the binding—everything must work together to give form and shape to what one hopes for, the perfect book.

Now the final choice of the illustrations has to be made. They must cover the most significant parts of the story without overwhelming it. They must also be distributed as evenly as possible throughout the text pages.

The artist decides on wood engraving as the most appropriate medium to carry the mood of the story. The drawings are rendered onto the woodblocks, then the engraving begins. Months go by in steady absorbing work; the pile of blocks begins to mount, waiting to be printed.

The proofing finally begins. The first prints are peeled off the inked blocks. Battle fatigue sets in; they are invariably disappointing. Corrections are made, new proofs are pulled, until finally one can't hold out any longer; the deadline is approaching. These are the final agonies of a working artist, to let go of his work knowing he could and should have done better. Then comes the great hangover. Your work is in the hands of the printer, and you know in your heart he is going to mistreat the fruits of your labors. Rare is the artist who does not suspect that the publisher will conspire with the compositor, the printer, and the

Sketches by Fritz Eichenberg, from among
the hundreds an artist accumulates for a book.

binder to cut corners and shatter the artist's dreams of the perfect book. Despite it all, the book is published and goes out into the world. And foolishly one feels like a proud old fossil when over the years people, young and old, begin to tell you how they grew up with your illustrations, which helped them to understand better what the Brontës, Dostoevsky, and others tried to express in prose. Then your head will swell to twice its size. Of course, you'll never hear from those people who despise illustrators and resent their interpretations.

Much of this is based on the plain fact that illustration has fallen on bad times. Too many vices of omission and incompetence have been committed. This becomes sadly evident when one looks back over the proud history of the book

The woodcut of the engraver (somewhat enlarged) is taken from Hartmann Schopper's well-known book devoted to various occupations and skills. The little volume, with numerous woodcuts executed by Jost Amman, appeared at Frankfurt-am-Main in 1568. (Rosenwald Collection)

which encompasses man's recorded history. Has the illuminator of today, the illustrator, the type designer, the printer improved upon Schedel's *Weltchronik,* Gutenberg's Bible, or Aldus Manutius's *Hypnerotomachia Poliphili,* made four centuries ago?

Where are the generous patrons of the arts who could commission great artists to create the *Weisskunig* and the *Theuerdank,* as Emperor Maximilian did 400 years ago, to his and the artists' eternal glory? There are a few oases in the cultural desolation of our century. Perhaps someone should have knighted Ambroise Vollard who earned his share of immortality through forty years of cajoling and inspiring France's great *peintres-graveurs* to produce the most beautiful books of our time.

The fine press book seems dead. Here and there we find some scattered notable efforts, comparable to the Cranach and the Bremer presses in Germany, to Tériade and Skira in France, to a few other printers and publishers in Switzerland, and a few in this country.

True, there are some enterprising publishers, galleries, and perhaps a few university presses who seem to be willing to experiment with illustrated books and portfolios à la Vollard, but they are too few and far between. At present some of the best books are published, produced, designed, and illustrated by a small group of artists who got tired of seeing the quality of their work compromised by indifferent handling.

If every responsible publisher in this country would venture to produce one really fine book a year—a book to be enjoyed in our time and to be left as a precious heritage to those who come after us—he would not only find a wealth of talented artists, gifted writers, good printers, and skilled designers willing and eager to cooperate, but he would also discover the venture to be a most rewarding experience culturally and, who knows, in the end economically as well. Fine books, in the long run, have proved to be more durable than stocks and bonds.

Max Beckmann—Day and Dream

BY KAREN F. BEALL

One of the commanding figures in twentieth-century art is Max Beckmann (1884–1950). His success began at a remarkably early age and at the time of his death he was widely honored internationally. Subjects for his pre-Expressionist paintings ranged from small portraits to current cataclysmic events and included mythological and religious themes as well. But service with the German medical corps during World War I affected him deeply. In the wards and operating rooms, horror confronted him daily, and he sketched what he saw. From that time on, his work underwent great stylistic changes—changes he himself saw reflected in his images when he said: "My pictures reproach God for his errors."

His life might be divided into three broad segments: 1884–1937, spent in his native Germany; the prewar, war, and immediate postwar years, spent in the Netherlands; and the last three years of his life, divided between St. Louis and New York City.

For Max Beckmann's work labels seem inappropriate. He was unyielding in his frank means of expression, and the iconography of his work is exceedingly complicated. Carl Zigrosser states it well in his brief paragraph on the artist published in *The Expressionists* in 1957, when he says that Beckmann's "all consuming passion for self-realization and self-expression [is] an expression of a very special kind: the projection of his own concept of the world he lived in. This intuition of his could not rest content with a mirror-image of outward appearance but must penetrate beyond to a universal reality." [1]

Beckmann related strongly to artists of the past. Among the first to influence him was Rembrandt van Rijn, but he studied masters of all periods including his immediate predecessors. By the time the First World War began—when he was only thirty—he had enjoyed considerable success and a monograph had been published listing some 125 of his painted works.[2]

Greater success followed during the 1920s. Another monograph appeared in 1924, the list of friends and patrons was growing and impressive, and his activity as artist and teacher was extraordinary. By the late twenties and early thirties he was dividing his time between teaching in Frankfurt and working in his studio in Paris. In 1931 the Museum of Modern Art in New York included eight of his works in an exhibition of German art. At the same time a second show was arranged in New York, at J. B. Neumann's, and a third at the Kestner Gesellschaft in Hanover. It was in this year, too, that the National Gallery in Berlin established a "Beckmann room," a rare honor, indeed.[3]

But 1933 brought Nazi power and with it the denunciation of Max Beckmann as one of the "degenerate artists," resulting in the loss of his post at the Städelsches Kunstinstitut. He left Frankfurt but remained in Germany, residing in relative seclusion in Berlin until 1937. During these tense and difficult years some five hundred of his works were removed from German museums.

On July 19, 1937, the day following Hitler's opening of the Grosse Deutsche Kunst Ausstellung (the great German art exhibition), an exhibition in Munich entitled Entartete Kunst (degenerate art) opened, which included ten of Beckmann's major works. Hitler had declared that artists 'distorting nature would do so either out of defiance against the state, in which case criminal punishment would be in order, or because of mechanical malfunctioning of the eye, which, being hereditary, would call for sterilization." [4] On July 20 Beckmann boarded a train for Amsterdam. He never returned.

The next ten years, also spent in relative isolation in his studio-residence, were highly productive ones. In 1938 Curt Valentin arranged an exhibition at the Buchholz Gallery in New York. The importance of Beckmann's alliance with Valentin, which was interrupted by the war and not resumed until 1945, will become apparent.

When Beckmann went to the Netherlands it was not his intention to remain permanently but to move on, either to Paris or to the United States. The outbreak of war prevented any move. There is a poignant note (here in translation as given by Selz) entered in the artist's diary on May 4, 1940: "America is waiting for me with a job in Chicago, yet the American consulate here issues no

Self-portrait from Day and Dream *(1946) by Max Beckmann. This and other reproductions from* Day and Dream *used with permission of Mrs. Max Beckmann.*

visa." [5] Within a few days the Nazis were in Amsterdam.

Beckmann remained in the Netherlands until 1947, when he left to accept a post teaching at Washington University in St. Louis. Following the summer of 1949, when he taught at the University of Colorado, he moved to New York City, where he spent the last year of his life teaching at the Brooklyn Museum Art School. A favorite pastime was walking in Central Park and it was there on the morning of December 27, 1950, on his daily walk, that Max Beckmann died.

In March 1967 Beckmann's widow offered to give to the Library of Congress the set of fifteen master lithographic sheets for the series "Day and Dream," originally called "Time-Motion." These are pen and tusche drawings made on transfer paper, a paper especially prepared with a coating of a soluble layer of starch and albumin. The stone to which the drawing on the paper is to be transferred is placed in a press and warmed. Then the surface is moistened and the transfer impressions are placed face down on top. With the correct degree of pressure the image adheres to the stone.[6] There is less spontaneity in the final lithographs than in the drawings, because the free pencil lines in the drawing and some of the lighter crayon strokes are lost in the transfer process.

The idea of a portfolio came from Curt Valentin, who had published a number of them for other artists. These were not designed to be great money-making ventures but rather were promotional in nature. Prints are an excellent vehicle for this purpose, for they are relatively inexpensive and permit greater distribution inasmuch as they are multiple originals. The nature of the portfolio's contents was left entirely to Beckmann. Valentin suggested a folio of ten or more prints, either lithographs or etchings. He offered in a letter of March 14, 1946, to supply the necessary copperplates should they be unavailable in the Netherlands and should the artist choose to etch the series. On April 5 Beckmann wrote that he was already working on the "lithos," referring to them as "Time-Motion." [7] On April 28 he wrote that they "promise to be very good," and on May 9 he wrote that they were drawn on transfer paper and that sample impressions were good. He asked if perhaps he should have them pulled in the Netherlands so that he could supervise the printing and urged that they be done quickly, as the fresher drawings print better. He asked for authorization to have the edition pulled without Valentin's having seen them, stressing that since each item had to be signed and numbered in pencil by him, printing them in New York would require two additional ocean crossings before the folios could be finally assembled. He said further that if given permission he would have the lithographic firm bill Valentin directly. By mid-May a cable came from

Detail from Weather-Vane *shows inking that was later lost in the transfer process.*

Valentin as follows: "Lithographs edition one hundred numbered and signed use best paper no special edition print in Holland will come in July." [8] A letter followed saying that the title page and table of contents were ready in New York.

There are a number of references to the portfolio in the Beckmann diaries. June 24, 1946: "Also, die Litho's, 'Time-Motion' 15 Stück endgültig fertig.—Na Gott sei Dank.—Glaube sind ganz gut geworden. . . ." [9] (So, the lithos "Time-Motion" finally finished. Thank God. Think they are quite good.) The entry on July 22 indicates that the printing has been completed, for he spent the entire day signing the lithographs: ". . . Sonst den ganzen Tag noch Litho's New York signiert. . . ." [10] Valentin visited the artist on July 14 but could not have picked up the completed sets. In a letter of October 11 Valentin wrote: "We are working on the portfolio but unfortunately, the lithographs are still at the customs

Weather-Vane *drawing*   Wather-Vane *lithograph*

and will probably remain there for a while due to the trucking strike. But in the meantime the covers will be finished, and the title page and index is already printed. I have forgotten how many sets you kept, please let me know so that I can send you the same amount of title pages and covers." [11] He evidently kept ten, as the edition is numbered 1–90.

On November 9 Valentin wrote: "For several reasons I have decided suddenly to show the *Actors* and *Death* and *Birth* beginning next Monday for three weeks—I hope you do not mind. It is not an exhibition which I expect to sell well, and I am not showing any other paintings, just the drawings, watercolors and fifteen lithographs. By the way, the cover and title page for *Day and Dream* will be mailed to you today." [12] This show opened on November 19. The small catalog which announced it stated: *"Day and Dream* has just been issued in an edition of 100 copies. Each lithograph is signed and numbered by the artist." The price of the portfolio was $125, an incredibly low figure in terms of today's market, on which not even one of the fifteen prints could be bought at that price.

To attempt to untangle the iconography of each image would be a difficult and uncertain thing. Harold Joachim is quoted as saying: "Beckmann's symbolism is completely expressed in pictorial terms which he himself found impossible to put into words." [13] To try to find continuity in the series is frustrating, and the attempt was abandoned after reading the artists's letter of February 28 and March 1, 1946, in which he responds to Valentin's initial suggestion of a portfolio. Beckmann proposes in the passage which follows that the prints be lithographs and says that he has many ideas from which one could make a series. He suggests that the motifs could be biblical, mythological, theatrical, or of circus or café life. Or, he adds, it could be an "all-in-one thing," a title for which could easily be found. Evidently this last idea is the one that was developed.

Der Grund aber weswegen ich die Feder ansetze sind die Lithos. Sie sind auf Umdruckpapier gezeichnet und ein Probedruck in der Technik in der ich eben arbeite, gab gute Resultate. Ich kann Ihnen die 10 Zeichnungen schicken und sie können sie in New York drucken lassen, aber sie sind dann nicht gezeichnet. Sie müssten also die gesamte Auflage wieder hierher senden, was bei den heutigen Dingen mit endlosen Schwierigkeiten verknüpft ist. Ebenso, das Rückschicken. Ausserdem ist es wichtig, dass die Zeichnungen bald und unter meiner Controlle gedruckt werden, je frischer um so besser komen sie im Druck. Probeabzüge kann ich nicht schicken ohne ihre [sic] Einwilligung, denn das heisst, dass die Umdrucke dann hier schon auf Stein sind—also nicht mehr transportfähig.[14]

Each sheet in the portfolio measures 40 by 30 centimeters. The table of contents lists fifteen lithographs as follows:

Self portrait I	I don't want to eat my soup VI	Morning XI
Weather-vane II	Dancing couple VII	Circus XII
Sleeping athlete III	King and demagogue VIII	Magic mirror XIII
Tango IV	The buck IX	The fall of man XIV
Crawling woman V	Dream of war X	Christ and Pilate XV

The Roman numerals appear on each sheet below the image at center. At the left, also below, is the edition note, in this case 23/90; each lithograph is signed "Beckmann" at the lower right. No marks of any other kind appear on either the recto or the verso of the sheets and none of the paper bears a watermark. (This is odd as Valentin expressly requested that each sheet be stamped "Printed in Holland.")

Subject matter includes all of the categories mentioned by Beckmann in his letter referred to earlier. "I don't want to eat my soup" illustrates the poem from Heinrich Hoffmann's *Struwelpeter* about the boy who didn't want to eat for four days and on the fifth day he was dead. Perhaps "Magic mirror" is Beckmann's interpretation of the Grimm brothers' story about Snow White. "Dream of war" is just that and carries the inscription "I came back" on the image. This is a reflection, just after World War II, on World War I. "Dancing couple" is a scene from café life, "Christ and Pilate" speaks for itself, as does "The fall of man" and, for the most part, the other titles. The subjects from this folio are a fair representation of Beckmann's choice throughout his career. He was not a landscapist or still life artist but dwelt rather on the not quite real world of people. On the whole, the set is cheerless and rather brooding. Perhaps Beckmann, no longer in the best of health, was looking back over his life and at the various elements that had, in one way or another, played some part in it.

They are strong drawings—in keeping with the artist's feeling that a drawing should be taken as a completed work of art and not merely a study for some more impressive work. The Library is happy to announce this important acquisition.

The thirteen drawings reproduced on the following pages complete the Day and Dream *portfolio.*

Left: Dancing couple

Above: Morning

Magic Mirror

Christ and Pilate

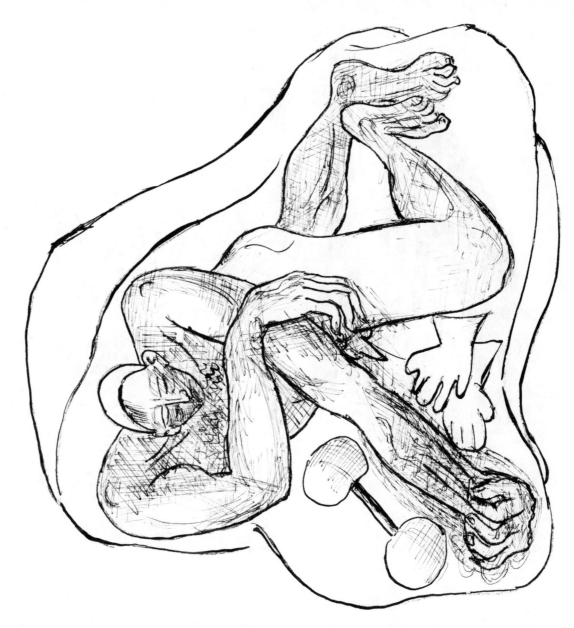

Sleeping athlete

The buck

Circus

I don't want to eat my soup

Dream of War

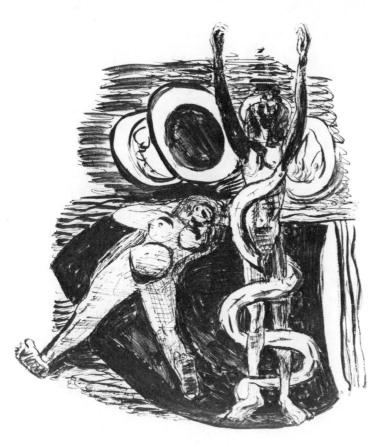

The fall of man

Crawling woman

King and demagogue

Tango

NOTES

1. Carl Zigrosser, *The Expressionists:* A Survey of Their Graphic Art, text by Carl Zigrosser (New York: 1957), p. 26.

2. Peter Selz, *Max Beckmann,* with contributions by Harold Joachim and Perry T. Rathbone (New York: 1964), p. 9.

3. Ibid., p. 47.

4. Ibid., p. 62.

5. Ibid., p. 73.

6. Felix Brunner, *A Handbook of Graphic Reproduction Processes* (New York: 1962), pp. 198–200.

7. Museum of Modern Art files.

8. Ibid.

9. Max Beckmann, *Tagebücher,* 1940–50, Zusammengestellt von Mathilde Q. Beckmann, Herausgegeben von Erhard Göpel (München: 1955), p. 155.

10. Ibid., p. 159.

11. Museum of Modern Art files.

12. Ibid.

13. Selz, p. 82.

14. Museum of Modern Art files.

Twentieth-Century Mexican Graphic Art

BY CHARLES HERRINGTON

One of the most vital artistic movements of the twentieth century springs from Mexico. A wave of creative productivity beginning about 1910 at the time of the Revolution has given leading Mexican artists international fame and an influence felt throughout the artistic world. The revived use of true fresco in the decoration of public buildings crowned the achievements of the major artists, and the resulting murals are considered by many to be the finest since the Italian Renaissance. The creative energy has not been restricted to painting, however; architecture, sculpture, and the graphic arts, particularly the woodcut and the lithograph, have all shared the same dramatic development.

Among recent acquisitions for the Joseph and Elizabeth Robins Pennell Collection of fine prints are nine examples of twentieth-century Mexican lithography. Six important artists are represented in this noteworthy addition to the collection: Diego Rivera, Francisco Dosamantes, Leopoldo Méndez, Jesús Escobedo, Alfredo Zalce, and Luis Arenal. The works of these artists, when combined with other prints already existing in the collections, not only relate the growth and development of contemporary Mexican graphic art but, because all Mexican art has been essentially social art, the prints also reveal the Mexican national consciousness in the most vivid terms. There is little concern shown for purely aesthetic values. Almost without exception, Mexican prints reveal man the revolutionary, the worker, the soldier, the subject of cruelty or brutality—always man in action.

As is true of all stylistic developments, modern Mexican art did not appear full-blown during the Revolution. The mature expression that we see today has

Suerte de Banderillas *by Posada*

Zapata *by Rivera*

its foundations in pre-Colombian times. During the colonial period the common art of Spain was imported into the New World, and an attempt was made to bury native expression with the idols of the pagan past. This measure succeeded for the most part until the nineteenth century and the advent of national consciousness, but as is so often the case, with freedom of thought, criticism, and creativity came a renaissance of native expression and the fusion of the two styles.

Certainly the most influential artist of the awakening period, particularly of those using the graphic media, was José Guadalupe Posada. Working for the publishing house of Vanegas Arroyo, he produced close to fifteen thousand prints mainly woodcuts and relief etchings, from about 1887 until his death in 1913. These prints are popular art par excellence, exploring all facets of Mexican life and customs in dynamic and moving compositions that are almost entirely free of foreign influence. The woodcut *Suerte de Banderillas* exemplifies Posada's innate sense of balance in composition and tone. No unessential elements clutter the central theme and a perfect equilibrium is established between light and shade. These principles were not necessarily learned from a foreign source as they are basic to all sophisticated pre-Conquest art.

Although the new tendencies were firmly established by Posada and other artists of the nineteenth century, their full impact was not felt until the Revolution, when Mexico emerged as a vigorous nation, experimenting with political, economic, and social reforms. Out of the turbulent strife of this period emerged the three great painters who founded a new era in monumental art—Diego Rivera, José Clemente Orozco, and David Alfaro Siqueiros.

Although most famous for their spectacular murals, these men have all contributed to graphic art. They did not, however, experiment with techniques in the manner of professional printmakers but more often used the popular medium to extend and reproduce their paintings. Rivera's lithograph *Zapata* is based upon a fresco at the Palace of Cortés in Cuernavaca. Similarly, the model for Orozco's lithograph *Franciscan* may be found on a vault in the National Preparatory School in Mexico City.

Diego Rivera, born in 1886 in Guanajuato, was a student of the French school. In Paris he responded particularly to the works of Ingres and Cézanne and was associated with Picasso during the second phase of cubism, but his mature and flexible style reflects the overpowering influence of his native Mexican heritage.

Above: Moises Saenz *by Siqueiros*

Right: The mood of the revolutionary period is continued in the cartoon-like lithographs of the second generation artists.

Nazi Pogrom *by Arenal.*

On the other hand, until 1932, Orozco had never been to Europe. His inspiration and school was the Revolution itself, the armies of which he followed into the field. His compassionate treatments of misery and suffering are statements of bitter protest.

Where Orozco's bitterness is seen in hauntingly beautiful compositions, the protestations of David Alfaro Siqueiros burst forth in brutal, swelling forms. In his portrait lithograph of Moises Saenz, the face looms on the paper. Power, not beauty, is the effect desired and achieved.

Marching Nazis and Fascists *by Méndez.*

There were three common elements that bound the works of these artists together, creating a mature Mexican school and establishing the trends of later decades. Each used his art to present social protest, whether in simple statements, skeptical examinations, or passionate outcries. Each was concerned mainly with what was to be said rather than with how to say it. In other words, content, not form, was the first consideration. In an overall view of the period, the third element is seen as an overpowering preoccupation with death, on the spirit of death, as if all of life were simply a preparation for it. Although particularly

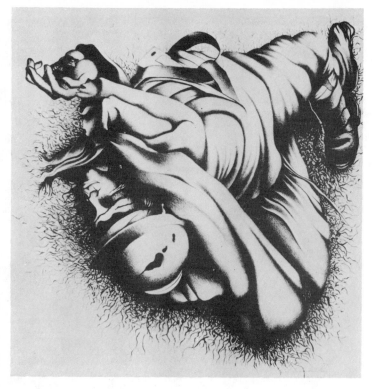

Oaxacan Mother, *left, and* Dead Soldier, *above, by Dosamantes*

noticeable in the first decade after the Revolution, this preoccupation is a continuous element in Mexican art from pre-Colombian times.

The incarnation of this spirit of death can be seen no better than in an early lithograph by Francisco Dosamantes, given the title *Dead Soldier*. Grotesquely foreshortened and twisted, stiff in agonized death, the figure is a universal statement of the horror of war.

As the revolutionary fervor began to subside in the 1930s, a new generation of artists cried out against social injustice, but this time with eyes turned toward

Europe and the growth of the Nazi and Fascist terrors. Thus, Méndez, Escobedo, Zalce, Arenal, and others joined the crusade of their predecessors. The prints of this period demonstrate the continuity of the Mexican school. The artists, having experimented little in techniques, still show a dominant interest in content.

In the 1950s, however, prints show a change in attitudes and interests. With the Revolution thirty years removed, there seems to be less concern with social protest, although the subjects continue for the most part to examine native Mexican life. The deathly gloom no longer prevails. The same Dosamantes who had conceived the *Dead Soldier* about 1930 later presents the *Oaxacan Mother*. A proud native figure, she expresses not death, but eternity.

A very recent print by one of Mexico's leading present-day artists, Rufino Tamayo, indicates that a break with past traditions has occurred. Here the first consideration is form, not content. The vigorous, seemingly dancing figure makes no obvious appeal or statement.

The continuing interest of the Library of Congress in Latin American culture is evidenced not only by the compilation of the Archives of Hispanic Culture and the activities of the Latin American, Portuguese, and Spanish Division but also by a noteworthy and growing collection of modern Mexican prints in the Prints and Photographs Division. A checklist of artists who are represented follows. (Birth and death dates are given where established.)

Aguilar, Carlos Maria R. de
Aguirre, Ignacio, 1900–
Alfaro Siqueiros, David, 1898–
Alvarado Lang, Carlos, 1905–
Amero, Emilio, 1900–
Arenal, Luis, 1908–
Avellano, José
Avila, Abelardo, 1907–
Baños, Luis
Beloff Camonen, Angelina
Beltrán, Alberto, 1923–
Bracho, Angel, 1911–
Calderón de la Barca, Celia, 1921–
Cantú, Federico, 1908–

Castro, Vita
Castro Pacheco, Fernando, 1918–
Charlot, Jean, 1898–
Chávez Morado, José, 1909–
Cortés Juárez, Erasto, 1900–
Dosamantes, Francisco, 1911–
Echauri, Manuel, 1914–
Escobedo, Jesús, 1918–
Franco, Antonio
García Maldonado, Alberto, 1920–
Garcin, Antonio
Gómez, Andrea, 1924–
Gutiérrez, Francisco, 1906–
Guzmán, Bulmaro, 1897–

Heller, Julio
Lugo, Amador, 1921–
Méndez, Leopoldo, 1903–
Monje, Luis L.
Mora, Francisco, 1922–
Moreno Capdevila, Francisco, 1926–
Núñez, Daniel
Ocampo, Isidoro, 1910–
Olvera, Jorge, 1915–
Alvera, Jorge, 1915–
Orozco, José Clemente, 1883–1949
Paredes, Mariano, 1912–
Paz Pérez, Gonzalo de la, 1910–

Peña, Feliciano, 1915–
Rabel [Rabinovich], Fanny, 1922–
Ramírez, Everardo, 1906–
Rivera, Diego, 1886–1957
Romero, Fernando
Romero, José
Tamayo, Rufino, 1900–
Trejo, Antonio, 1922–
Valadez, Emiliano
Vázquez, J. Francisco, 1904–
Yampolsky, Mariana, 1925–
Zalce, Alfredo, 1908–
Zamarripa, Angel, 1912–

Tamayo's dancing figure

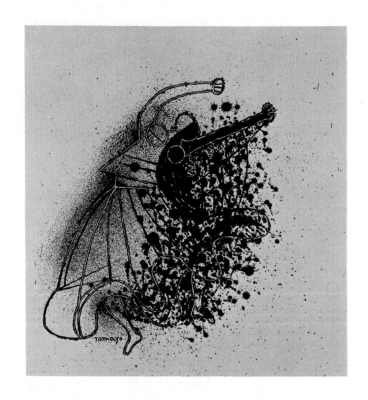

A Rare Film Poster

BY ELENA G. MILLIE

The Prints and Photographs Division has acquired for its collections an interesting French poster by the artist August Leymarie entitled *Charlot—"L'as des comiques,"* published in Paris by L'Agence Générale Cinématographique.

Charlie Chaplin, wearing his famous baggy pants, floppy shoes, cane, moustache, and derby, is shown stepping from America to France with suitcase in hand. Here the mystery begins, because the occasion for which the poster was designed, the date of its execution, and the identity of the artist, beyond his name, seem unrecorded in published histories of the poster and the motion picture.

It is known, however, that Chaplin, or "Charlot" as the French affectionately called him, traveled abroad in September 1921. He had just divorced his first wife, Mildred Harris, and decided a trip to Europe would be an excellent escape from reporters and from publicity. His native England, France, and Germany were on his intended itinerary.

His first stop was London. Chaplin relates in his book *My Trip Abroad* that on arriving at Southampton, he was overwhelmed by the huge and enthusiastic crowd on hand to greet him. It seemed to follow him everywhere, leaving him without a moment's peace. At the end of a week he made a quick departure to Paris, hoping to find that peace. On reaching the French shore, however, he saw that he was "out of the frying pan" into the fire. Nevertheless, Chaplin loved Paris. The crowds kept their distance during most of his visit, and Paris turned out to be one of his favorite cities on the tour.[1]

A drawing of his hat, cane, and boots, Charlie's favorite autograph, appears in Charlie Chaplin, King of Tragedy, *where it is identified as an autographed crest given to the writer. © 1940, The Caxton Printers, Ltd., Caldwell, Idaho. Reproduced by permission.*

Left: This colored lithograph poster by August Leymarie shows Charlie Chaplin dressed in green trousers and a maroon coat and topped by his brown derby. It was published by L'Agence Générale Cinématographique in Paris and measures approximately 61 by 45 inches.

Charlie Chaplin had been a longtime favorite of the French. In 1914 his first movies, *Fatty* and *Caught in a Cabaret,* were shown in Paris. When the war broke out, his films were shown at the front and did much to lift the morale of the soldiers. Therefore, to the French, Charlot was indeed "L'as des comiques."

One morning during his stay in Paris, Chaplin was cornered by J. P. Morgan's daughter, Anne, with a request to show his latest film, *The Kid,* at a gala to raise funds for the rebuilding of devastated France.[2] She said that if he would appear in person, she was sure he would be decorated. Feeling mischievous, Chaplin promised her, and the date was set. This was the only time on his trip that he consented to make a formal appearance in connection with one his films,[3] and it is conceivable that the poster was produced for this occasion.

The poster was published by a large film distributing company in Paris, L'Agence Générale Cinématographique, which might seem to indicate that it was designed for a showing of a Chaplin film. However, it names no film in particular, and since it pictures Charles carrying his suitcase, a personal appearance by the star in France is suggested. It is, therefore, likely that the poster was used to announce his appearance in Paris at the Trocadéro for the showing of *The Kid,* where Chaplin was presented with a medal making him an Officier de l'Instruction Publique.[4]

This unusual French poster, formerly in the possession of a dealer in London, was purchased for the Library of Congress with funds from the bequest of Mrs. Gardiner Greene Hubbard.

NOTES

1. Charles Chaplin, *My Trip Abroad* (New York: 1922), pp. 104–5.
2. Charles Chaplin, *My Autobiography* (New York: 1964), p. 277.
3. Pierre Leprohon, *Charles Chaplin* (Paris: 1957), p. 280.
4. Gerith von Ulm, *Charlie Chaplin, King of Tragedy* (Caldwell, Idaho: 1940), p. 161.

Architectural Collections of the Library of Congress

BY C. FORD PEATROSS

The now various roofs of the Library of Congress shelter a unique aggregation of documents relating to the history of architecture and the associated disciplines of engineering, landscape and interior design, and city planning. America's built tradition, in a sense its physical plant—consisting of houses, office and government buildings, schools and colleges, places of worship, theaters, sports arenas, hotels, garages, factories, bridges, dams, and even gardens, parks, and public squares—represents the continuing investment of its citizens, both individually and communally, in their nation's development. There can be no more tangible record of the sources, aspirations, and achievements of American civilization than this built tradition, which embodies the commitment of both labor and capital to a building purpose, whether symbolic or functional, whether a war memorial or a steel foundry.

For those who wish to study our nation's development through its architectural expression, the Library of Congress offers magnificent resources not only in its book and periodical collections but also in complementary and often unique documents and reference aids in such special collections as those to be found in the Geography and Map Division, the Local History and Genealogy Room, the Microform Reading Room, the Manuscript Division, the Rare Book and Special Collections Division, and especially in the Prints and Photographs Division. Researchers in no other country enjoy the benefits of having all of these necessary and related resources for the study of architecture so assembled, thus facilitating their use and comparison.

Workmen applying the finishing decorative touches on the galleries of the theater; from B. Henry
Latrobe's album of drawings for "Designs of a Building to be Erected at Richmond in Virginia, to
Contain a Theatre, Assembly-rooms, and an Hotel," 1797–98. The project was never carried out. In the
Library's extensive collection of original architectural drawings, the over two hundred Latrobe drawings
represent the finest examples of that art, for Latrobe was a superb draftsman as well as one of the
finest architects of his age. Pen and ink with colored washes. LC–USZ62–1221; LC–
USZC4–92 (color)

My purpose here is to reveal something of the history, nature, scope, and ways of using the various architectural collections in the Library's Prints and Photographs Division, both those collections which are exclusively architectural and those which, although not primarily architectural, include important related documents. As its name does not reveal, the Prints and Photographs Division has been for nearly fifty years our national buildings archive, serving as the principal repository for the photographic prints and negatives, measured and other drawings, and historical, architectural, and technological information documenting structures and sites in the United States and its territories and possessions. During this half century it was only natural that such an established archive should attract many supplementary architectural documents; these have come to the Library through purchase, gift, and loan from architectural photographers, scholars, students, universities, historical societies, and ordinary citizens. In addition, the division's vast collections of historical photographs and prints have been arranged and indexed both by subject (often architectural) and by geographic location, thus making them more easily accessible to architectural researchers.

Mere chance did not bring this remarkable body of architectural documentation to the Library of Congress. The Library was a pioneer both in realizing the importance of a vanishing architectural heritage and in taking steps to see that that heritage was properly recorded and made available for study. During the 1930s the Library was instrumental in the creation and organization of three important collections: the Pictorial Archives of Early American Architecture (PAEAA), the Carnegie Survey of the Architecture of the South (CSAS), and the Historic American Buildings Survey (HABS). These major groups formed the core of the present collections. Before that time, architecture fell within the purview of the old Division of Prints, which was "devoted to the subject of the fine arts (including architecture)," [1] and related documents were acquired sporadically through purchase, gift, transfer, and copyright deposit. The Library's collecting energies in the subject of architecture did not receive concentrated direction until 1929, when Leicester B. Holland of Philadelphia, an architect and historian of architecture and landscape design, was named to head the newly formed Fine Arts Division.

Dr. Holland's initiative, coupled with sizable gifts of architectural photographs in 1929 and 1930, prompted the Library to establish "a national repository for photographic negatives of early American architecture, to preserve and make available to students of history and others, pictorial records of our rapidly disappearing ancestral homes." [2] This project was begun with a $5,000 grant from the Carnegie Corporation. The amount had grown to $26,000 by 1939,[3] when over ten thousand negatives had been acquired by purchase, loan, and gift from all across the country. The Library had actively sought out these negatives through national solicitation in newspapers and magazines and circular letters sent to the chapters of the American Institute of Architects and to various historical and photographic societies.[4] Donations still come in as a result of those early efforts. As late as last November the division received a snapshot of an old home at Staten Island, New York, attached to a yellowed clipping from a 1930s *New York Times* with the heading "Library of Congress Seeks Photographs of Historic Buildings."

The Pictorial Archives of Early American Architecture, as this collection came to be called, had been given early encouragement by one of the nation's finest architectural photographers, Frances Benjamin Johnston. In 1929 she deposited in the Library "between 5,000 and 6,000 photographic negatives, largely of gardens and architectural subjects, . . . ultimately to become the property of the Library," for, in her words, "the purpose of creating a nucleus for a national foundation for the study of early American architecture and of garden design." [5] These were later supplemented by further gifts from Miss Johnston and by commissions to her from the Carnegie Corporation between 1930 and 1943, of approximately eight thousand photographs of buildings in Maryland, Virginia, North Carolina, South Carolina, Georgia, Florida, Alabama, Mississippi, and Louisiana. Called the Carnegie Survey of the Architecture of the South, the magnificent images in this collection alone have provided the inspiration for several books, including Henry Irving Brock's *Colonial Churches in Virginia,* Samuel Gaillard Stoney's *Plantations of the Carolina Low Country,* Thomas T. Waterman's *The Early Architecture of North Carolina, Mansions of Virginia,* and *Dwellings of Colonial America,* and Frederick D. Nichols's *The Early Architecture of Georgia.*[6]

Miss Johnston's expert photographs not only displayed her own skill and artistry but also revealed a prescient interest in vernacular architecture. She was among the first to realize the beauty and significance of these humbler and rapidly disappearing structures. She also set an important precedent by giving the body of her architectural photography to the Library, a practice since followed by other architectural photographers, including Robert Tebbs and Theodore Horydczak.

To make the materials which it was collecting available to and usable by researchers, the Library developed a unique system called the Shelf-List Index. That system assigns an identifying number to a building or site and to all the records which document it: photographic negatives and prints, historical information, etc. The organizational basis of the system is geographic: state, country, and city or vicinity. Buildings or sites are thus assigned a coded prefix—indicating the state, county, and city—plus their own number; the records accordingly are arranged by geographic code and then numerically. The index cards which provide access to those records, however, are filed alphabetically after the geographic code, to simplify the researcher's task, especially when the building or site is located in a large city.

Thus, the materials we have for the Singer Tower in New York City, for example, are assigned the following Shelf-List number: NY,31–NEYO,71– . This includes an abbreviation for the state (New York); the number of the county, according to its alphabetical sequence (New York County); an abbreviation for the city or vicinity (New York City); and the number assigned to the individual building or site (Singer Tower) when material relating to it was first received at the Library and cataloged.

Because all of the photographic prints and negatives for Shelf-Listed buildings and sites are also numbered sequentially, one need only note the entire code to order a copy from the Photoduplication Service or to call for a reference print of a specific photograph. The order number for the HABS photograph showing the demolition of the Singer Tower would be NY,31–NEYO,71–4, since it is the fourth of the twenty HABS photographs of that building. Measured drawings and data pages are also numbered separately and may be ordered in the same way.

Unfortunately, the somewhat tedious explanation of this system can only partially reveal the many benefits it affords to researchers. Those are best discovered by using the records. One principal advantage of the geographic arrangement is that a researcher who is interested in all of the buildings in a particular state, county, city, or rural neighborhood rather than in a particular structure will find their records already grouped together. The fact that those units are also political is important because of the parallel organization of related official documents, including deeds, building permits, tax records, and wills. Finally, those same geographical units are the key to a vast corresponding body of published materials, including city directories and local histories. It was therefore a logical development that the Shelf-List Index, originally designed by the Library for its Pictorial Archives of Early American Architecture, was extended to include the records of the Historic American Buildings Survey. In fact, the system was an important reason why the Library was planned as the repository for the HABS collection.[7]

Devised largely through the efforts of Charles E. Peterson of the National Park Service, HABS began in 1933 "as a work relief project under the Civil Works Administration, to aid unemployed architects and draftsmen and at the same time to produce a detailed record of such early American architecture as was in immediate danger of destruction."[8] From the beginning, the Library of Congress "was obviously indicated as the institution best fitted to have permanent care and administration of the completed records"[9] which HABS produced and which became "an integral part of the Pictorial Archives of Early American Architecture."[10] HABS achieved more permanent status in 1935 under a tripartite agreement signed by the National Park Service, the American Institute of Architects (AIA), and the Library of Congress, and it continued after that date with funds from the Works Progress Administration.[11]

The Library essentially wore two hats in this arrangement, for Dr. Holland functioned not only as the Library's representative, approving and signing each deposited measured drawing and supervising the organization and service of the collection to the public, but he also represented the AIA, serving as chairman of its national Committee on the Preservation of Historic Buildings. Both HABS and PAEAA reached a peak of activity in 1934–35, during which over 750 architects employed by HABS were busy recording structures and sites all across the country, while at the Library Dr. Holland, Natalie Plunkett, and Virginia Daiker were accessioning and cataloging the records pouring into the two collections as well as preparing an architectural subject index with over five hundred headings. Simultaneously, six architects assigned to the Library's Fine Arts Division from the Park Service were busy indexing (geographically, of course) the illustrations in 128 architectural books in the division's reference collection.[12] That project became known as the Index of Illustrations of Early American Architecture.

The operations of HABS itself were stilled by the manpower necessities of World War II, and its recording activities were not resumed until 1957. At present it has documented almost seventeen thousand structures in 34,750 measured drawings, 44,800 photographs, and 15,450 pages of historical and architectural information. Add to this the work accomplished by the Historic American Engineering Record (HAER), which in 1969 began to similarly document monuments of American engineering skill, and the number of structures represented in these two deposit collections at the Library approaches twenty thousand. Both collections are created by professional staffs within the Heritage Conservation and Recreation Service of the U.S. Department of the Interior, but the Library of Congress is responsible for their care, preservation, and public service.

It should be noted that as the Library's largest and most important architectural collection, HABS has enjoyed an often unfair dominance over the many smaller and less publicized architectural collections in the Prints and Photographs Division. A dismaying number of researchers think it represents the Library's only architectural material. HABS is, of course, along with PAEAA and HAER, the key from which one works—through the Shelf-List Index system and supplemental card indexes—to get at the valuable documents in those adjunct collections. However, the approximately twenty thousand buildings surveyed by HABS and HAER collectively represent less than half of the structures and sites indexed in all of the card files and only a fraction of those documented in other collections in the division but not individually indexed. PAEAA and HABS are the backbone from which has developed a complex synaptic network allowing the retrieval of related architectural illustrations in hundreds of other collections.

For instance, there are many groups of materials in the division's collections which are kept together for various reasons—such as common donor or medium—including eleven thousand groups cataloged according to the "lot" system. These are indexed by subject and the largest are subdivided geographically. Thus the reference copies for the Historical Print Collection, the mounted photographs (including gifts, purchases, and copyright deposits), the panoramas and stereopticon views, and the large collections from a single source, like the Detroit Publishing Company (over thirty thousand photographs) and the Farm Security Administration (over seventy-five thousand photographs), are arranged geographically. Even the subject files, whether they comprise card indexes to original materials or to copy negatives or consist of mounted original photographs, are secondarily arranged according to geographical location, e.g., Theaters: U.S.—California—San Francisco. The obverse applies to geographic files, which are secondarily arranged by subject, e.g., U.S.—California—San Francisco: Theaters.

The manner in which these subject/geographic synapses function should become evident in the examples which follow demonstrating the location of relevant materials on a variety of subjects: a building type (theaters), an engineering form (bridges), a single structure (Singer Tower), architectural styles (Gothic, French), design details (onion-shaped cupolas), an individual architect or firm (Frank Lloyd Wright), and vernacular structures (domestic, commercial). For the sake of simplicity, the examples are limited to American architecture, although the collections contain outstanding documentation of architecture throughout the world, of obvious importance in investigating the origins of and foreign influences on American design.[13]

This survey of illustrations of American theaters encapsulizes the history of that form according to changing needs and technological and stylistic developments. Almost all were readily located by searching for theaters in several different subject and geographical files, as discussed above. They include original and measured drawings, historical prints, and various types of photographs, spanning the period between 1798 and 1960.

Through most of the history of the American theater, potential commercial success has played a significant role in the design of its buildings. Both spatial and decorative extravagance have been key factors in attracting theatergoers; therefore both the interiors and, later, the exteriors of American theaters have not infrequently proved more dramatic than the performances they hosted. One of the most ambitious and elegant early American theater schemes was B. Henry Latrobe's projected building combining a theater, assembly rooms, and a hotel, proposed for Richmond, Virginia, in 1797–98. Perhaps too ambitious, it was never built, but the project is represented by one of the beautiful watercolor drawings in Latrobe's album, part of the Library's extensive collection of original American architectural drawings. That rendering shows Latrobe himself, standing on the rail of the gallery, directing the workmen who are applying the finishing decorative touches to the interior of his theater.

Another elegant but ultimately more successful project was the Chestnut Street Theatre in Philadelphia, which was designed by a student of Latrobe's, William Strickland, in 1822–24. Destroyed in 1856, its facade, exhibiting affinities to the English Regency style, is fortunately preserved in one of the division's historic photographs. Such a facade was soon considered unfashionable by advocates of the new rage, the Greek Revival. Such an advocate was Alexander Jackson Davis, who depicted the use of a Greek Revival facade in his 1828 engraving of New York City's Bowery Theatre, from the Historical Print Collection. The Greek Revival itself soon gave way to the Italianate and Second Empire forms seen in the 1871 lithograph *Crescite et Multiplicamini*. This lithograph also shows an early example of a development which would have lasting effects on both the architecture and the structure of the performing arts in America, that being the establishment of a circuit of theaters by impresario John T. Ford.

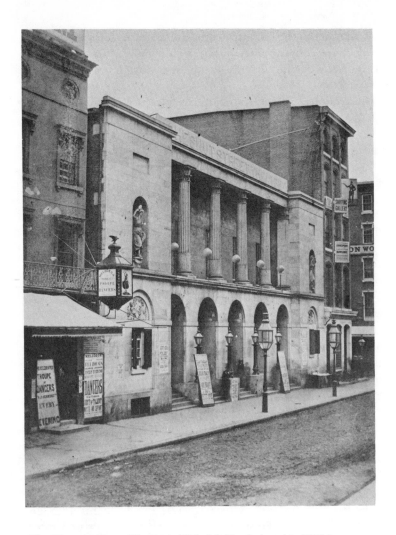

View of the Bowery Theatre, New York, "drawn and engraved expressly for the New-York Mirror" by Alexander Jackson Davis, 1828; from the Historical Print Collection. That the Greek Revival was primarily a "facade style" is well, if not intentionally, argued in this view of the theater, designed by J. Sera to replace the 1825 design of Ithiel Town. The engulfing clouds do less to relieve the heavy Doric order than to recall, unfortunately, the fire that destroyed its short-lived predecessor. LC–USZ62–32484

Facing page: Lithograph by A. Hoen and Company of Baltimore, 1873, from the Historical Print Collection. No less than eight strategically placed muses present the various architectural glories of John T. Ford's small theatrical empire. The showpiece in the center panel is Ford's Grand Opera House in Baltimore, surrounded by the just completed Opera House in Washington, the Holliday Street Theatre in Baltimore, Ford's own residence in Baltimore, and the now famous Ford's Theatre in Washington, shown here serving as the United States Medical Museum, having closed as a theater soon after the assassination of President Lincoln during a performance of Our American Cousin. LC–USZ62–15672

The Chestnut Street Theatre in Philadelphia, designed in 1822 by William Strickland and demolished in 1856. This photograph by McClees is filed among the Miscellaneous Oversize Historic Photographs (A size), No. 46. The Chestnut Street Theatre and thousands of other important American buildings are represented in the Library's nineteenth- and early twentieth-century photographs, many of which were copyright deposits. LC–USZ62–11636

CRESCITE ET MULTIPLICAMINI.

OPERA HOUSE.

CALLIOPE.

CLIO.

NEW OPERA HOUSE, WASHINGTON.
ERECTED 1873.

HOLLIDAY ST. THEATRE, BALTO.
ORIGINALLY BUILT 1794.

FORD'S GRAND OPERA HOUSE.
BALTIMORE.
1871

FORD'S THEATRE, 10TH ST, WASHINGTON
NOW U.S. MEDICAL MUSEUM.
ORIGINALLY ERECTED 1863.

JOHN T. FORD'S RESIDENCE,
BALTIMORE 1869.

Another early theatrical promoter, a Mr. Niblo of New York City, in 1853 opened a building combining theater and assembly rooms, not unlike that envisaged by Latrobe some fifty years before. The many pleasures of Niblo's Garden were detailed in a popular illustrated magazine, *Gleason's Pictorial Drawing-Room Companion,* of May 14, 1853. Many such clippings from magazines like *Harper's, Leslie's,* and the *Illustrated London News* form a useful part of our Historical Print Collection.

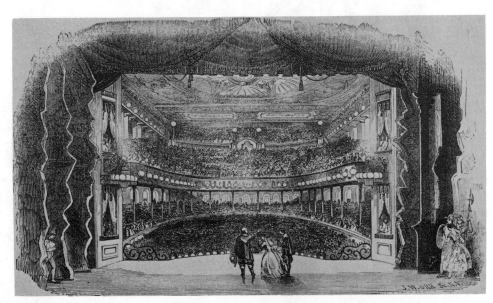

Three views of the interior of Niblo's Garden, New York, engraved by J. W. Orr for Gleason's Pictorial Drawing-Room Companion, *May 14, 1853. "Unsurpassed even in Europe" according to the accompanying article, Niblo's also included "a splendid concert hall, and ball-room, with richly furnished reception parlors, drawing-rooms, dressing-rooms, and a supper saloon sufficiently capacious to accommodate upwards of a thousand guests. Independent of these, . . . the entrance halls and lobbies are sufficiently spacious to afford accommodation for an entire audience at one time, and even these are decorated in a style of splendor equal to the interior of our most sumptuous dwellings." Located among the reference copies of the Historical Print Collection under Theaters (Exteriors and Interiors). LC–USZ62–2647*

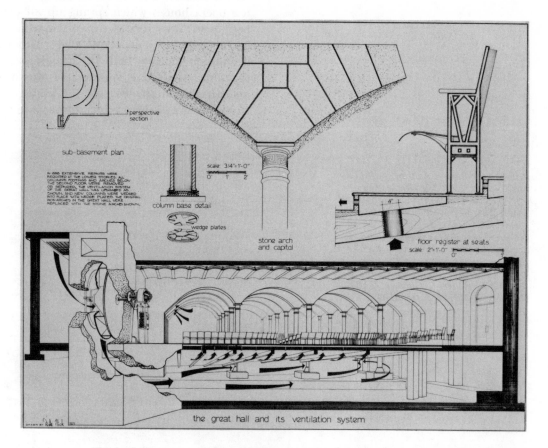

In the drawing:
- perspective section
- sub-basement plan
- scale 3/4"=1'-0"
- column base detail
- wedge plates
- stone arch and capital
- floor register at seats
- scale 2"=1'-0"
- the great hall and its ventilation system
- DRAWN BY Dale Flick

Cross section and details showing changes made in the structure and ventilation system of the Great Hall of the Cooper Union for the Advancement of Science and Art in New York City, ca. 1888. 1971 drawing by Dale Flick, HAER. (HAER NY–20) NY,31–NEYO,81–sheet 20

With the increase in the complexity and size of productions and audiences, theater auditoriums required technological advances in such areas as acoustics and ventilation. Recognized achievements in both of those sciences are documented in measured drawings in the HAER and HABS collections. One was the improvement of the ventilation system of the Great Hall of the Cooper Union in New York City about 1888, drawn by HAER; another was the acoustical perfection of Adler and Sullivan's huge Auditorium in Chicago in 1887–89, the design of which is shown in a longitudinal section by HABS.

Operatic productions, increasingly popular after the middle of the nineteenth century, dictated elaborate theaters like the Auditorium. Of the number-less opera houses which sprang up all over the country, the most famous has been New York City's Metropolitan, which was originally built in 1883 according to the designs of J. Cleveland Cady. Although HABS recorded the Met before its demolition in 1966, both the building's exterior and its neighborhood had by that time undergone considerable alteration. The excellent turn-of-the-century photographs in the Detroit Publishing Company collection provide a much better picture of the original appearance and setting of the building.

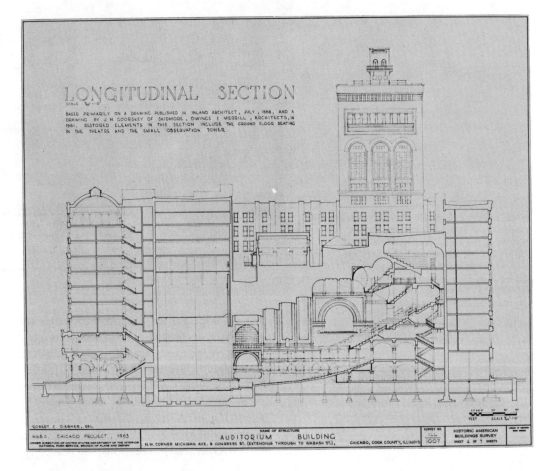

Adler and Sullivan's Auditorium Building, Chicago, built 1887–89. Seating 4,237 people, the Auditorium supplanted New York's Metropolitan as the largest theater in America. It incorporated numerous technological innovations and its acoustical design has often been hailed as the finest of any theater in the world, especially for operatic productions. 1963 drawing by Robert C. Giebner, HABS. (HABS ILL–1007) ILL,16–CHIG,39–sheet 4

The Metropolitan Opera House, New York City, from the southeast. The view above shows its appearance around 1905; the HABS photograph on the right was taken by Jack E. Boucher in May 1966, shortly before the Met's demolition. Built to the design of J. Cleveland Cady in 1883, the Met was the greatest theater in America in its day, but it had undergone many changes by the time of the later Photograph. Besides the modern refacing of the ground story and the alterations in the roofline, the neighborhood had changed so that it reflected little of the original relation of the building to its site. The earlier photograph is one of more than thirty thousand views of American cities, towns, buildings, and scenery, ca. 1898–1914, from the Detroit Publishing Company collection. The company's 8" x 10" glass plate negatives for sites east of the Mississippi are also in the Library's collections. Above: LC–D4–18310; right: (HABS NY–5486) NY,31–NEYO,79–1

Many other late nineteenth- and early twentieth-century American theaters are illustrated in the Single Subject File under that subject category. The Bradford Theatre, otherwise unidentified, exhibited a typical auditorium form for that period, not unlike the one shown in an advertisement for "Lyman Howe's New Marvels in Moving Pictures" from the collection of American theatrical posters. With the advent of motion pictures, theaters like the Bradford often saw their live performances replaced by films.

Motion pictures, perhaps more than any other medium, took advantage of the audience-attracting features inherent in theater architecture. In Sidney Lust's Leader Theater in Washington, D.C., about 1920, the building itself has become

Interior view of the Bradford Theater, in a 1907 copyright deposit photograph by Frank Robbins from the Single Photo File under Theaters—Miscellaneous (no location given). The Single Photo File contains thoussands of gift and duplicate copyright deposit photographs filed according to the subjects they represent, many of which are architectural. Within those subject categories they are arranged alphabetically by geographical location, when it is known. LC–USZ62–62049

In this poster for "Lyman H. Howe's New Marvels in Moving Pictures," Howe graphically assaults his audience with ships of the Spanish-American War. Such "legitimate" subjects were part of the attempt of early motion picture entrepreneurs to attract a "high-class" clientele, and here the attentive, prosperous, and surprisingly calm audience occupies seats in a "legitimate" theater very similar to the Bradford. Found in the Historical Print Collection reference file under the category Theaters—Motion Picture. The original lithograph by Courier (1898) is in the division's Poster Collection under Entertainment. LC–USZ62–62048

a form of theater, with its caryatid-flanked facade transformed into a proscenium framing a changeable set, here extolling the rustic virtues of the feature attraction. The role of such advertising in the design of theater facades included the "architecture in light" of illuminated marquees like that of Washington's Loew's Palace. By the early 1930s the marquee and the facade had become almost completely integrated, as in the "moderne" design of the Trans-Lux Theatre at 58th Street and Madison Avenue in New York City. Meanwhile, the interiors of such theaters began to fulfill the promise of the "motion picture palace," as is evident in an interior view of the grandest from the 1920s, the Roxy in New York City, where vast spaces combined with profuse Plateresque decoration to overwhelm the moviegoer.

Sidney Lust's Leader Theater, Washington, D.C., about 1920, below, and the illuminated marquee of Loew's Palace Theater, also in Washington, about 1924, below right. Both photographs by the National Photo Company (a gift collection), from the Single Photo File under Theaters: United States—D.C. Right: LC–F82–5360; below: LC–USZ62–62050

The Trans-Lux Theatre, 58th Street and Madison Avenue, New York City, about 1931. Rather than appearing to be merely tacked onto an existing building, the marquee here has become an integral part of the design, functioning as a combination frieze and string course in one of the sophisticated designs for which the Trans-Lux chain was notable. From the Single Photo File under Theaters: United States—New York City. LC–USZ62–62051

Interior view of the Roxy, New York City, around 1927, now demolished. Planned as a "total experience" for theatergoers by its promoter, S. L. Rothafel, the Roxy purportedly cost over $15 million and seated over six thousand. Its oval lobby alone could hold three thousand people. Copyright deposit photograph from the Geographic File, New York—New York City: Theaters—the Roxy. LC–USZ62–62052

*Model of the Lincoln Center for the Perform-
ing Arts, New York City, with its planners:
standing in center, Wallace K. Harrison, chief
architect; from left, Edward Mathews, Philip
Johnson, Jo Mielziner, John D. Rockefeller III
(president of the Center), Eero Saarinen,
Gordon Bunshaft, Max Abramovitz, and
Pietro Belluschi. This photograph by Arnold
Newman is from an article entitled "Culture
City" in the January 19, 1960, issue of* Look
*and is in the extensive negative files of the
magazine, 1937–71, which form one of the
division's collections. For noncommercial use
only. LC-L9–21806*

That type of theater had reached the apogee of its development, however, and after television began to steal away a large section of the audience in the early 1950s, the great theaters became increasingly obsolescent. The principal new theater form that developed in this country during the 1950s and 1960s was the cultural center. One of the most important of these is New York City's Lincoln Center, made up of four theaters, including the new home of the Metropolitan Opera, for four different types of performances. Several of the nation's leading architects, shown lounging about the model of the Center in a photograph from the *Look* magazine collection, pooled their talents for an influential, if not completely successful, design. It brings us full circle from Latrobe directing the building of his proposed scheme for an entertainment complex and completes this visual survey of what can be assembled from the Library's architectural collections on a specific building type.

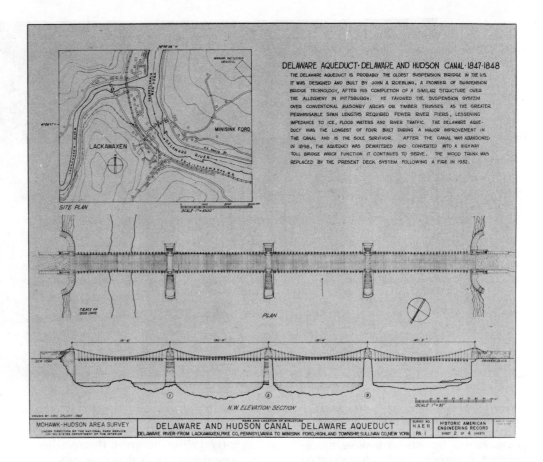

Site map, plan, and elevation of the Delaware Aqueduct of the Delaware and Hudson Canal, built 1847–48 and spanning the Delaware River from Lackawaxen, Pennsylvania, to Minisink Ford, New York. 1969 drawing by Eric Delony, HAER. (HAER PA–1) PA,52–LACK,1–sheet 2

The same approach can be taken in using the division's collections to survey the development of American bridges in their various forms and methods of construction. HABS recorded more than fifty bridges before 1969, but since that time the Historic American Engineering Record has assumed those responsibilities. The site, plan, and elevation of one of the earliest American suspension bridges, the Delaware and Hudson Canal's Delaware Aqueduct, are all depicted in a single HAER drawing from 1969. This type of material is supplemented by historical photographs in the collections, like the 1860s view of a combination truss spanning the Cumberland River at Nashville, Tennessee, found under the category "railroad bridges" in reference prints of the Brady-Handy Collection; it is also indexed in our subject file for bridges. Other remarkable documents are to be found in the Historical Print Collection, including manufacturer's advertisements like that of the Wrought Iron Bridge Company of Canton, Ohio, dating from the 1870s, and views like the 1871 lithograph showing the engineer, phases of construction, and finished appearance of St. Louis's Eads Bridge. At the time of its erection, 1867–74, the Eads Bridge was notable for the largest fixed-end steel arches ever constructed. One can even set about recreating the construction of some bridges from photographs in various collections; a good example is the Williamsburg Bridge over the East River in New York, 1896–1903.

Bridge across the Cumberland River at Nashville, Tennessee. The Brady-Handy Collection contains hundreds of excellent views of buildings—and bridges—from the 1860s, few of which structures survived even into this century. The collection has divisions according both to cities and to building types; this photograph was under the category Railroad Bridges (Lot 4177). LC–B811–2642

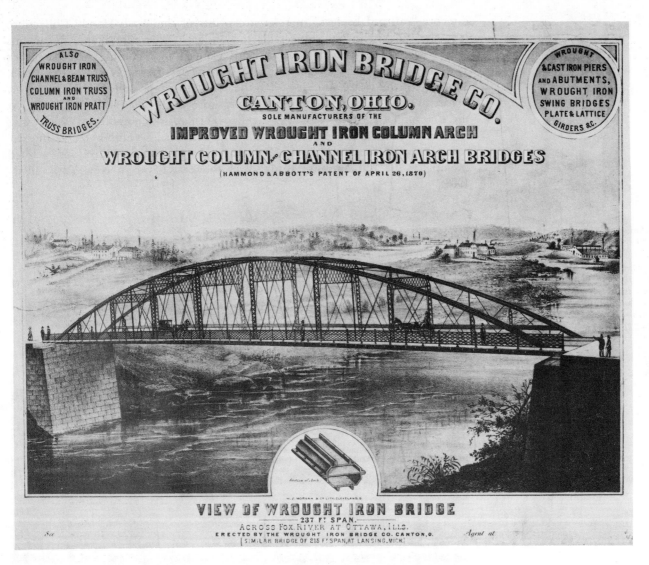

An 1870s lithographic advertisement executed by W. J. Morgan and Company, found in the Historical Print Collection (B size). Documents like this are invaluable in the study of American engineering. This one not only shows the product and name and location of the manufacturer, but also provides a cross section of its principal structural unit and identifies its patent. LC–USZ62–54648

338 / *Prints, Drawings, and Paintings from the Turn of the Century to the Sixties*

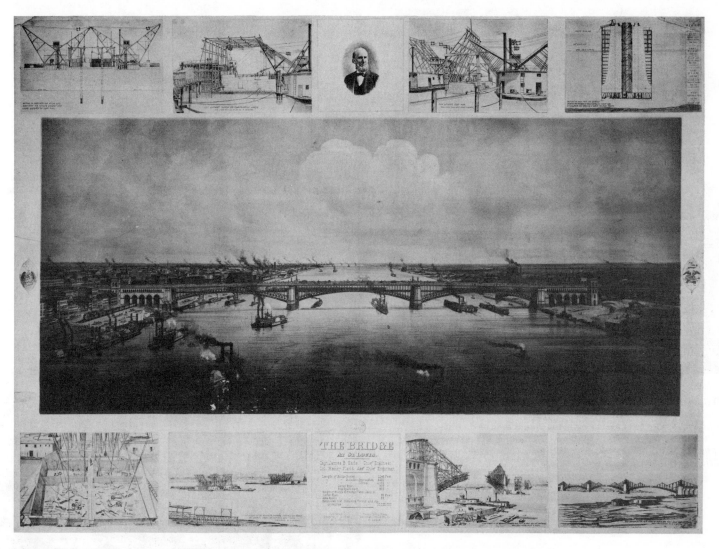

Above: View of the Eads Bridge across the Mississippi at St. Louis, constructed 1867–74. Vignettes provide details of the progress of its innovative construction and a portrait of its chief engineer, James E. Eads. This 1874 lithograph, after a drawing by F. Welcker, was deposited for copyright by the Democrat Lithography and Printing Company and is now in the Historical Print Collection (D size). Its copy negative was indexed under Bridges, and a reference copy placed with others relating to Missouri. LC–US–Z62–1032

The Williamsburg Bridge across the East River, New York City, under construction about 1903; from a stereoscopic view deposited for copyright by the Keystone View Company. Thousands of such stereo views make up an independent reference collection which is arranged geographically. This photograph was filed under New York—New York City: Bridges—Williamsburg. LC–USZ62–62053

Below: The Williamsburg Bridge and its approaches after completion, in a 1919 copyright deposit by Irving Underhill found in the Geographic File (mounted photographs) under New York—New York City: Street Views. This view of the original neighborhood and the bustle of vehicular and pedestrian traffic conveys the vital importance of the bridge to the city as no modern photograph could. LC–USZ62–35807

Nighttime festivities at the opening of the Williamsburg Bridge. Photograph deposited for copright in 1903 by C. O. Wiesemann and found in the Geographic File (mounted photographs) under New York—New York City: Bridges—Williamsburg. LC–USZ62–62054

The same type of visual history may be assembled for specific structures, such as the Singer Tower in New York City, a remarkable Beaux-Arts skyscraper designed by Ernest Flagg and built between 1906 and 1908. Using the HABS records, the supplemental card indexes, and geographic files, one can document its construction, contemporary portrayal by an artist, and demolition. It is even possible to examine the social history of such building forms as the skyscraper in our collections of popular American illustration. Both the 1907 cartoon from *Puck* magazine and a Reginald Marsh drawing for *The New Yorker* in the 1930s comment effectively on the new problems of scale introduced into the urban landscape by the tall buildings.

The Singer Tower, 149 Broadway, New York City, under construction about 1908. Detroit Publishing Company collection, Lot 9150–M. New York City–Named Buildings (arranged alphabetically). LC–D4–70745

E. C. Peixotto's pen-and-wash drawing of the Singer Tower was done in 1909, just after the building's completion, and published in Scribner's Magazine, *September 1909. Found by using the architectural collections' supplemental index to buildings, it is filed in Cabinet of American Illustration (B size). LC–USZ62–58650*

The Singer Tower from the northwest during its demolition, September 1967. Photo by Jack E. Boucher, HABS. (HABS NY–5463) NY,31–NEYO,71–4

"The Future of Trinity Church" according to a wood engraving by
Albert Levering published in Puck, March 6, 1907. Photocopies of
published materials in the general collections are filed under subject
categories, with the reference copies in the Historical Print Collection.
They are also separately listed by subject and geographic location in the
index to copy negatives. LC–USZ62–59235

"Pretty, isn't it"—original crayon drawing by Reginald Marsh for
The New Yorker, showing two tiny figures taking in the Brobdingnagian
structures of lower Manhattan. Filed in Lot 9222, it was found by
looking in the division's general subject index under New York City—
Caricatures and Cartoons. LC–USZ62–62055

344 / Prints, Drawings, and Paintings from the Turn of the Century to the Sixties

Architectural styles have been a source of both inspiration and debate for most of the history of American architecture. Numerous citations for "Gothic" buildings can be found in the architectural subject index, but two fantastic examples of the commercial application of that style—fifty years apart—were found by looking through the commercial buildings in New York City represented in the Historical Print Collection and the Geographical File of mounted photographs. Similarly, instances of "French" influence in interior design, almost fifty years apart, were found in the Historical Print Collection and the Single Subject File.

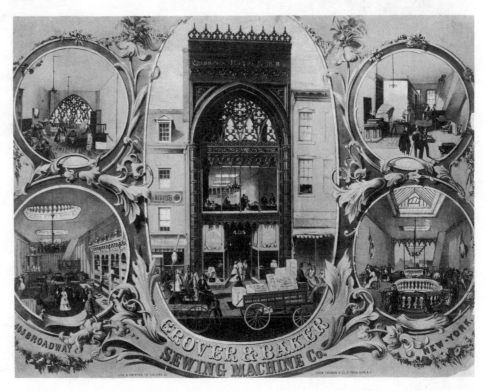

Color lithograph from 1861, showing the busy premises of the Grover and Baker Sewing Machine Company in New York City, where Gothic details were translated into the then modern idiom of cast iron and plate glass. Lithograph by Crow, Thomas and Company, in the Historical Print Collection (C size). LC–USZ62–13217

"A Parlor View in a New York Dwelling House," about 1854, a woodcut from a contemporary illustrated magazine. A parlor "in the French taste" in the 1850s apparently consisted of a rather bizarre combination of Louis XIV and Louis XV motifs and pointed perhaps more to its owners' prosperity than to their artistic sensibilities. From the Historical Print Collection under New York—New York City: Private Homes and Mansions. LC-USZ62–62057

The parlor in the Presidential Suite of Philadelphia's Bellevue-Stratford Hotel, showing a turn-of-the-century American interpretation of a French interior. Although a bit purer in its largely Louis XV inspiration than the earlier example, fashionable anachronisms like the lamp on the center table render it less successful. Copyright deposit photograph by William H. Raw, ca. 1910, in the Single Photo File under Hotels, Taverns, etc.—Interiors: United States—Pennsylvania. LC-USZ62-62058

If one wishes to investigate details of design, hundreds are indexed in the architectural subject files, and a number of illustrations can be found under such a heading as "Cupolas." A still broader sample can quickly be assembled by scanning various geographic files for building types in areas likely to have onion domes. A combination of these methods produced a survey of onion-shaped cupolas from Alaska to Texas, dating from the beginning to the end of the nineteenth century, showing them gracing a church, residences, and resort buildings.

A HABS measured drawing by Robert G. Higginbotham of a section through St. Michael's Cathedral in Sitka, Alaska, first built around 1817 and rebuilt in 1848. Its onion-shaped cuploas are of a type often used on Russian Orthodox churches and are indexed in the Architectural Subject Index. This and other HABS drawings were used to rebuild St. Michael's a second time after it was destroyed by fire in 1966. (HABS ALAS–1) ALAS,5–SITKA,1–sheet 5

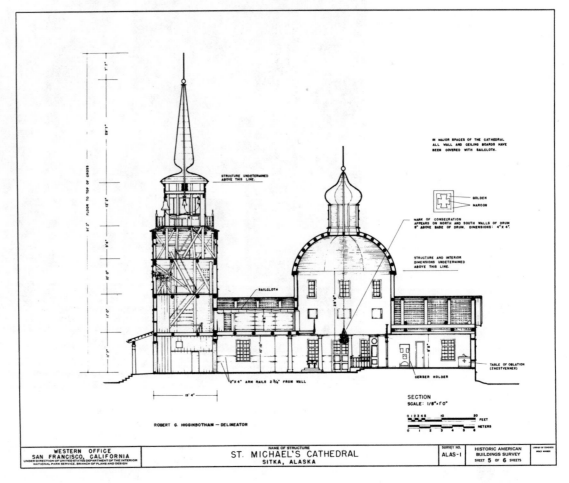

*"Oriental Villa" from Sloan's Homestead Archi-
tecture, by Samuel Sloan (Philadelphia: J. B.
Lippincott, 1861). The onion cupola is a
prominent feature of this octagonal design for a
residence, found under the general category
Architecture with other reference copies from the
Historical Print Collection. When copy negatives are
made from illustrations in the Library's American
architectural books and periodicals, they are
indexed by subject and reference copies are placed
in the appropriate subject and geographic files.*
LC–USZ62–53305

*Almost identical to Sloan's "Oriental Villa" is Longwood, near Natchez,
Mississippi, which he designed about 1860 for Haller Nutt. Left unfinished since
the beginning of the Civil War, Longwood remains one of the outstanding
applications to a domestic structure of what the nineteenth century called the
"Moorish style." This image was found in the Single Photo File under
Dwellings: United States—Mississippi and is one of the more than twenty-five
thousand photographic views of American cities, towns, buildings, and scenery
produced or collected by the Wittemann Brothers (later the Albertype Company)
of Brooklyn, New York, and given to the Library by Mrs. Gladys G. Wittemann
in 1953.* LC–USZ62–46823

Another house with a "Moorish" onion cupola, this one in Dallas, Texas. In the Single Photo File under Dwellings: United States—Texas; also from the Wittemann bequest. LC–USZ62–62059

A "Moorish" bathing pavilion at Salt Lake City, Utah. Resort areas and exotic architectural styles have often exhibited a natural affinity for one another. From a stereoscopic view deposited for copyright in 1906 and located in the Stereo File under Utah—Salt Lake. LC–USZ62–62060

Facing page: Also sporting onion cupolas was the huge Tampa Bay Hotel, in Tampa, Florida, finished in 1891 and now a university building. From the Detroit Publishing Company collection, Lot 9083: Florida. LC–D4–05846

Above: Frank Lloyd Wright (1867–1959), one of America's most original, controversial, and influential architects. Thousands of notable Americans, including architects and engineers, are represented in the division's Portrait File, where this image, a 1926 copyright deposit, was found. LC–USZ62–36384

The careers of individual architects and firms may also be traced through various groups of material. A quick check of two probable sources, the Portrait File and the *Look* Collection, produced photographs of Frank Lloyd Wright, both early and late in his career, the latter showing him at work with his students at Taliesin West in 1951. As for his buildings, thirteen have been surveyed by HABS alone, often with measured drawings like those for the influential Robie House in Chicago. By chance, among the oversize architectural drawings we discovered a significant unpublished version of his design for a United States embassy complex in Tokyo, Japan. Deposited for copyright in 1914, it represents a telling link between Wright's Prairie Houses and his important design for

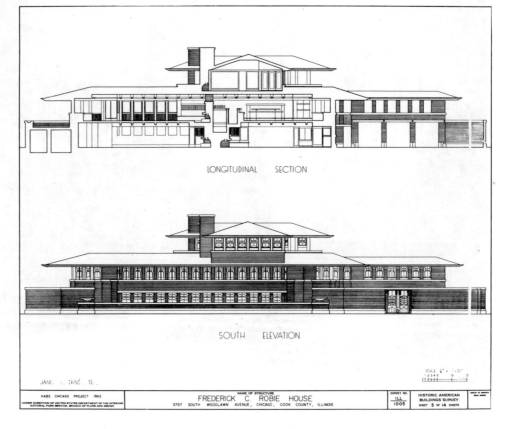

LONGITUDINAL SECTION

SOUTH ELEVATION

| HABS CHICAGO PROJECT 1963 | NAME OF STRUCTURE | SURVEY NO. | HISTORIC AMERICAN |
| UNDER DIRECTION OF UNITED STATES DEPARTMENT OF THE INTERIOR NATIONAL PARK SERVICE, BRANCH OF PLANS AND DESIGN | FREDERICK C. ROBIE HOUSE 5757 SOUTH WOODLAWN AVENUE, CHICAGO, COOK COUNTY, ILLINOIS | ILL 1005 | BUILDINGS SURVEY SHEET 5 OF 14 SHEETS |

Scale drawing of the south elevation of Wright's famous Robie House in Chicago, built 1908–10. HABS has recorded thirteen of Wright's buildings in photographs and measured drawings. 1963 drawing by Janis J. Erins, HABS. (HABS ILL–1005) ILL,16– CHIG,33–sheet 5

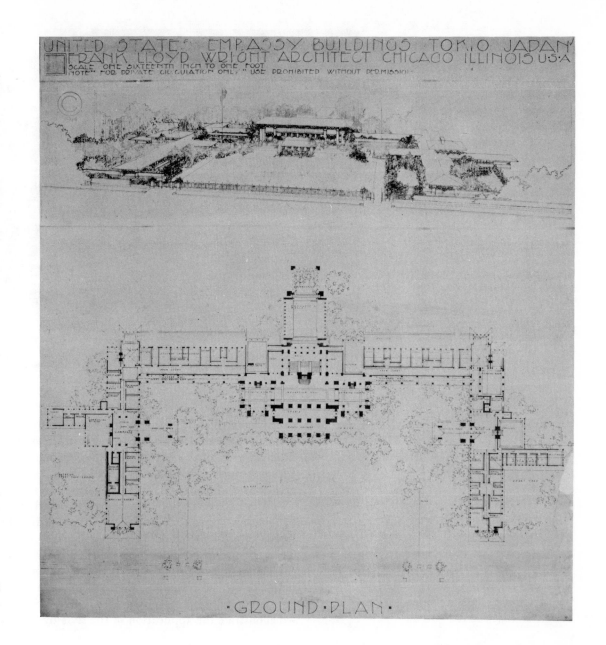

Wright's 1914 copyright deposit design for U.S. embassy in Tokyo. Heliotype highlighted with colored pencil and including alterations in black ink. LC–USZ62–62061

Tokyo's Imperial Hotel, commissioned in the same year. The many such schemes which have come into the Library's collections through copyright deposits are often the only evidence of some stages in the design of a building, or of a project never carried out. They promise to be one of the division's most important future resources for scholarly investigation, especially of the works of individual architects and firms.

Another especially rich resource is found in our unmatched documentation of America's vernacular structures. A familiar building type throughout the low-lying areas of the South is characterized by high basements, shading verandas, and spreading roofs. First credited to the French in the Illinois Territory, the design took advantage of available materials and building skills and combatted certain clear disadvantages of climate and terrain. Examples of both grand and humble dwellings—drawn with equal facility from three different collections—demonstrate the application of the style over one hundred years.

Above: Engraving of a "French Habitation in the Country of the Illinois" from Collot's Voyage dans l'Amerique Septentrionale (Paris, 1826). The reference copy of this early view of an important American vernacular building type is included in the Historical Print Collection under Illinois. LC–USZ62–33765

Above right: Virtually an exact continuation of the building design illustrated by Collot is this cabin near Edgard, St. John the Baptist Parish, Louisiana. This view, typical of Frances Benjamin Johnston's excellent photographs of American vernacular architecture, was made in 1938 as part of the Carnegie Survey of the Architecture of the South. LC–J7–LA1209

Right: The Octave J. Darby Home in New Iberia, Louisiana, originally built by François St. Marc Darby in 1813, exhibits the same characteristics but on the larger and more elegant scale of a plantation house. This photograph is from the Single Photo File under Dwellings: United States—Louisiana, and was part of the Wittemann bequest. LC–USZ62–62062

Another type of structure, also peculiarly American in its symbolic hucksterism, might be classified as the "commercial vernacular"; it is well represented by such examples as Lucy, the Margate Elephant, and a 1930s eating establishment which disallows any conjecture as to its function.

Left: Lucy, the Margate Elephant, served as a tourist attraction and for a short time as a hotel in Margate, New Jersey; it has recently been restored. This view comes from the Single Photo File under the heading Hotel, Taverns, etc.: United States—New Jersey, and was part of the Wittemann bequest. LC–USZ62–59150

A roadside ice cream stand near Berlin, Connecticut, October 1939. The FSA/OWI collection is rich in examples of such American commercial vernaular types. During the 1930s, when most of this collection was created, the independent businessman, rather than the chain, was still supreme along our highways, and he often used such overblown symbolism to advertise both his wares and his individuality. Photographs by Russell Lee filed in the Northeastern Region of the FSA/OWI collection under Lunchrooms, Diners. LC–USF33–12442–M3

The Prints and Photographs Division also offers important resources for the study of America's urban development. Among the most significant of these are the "bird's-eye" views in the Historic Print Collection, like the one for Virginia City of 1861, and the photographic panoramas. Our geographic files include such items as an 1869 scheme to alleviate New York City's traffic problems by means of an arcaded railway, and such later alternatives to urban congestion as the "new towns" of the 1930s. The development of Greenbelt, Maryland, for instance, is well documented in the files of the Farm Security Administration/Office of War Information Collection.

Bird's eye view of Virginia City, Nevada Territory, with vignettes of individual buildings around the border. The value of such documents for the study of the development of a town or city and its architecture is clear. This view, drawn by Grafton T. Brown, lithographed by C. C. Kuchel, and published by Britton and Company, 1861, comes from the Historical Print Collection (D size, Kuchel). LC–USZ62–7743

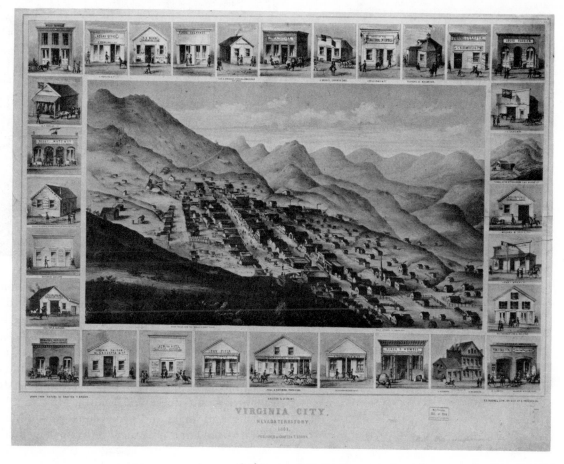

"Proposed Arcade Railway under Broadway, 1869." This predecessor of the subway showed an early attempt at separating vehicular and individual traffic from mass rail transportation. A 1905 copyright deposit, it was found in the Geographic File (mounted photographs) under New York—New York City: Street Views— Broadway. LC–USZ62–62063

Perhaps these samplings have provided some idea of the scope and wealth of the Library's architectural collections. Not discussed were the important complementary collections in the custody of other branches of the Library. The materials on urban development used as examples only hint at the related resources in the Geography and Map Division. Further, the Library's Manuscript Division houses the papers of an impressive cross section of American architects and engineers, including those of William Thornton, Montgomery Meigs, Frederick Law Olmsted, Cass Gilbert, and Ludwig Mies van der Rohe. The range of American architectural books and professional and trade publications to be found in the Library's book and periodical collections is equally impressive.

Panoramic view of San Francisco, California, in 1877, with a key identifying the numbered buildings and landmarks. Its creator, Eadweard J. Muybridge, identified himself as a "landscape, marine, architectural, and engineering photographer," although he later became more famous for the pioneering photographic studies of movement which he began in the same year. The importance of such documents is similar to that of bird's-eye views, and the majority of the Library's extensive collection of such panoramas came to it through copyright deposit. Most are arranged by geographic location. LC-USZ62-24754

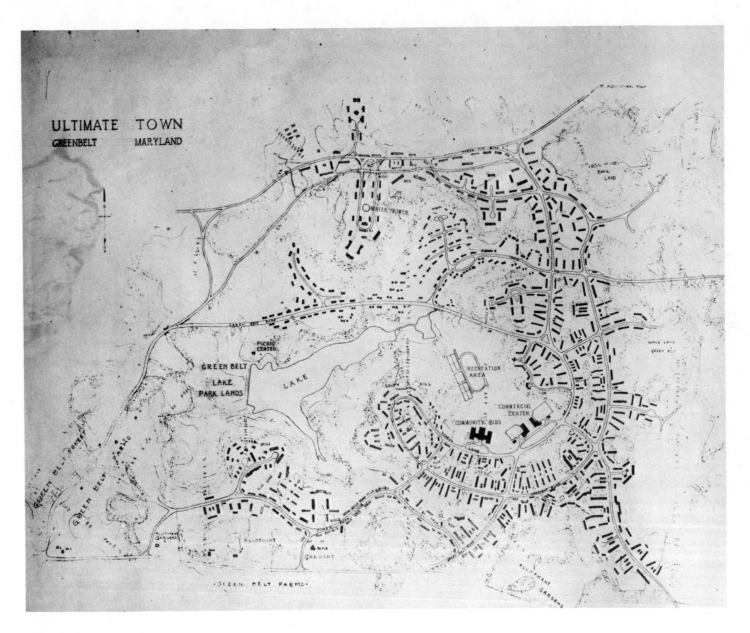

ULTIMATE TOWN

GREENBELT MARYLAND

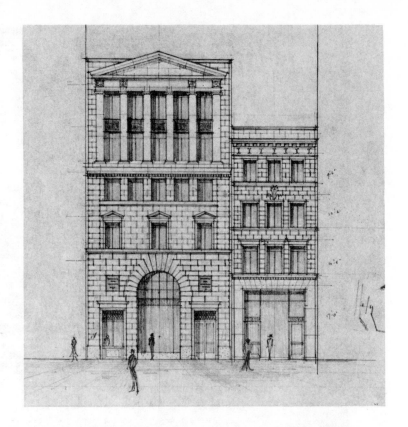

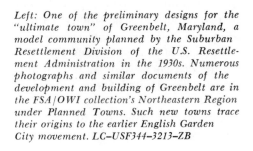

The Library of Congress also enjoys a valuable array of support services and expertise applicable to the preservation and use of its architectural collections. The Restoration Office has beautifully restored many of the Library's architectural drawings, most recently and notably the Bulfinch Sketchbook. Requests by museums and historical societies across the country for original items from the collections are handled by the Exhibits Office. For the students, scholars, preservationists, and others who order thousands of copies of the materials each year, the Photoduplication Service answers their needs.

The architectural collections have grown steadily, if not rapidly, since 1944, when the Fine Arts Division was transformed into the present Prints and Photographs Division. Much of the credit for their continuing development must go to Virginia Daiker, who retired in 1975 after forty years of admirable and knowl-

A recent and important addition to the Library's collection of early American architectural drawings is this beautiful sectional elevation of Stephen Hallet's influential entry in the competition to design the United States Capitol. Drawn sometime after March 1793, it complements three other drawings of the French-trained architect's final or "E" scheme that were already in the collection. LC–USZ62–59240; LC–USZC4–596 (color).

edgeable service to the collections. The regular deposits of records by HABS and HAER have recently been supplemented by two important acquisitions: a collection of approximately sixteen thousand drawings and documents representing the work of the Washington, D.C., architectural firm of Waggaman and Ray from 1907 to 1930, given to the Library by the family of George N. Ray, and the purchase of an important competition drawing for the United States Capitol by Stephen Hallet.

America's built heritage is here documented and available for study by building type; by design discipline, including architecture and landscape architecture, city planning, and interior design; and by medium, including original and measured drawings, prints, and photographic prints and negatives, many incorporating photogrammetric and stereographic techniques. This special mix of comprehensive collections and established services constitutes a genuine national treasure, approaching in reality the ideal envisioned by Dr. Holland almost fifty years ago.

NOTES

1. U.S., Library of Congress, *Annual Report of the Librarian of Congress* (hereafter cited as *ARLC*), 1927, p. 132.

2. *ARLC*, 1930, p. 235.

3. Virginia Daiker, "Pictorial Archives of Early American Architecture," undated historical explanation of the collection; PAEAA File, Architectural Collections, Prints and Photographs Division.

4. Leicester B. Holland, "Report on the Pictorial Archives of Early American Architecture," May 7, 1932, p. 1; PAEAA file. As part of these efforts, Dr. Holland even gave a radio talk on the NBC network, September 27, 1933, entitled "The Romance of Preserving Old Buildings," a typescript of which survives in our files.

5. *ARLC*, 1930, p. 229.

6. Paul Vanderbilt, *Guide to the Special Collections of Prints & Photographs in the Library of Congress* (Washington: Library of Congress, 1955), p. 87.

7. Leicester B. Holland, "Report on the Pictorial Archives of Early American Architecture," December 31, 1935, pp. 1–3; PAEAA file.

8. Ibid., p. 1.

9. Ibid.

10. *ARLC*, 1934, p. 137.

11. *ARLC*, 1936, pp. 160–61. The Historic Sites Act of 1935 was the legal instrument establishing the long-range program.

12. Leicester B. Holland, "Report on the Pictorial Archives of Early American Architecture," April 24, 1934, p. 2; PAEAA file.

13. Collections of foreign architectural documentation usually are also geographically indexed, arranged, and subdivided and include a broad range of media. The scope of the foreign material is nearly encyclopedic, including examples representative of almost every historic or national building tradition.

About the Authors

Karen F. Beall, curator of fine prints, came to the Prints and Photographs Division in 1964. A native of the Washington, D.C., area, she completed her undergraduate studies at American University and did graduate work there and at Johns Hopkins University. In addition to the articles she has published in *Quarterly Journal* and in *Philobiblon,* Mrs. Beall has compiled *American Prints in the Library of Congress,* contributed notes on fine prints to *Viewpoints,* and is the author of *Cries and Itinerant Trades,* which she undertook with the aid of a grant from the American Philosophical Society.

Edgar Breitenbach was chief of the Prints and Photographs Division from 1956 to 1973. A native of Germany, he received a doctor's degree in the history of art from the University of Hamburg in 1927 and a library diploma for research libraries from the University of Berlin in 1929. He has taught art history at Mills Fine Arts Center in Colorado Springs, worked for the Federal Communications Commission and the Office of War Information in Washington, and spent ten years in Europe working for the Monuments, Fine Arts, and Archives Section of OMGUS, and the American Memorial Library in Berlin. Among Dr. Breitenbach's publications are *Speculum humanae salvationis, The American Poster, Santos, the Religious Folk Art of New Mexico,* and numerous essays in the field of art history.

Virginia Daiker retired in 1975 after completing more than forty years of service in the Library's Prints and Photographs Division and its predecessor, the

Fine Arts Division, as indexer, cataloger, head of the reference section, and specialist in American architecture. A native Washingtonian, she received her B.A. in education from Maryland University and her B.A. in library science from the George Washington University. Miss Daiker was honored by awards from the *American Scenic and Historic Preservation Society* and the *National Trust for Historic Preservation* for her work on the Historic American Buildings Survey.

Fritz Eichenberg, an illustrator and printmaker, served as a member of the Library of Congress's Pennell Committee from 1959 to 1965. A native of Cologne, Germany, he graduated from the State Academy for Graphic Arts in Leipzig in 1923. He was chairman of the Art Department at Pratt Institute from 1956 to 1963 and was on the faculty of the Department of Art at the University of Rhode Island from 1966 to 1972, serving as chairman of the department from 1966 to 1969. In 1972 he began teaching at Albertus Magnus College. Mr. Eichenberg has illustrated over a hundred books. His graphic work is included in the major print collections in the United States and Europe.

Alan M. Fern, director of the Research Department in the Library of Congress, joined the Library staff in 1961. Before being appointed to his present position in 1976, he served in the Prints and Photographs Division as assistant curator of fine prints, curator of fine prints, assistant chief, and chief. Dr. Fern received his A.B. degree in 1950 from the University of Chicago. He continued his studies in the history of art at the same university and received his M.A. in 1954 and his Ph.D. in 1960. Before coming to the Library, Dr. Fern taught at the University of Chicago, the Art Institute of Chicago, the Institute of Design, the University of Maryland, and Pratt Institute. He has published extensively in the field of art and printmaking.

Charles A. Herrington worked in reference and cataloging in the Library's Prints and Photographs Division from 1965 to 1967. Having received a B.A. degree from Tulane University in 1964 with emphasis on art history and French, he left the Library of Congress to enter graduate school at the University of Wisconsin, where he was awarded an M.A. in art history. Mr. Herrington continued his graduate study at the University of Michigan, specializing in architectural history. Since 1973, he has been employed by the Department of the Interior as chief of registration for the National Register of Historic Places.

Milton Kaplan, retired curator of historical prints in the Prints and Photographs Division of the Library of Congress, came to the Library in 1941, after graduating from the College of William and Mary in 1940. He organized several major exhibits at the Library, among them "Hair," "Advertising in Nineteenth-Century America," and "The Performing Arts in Nineteenth-Century America." He compiled the book *Pictorial Americana* and coauthored *Charles Fenderich, Lithographer of American Statemen* and *Viewpoints,* all Library of Congress publications. Mr. Kaplan also coauthored a number of illustrated books in American history: *Presidents on Parade* (1948), *Divided We Fought* (1952), *The Story of the Declaration of Independence* (1954, 1975), and *The Ungentlemanly Art* (1968, 1975).

Fiske Kimball (1888–1955) was director of the Philadelphia Museum of Art from 1925 to 1955. A native of Massachusetts, he received bachelor's and master's degrees from Harvard and a doctor's degree from the University of Michigan. He taught art and architecture at the universities of Illinois, Michigan, and Virginia from 1912 to 1923. His published writings include *The Creation of the Rococo* as well as articles in various art and architecture journals. Dr. Kimball served on the advisory board for the restoration of Colonial Williamsburg.

Mary R. Mearns, a retired staff member of the Library of Congress, attended George Washington and Benjamin Franklin Universities. She served the Library for thirty years—in the Card Division, Chief Clerk's Office, and Reading Rooms. As an administrative assistant, she aided in the organization of the Reference Department. Mrs. Mearns reports that the interview with Clifford Berryman was one of the happiest events of her Library days.

Elena G. Millie came to the Library of Congress in 1964. She received her B.A. from the University of North Carolina, where she also did graduate work in art history, and worked for a year at the National Gallery of Art before joining the staff of the Prints and Photographs Division as a cataloger. She is now curator of the Poster Collection and is also responsible for the British and French Political Cartoon Collection and the J. and E. R. Pennell Collection of Whistleriana. Mrs. Millie has compiled a checklist of the British political cartoon holdings in the Library of Congress for publication.

C. Ford Peatross, curator of the architectural collections, joined the Prints and Photographs Division in 1976. A native of North Carolina, he received his B.B.A. degree in business administration from Wake Forest University in 1969. A Ph.D. Candidate at the University of North Carolina at Chapel Hill, he has specialized in architectural history and nineteenth-century painting and graphic art. During 1974–75 he was a Samuel H. Kress Fellow at the National Gallery of Art, and in 1975 and 1976 attended summer schools on Austrian and Roman baroque architecture sponsored by the University of London's Courtauld Institute. He has delivered papers before various professional societies, his work on Théodore Géricault appearing in *Studies in Art History*. Before coming to the Library, he was a researcher for *The Architecture of Washington, D.C.,* published by the Dunlap Society.

Renata V. Shaw, bibliographic specialist in the Prints and Photographs Division, joined the Library staff in 1962. A native of Finland, she received an M.A. in art history from the University of Chicago (1949), the Magister Philosophiae at the University of Helsinki (1951), and a diploma in museology at the Ecole de Louvre in Paris (1952). After two additional years of postgraduate work at the Sorbonne and the Ecole de Chartes, Mrs. Shaw taught French in Washington, D. C., and worked at the National Gallery of Art. She continued her graduate studies at Catholic University, receiving an M.S. in library science in 1962. Mrs. Shaw has written several articles in the field of graphic arts and visual librarianship. In 1973 she published a bibliography entitled *Picture Searching*.

Raymond L. Stehle, a pharmacologist by profession, earned his Ph.D. at Yale University in 1915. He taught physiological chemistry at the University of Pennsylvania until 1921, when he accepted an appointment at McGill University in Montreal. In 1924 he became a full professor and chairman of the department of pharmacology, a position he held until 1953, when he became professor emeritus. Upon his retirement he spent nearly a year in Europe and, on his return, eventually settled in Washington, D. C. Dr. Stehle has contributed numerous articles to scientific journals and, since his retirement, has published several studies of artist Emanuel Leutze.

☆ U. S. GOVERNMENT PRINTING OFFICE : 1979 O - 247-861